KENNEDY BABYLON

A Century of Scandal and Depravity

Volume 2

HOWIE CARR

Howie Carr

TABLE OF CONTENTS

ACKNOWLEDGMENTS

WRITING A BOOK LIKE this is always a team effort, and I am grateful to everyone who helped me put it together in time for the Christmas 2018 season.

First of all, thanks to my beautiful wife, Kathy, who once again flawlessly handled the business side of production, with help from John Murray, my network's vice president for finances.

The staff of my radio show provided invaluable assistance. Producer Grace Curley kept track of more than 100 photographs, handled the computer chores, and came up with the color scheme for the cover, which hopefully makes it easy for readers to distinguish between this book and *Kennedy Babylon,* Volume 1.

Steve Robinson, my executive producer, bought rights to the photographs from the Associated Press that we used to supplement those I obtained from my newspaper, the *Boston Herald.*

The *Herald's* new owner, Digital First Media, continued to allow me full access to the paper's photo files, and chief photographer James Mahoney provided whatever pictures I asked for. Joe Dwinell, one of the editors, diligently searched the archives for my old columns, especially the ones I used for the "In His Own Word" chapters. (Basically that task required Joe to type the name of a Kennedy into the search engine along with another word or words, usually "uh," "um," or "you know.")

At Bookmasters in Ashland, Ohio, Jen Welsch did her usual great job pulling together the host of production details. Allison Barrows added some excellent new caricatures to the cover, which was designed by our web guy, Josh Phelps. With her skillful copyediting, Chris Wrona once again saved me from numerous grammatical and factual errors.

Thanks again to all of my radio affiliates. Some have corporate ownership—iHeart, Saga, Townsquare, Blueberry Broadcasting—and others are independently owned. AM or FM, I love them all. Also thanks to Chris Ruddy at Newsmax. Being on national cable television for two hours a day is such a pleasure.

Thanks also to Bob Maynes of Mathews Brothers, which as my listeners know has been making windows in Maine since 1854. Bob and Mathews Brothers were with us on the network from the beginning, and we continue to have a lot of fun working together. Those gray Mathews Brothers notebooks came in very handy—23 chapters, 23 notebooks. That's Mathews Brothers with one T.

Over the years, I've received much information about the Kennedys, not to mention photographs, from my listeners and readers. This book wouldn't have been possible without your assistance.

And to every one of my listeners, readers, and viewers, I want to express my sincerest gratitude for your support and friendship over the years, because I couldn't have done anything without you.

I hope you enjoy this second and final volume of *Kennedy Babylon.*

CHAPTER ONE

INTRODUCTION: "I'M DRUNK . . .
I KNOW THAT!"

I F MATTHEW MAXWELL ("MAX") Taylor Kennedy and his daughter Caroline hadn't been Kennedys, the Barnstable Police would have had probable cause to charge them with impersonating members of the family.

According to the arrest report on the morning of August 20, 2017, the 52-year-old Kennedy had refused to identify himself or provide identification to officers who were responding to numerous complaints of excessive noise at 1:20 on a Sunday morning in Hyannis Port.

The Kennedys' version of Bring Your Daughter to Work Day was about to unfold. But since Kennedys don't work, this would be Bring Your Daughter to Jail Day.

The scene was a rented house at 172 Irving Avenue, around

Max poses with his book about World War II.

the corner from the Kennedys' famous compound. Max had sold his own house in Hyannis Port a few years earlier for $5.9 million, after a series of run-ins with the local conservation commission over his "improvements"—also known as zoning violations—ironic, considering Max's long advocacy, as the Kennedys call it, of environmental issues at something called the Watershed Institute.

But it could hardly be summer for any Kennedy without some "cottage" to crash at within staggering distance of the family's storied Cape compound. And so it was that yet another Kennedy house party was in full swing that night.

The local rent-a-cops from Hyannis Port Security had already responded to several complaint calls, stopping the drunken revelers from throwing firecrackers off a nearby pier, politely asking the partygoers to turn down the music, and in response generally getting told to go fuck themselves.

Finally, the Barnstable Police had been called, and now they were themselves getting the royal treatment from the drunken crew that had once been known as America's First Family.

Officer Armando Feliciano wrote the initial incident report.

After being asked for some identification at the front door of the house, Max Kennedy turned his back on the cop and "then pushed his way through the group of people who were listening to me and grabbed hold of this male pulling him back into the house in an aggressive manner."

Officer Feliciano again asked Kennedy for some identification.

"He became even more irate with me. I observed Kennedy to have noticeably bloodshot and glassy eyes and he was sweating profusely during our conversation. Kennedy was yelling at me not to enter the house as I moved closer to the door."

Same as it ever was . . .

"Kennedy continued to yell and scream at me and refused any cooperation whatsoever. He told me to leave. He appeared to be very unsteady on his feet and his movements were erratic . . . Kennedy only pointed his finger at my chest and refused any sort of civil communications. Neither Kennedy, nor the other party guests, made any effort whatsoever to stop the disturbance (only turning the music back up during our conversation). The disturbance only grew worse . . ."

Max Kennedy was a sort of Everyman Kennedy of his generation—the ninth of RFK's 11 children, born in 1965, named after a famous Cold War general by his "liberal" father. Like six of his siblings, he'd already been arrested at least once—in his case, for assaulting a Harvard University cop in Cambridge at the age of 17.

Kennedys are always getting arrested, but Max's embarrassment was who he'd been arrested with—his cousin, Michael Skakel, then already a suspect in the savage murder of his 15-year-old female neighbor in Connecticut in 1975. He was eventually convicted and sent to prison (and later released when his conviction was overturned by the state supreme court).

It was that revelation about his arrest with Skakel in the *Boston Herald* that had finally forced him out of the race for the U.S. House seat previously held by the late Joe Moakley in 2001.

It was just another in a string of electoral disasters that had befallen his once-invincible family. His eldest sister had been defeated in her bid to become governor of Maryland; his eldest brother had been driven out of the Massachusetts race for governor by a sex scandal involving yet another brother.

A few years later his cousin Caroline's bid to replace Hillary Clinton as senator from New York would founder after a pathetic series of tongue-tied interviews with the New York newspapers (see Chapter 15). His cousin Patrick would leave the House of Representatives following an embarrassing string of drug- and alcohol-related mishaps (see Chapter 5).

Even as Max was about to be arrested again, another of his brothers, Christopher, was struggling in his own race to become governor of Illinois. And this time, the circumstances would be particularly ironic—Chris would be outspent by Jay Pritzker, the scion of an even more fabulously wealthy family than the Kennedys. Months later, Chris wouldn't just lose the Democratic primary, he would finish . . . third.

In 2001, Max had mounted his own comically inept campaign for Congress. He entered the race as the overwhelming favorite, even though he didn't live in the district and had accomplished precisely nothing in his life.

His listed profession: "co-director of a non-profit environmental organization." In other words, he didn't work. You couldn't get much more new-generation Kennedy than that.

A generally favorable piece in the *New York Times* noted how many traits Max shared with other male members of his family down through the generations: He never carried cash, relying on others to pick up the tab. He dressed like a hobo, favoring, in his case, Hawaiian shirts, chinos, and sneakers with no socks.

Like his older brothers Joe and Michael before him, he had "managed" his uncle's reelection campaign in 2000. Like his father, his uncles, and his brother Michael, he drove a convertible—a green Chrysler Sebring. He was a recovering alcoholic, noting in understatement, "Some people say there's an alcohol gene in my family."

In summation, he was a Kennedy—by definition not a serious person, and he knew it. Asked by the *Times* reporter how he passed his time, Max replied, "Lately, I've been into astrology."

Nonetheless, Max was expected to cruise to an easy victory in the working-class suburban-Boston congressional district. He even deigned to buy a house in the district, in West Roxbury, where he planned to move with his wife and three young children, including 6-year-old Caroline, known to the family as "Summer."

But Max faced a number of problems his father and uncle had never encountered. For one thing, this was to be a special election, in an off year, to replace the dying Moakley. That meant that it was a "free shot" for incumbents in the district. They would not have to give up their legislative seats to run for higher office.

The candidates included state Sen. Steve Lynch, an ironworker from South Boston who had already vanquished one minor Boston political dynasty—the Bulgers, when Senate President William Bulger attempted to place his feckless namesake, Billy Jr., in the seat he resigned from to become president of the University of Massachusetts.

Another candidate was Sen. Brian Joyce of Milton, a crooked suburban pol who was such a political opportunist that his nickname was "Multiple Choice." He would later be found dead in the fall of 2018 at the age of 56 after being indicted in federal court in Boston on 113 counts of racketeering and extortion.

Max was to begin his campaign officially on May 17, 2001, at a fund-raising breakfast for one of his father's charities, the Robert F. Kennedy Children's Action Corps. As he walked in, Max was confronted by a local TV crew demanding a response to the just-released video footage of him kicking a dog. It turned out that Max had merely been trying to break up a dogfight in his neighborhood, but the shouted questions spooked him.

Once inside, as he began his speech, Max appeared confused. He lost his train of thought, giggled at inopportune moments, and made one misstatement after another. He said that Byron "Whizzer" White, an appointee of his uncle to the U.S. Supreme Court, was still a justice. (He'd retired in 1993.) He said that Burke Marshall, one of Ted Kennedy's lawyers during Chappaquiddick, "is now in charge of Yale" University. (He was a law professor.)

He tried to hit on all the Democratic hot buttons, like global warming.

"Last Tuesday was the hottest earliest day on record," he stammered. "It was seven degrees hotter than the hottest day, hottest earliest day prior."

How hot was it, Max?

Repeating variations of a single word over and over reminded everyone of his cousin, Patrick, the tongue-tied Rhode Island congressman. He mentioned his career as an assistant district attorney—how very Uncle Ted–like. Sen. Kennedy had been an assistant district attorney in Suffolk County, of which West Roxbury is a part, back in the 1960s, taking time out only for "fact-finding missions" to South America, where in Peru Teddy had rented a brothel for an entire night, just for himself and his chauffeur.

Now, 40 years later, his nephew was recounting his experiences as a local prosecutor in Philadelphia. Or trying to.

"Um, I remember . . . uh . . . I remember not—could tell you a number of just . . . uh . . . horrify—absolutely horrifying stories. I'll just tell you one. Um . . . I was . . . uh . . . I had a case . . . um . . . where the police were received a radio call . . ."

Another vexing problem for the newer generation of Kennedys was their inability to comprehend the political geography of Massachusetts. Granted, this was a common problem among many Massachusetts Democrats, so many of whom had drifted into the state from elsewhere to "teach" at Harvard University.

Robert B. Reich, an unsuccessful candidate for governor in 2002, drew a complete blank during his campaign when asked to name the westernmost county in the state (Berkshire County). Elizabeth Warren, another out-of-state Harvard professor, referred in her initial campaign for the Senate to the "west coast of Massachusetts." (Was she referring to the banks of the Connecticut River?) In a 2018 debate, she mispronounced the name of the town Bourne as "Bern."

Max's older brother Joe Kennedy had the same problem in 1986 when he first ran for Tip O'Neill's House seat. (Although the Kennedys no doubt still considered it JFK's seat, even though he hadn't run in the district since 1950.)

When JFK ran, the North End was part of the district. But Tip O'Neill had always worried about an Italian challenger taking him out, so over the decades he'd trimmed out some of the heavily Italian neighborhoods, such as the North End of Boston, Ward 3.

But when Joe began his campaign in 1985, no one bothered to check the district's new boundaries. He spent several weekends going door-to-door and shaking hands around Hanover Street before someone finally informed him of the district's new boundaries. But Joe, of course, had an excuse—he hadn't lived in the district until he decided to represent it in Congress.

The joke in 1986 had been that if Joe Kennedy's moving van broke down on the way from Cohasset on the South Shore to his new house in the district, in Brighton, then Joe Moakley would have found himself with a primary opponent named Kennedy.

Now, Moakley was dying, and, sure enough, a Kennedy was moving into his district. But Max was as shaky on Bay State geography and politics as his older brother Joe.

Running for office, any office, a candidate cannot neglect any part of the area, in or outside of the district. So Max's speechwriters threw in the obligatory reference to "cities like Cambridge and Stoughton and Needham and Brockton and Braintree."

The only problem was that Stoughton and Needham and Braintree aren't cities, they're towns, as any candidate for state representative could have told Max. But then, the last Kennedy to run for the state legislature was Max's great-grandfather, Patrick, back in 1892. (He won.)

These days the Kennedys assume that most voters know absolutely nothing about the family's past. For instance, Max Kennedy's father, after graduating from law school, had gone almost immediately to work for Sen. Joseph McCarthy of Wisconsin, the Communist hunter now reviled in all polite Democratic circles.

Not that Max would mention any of this, of course.

"Somewhere around the time he began law school," Max continued, "I think my father began to believe there were things about our country that were troubling and needed to be addressed."

Namely, Communists. Communists and labor unions controlled by gangsters. Those were RFK's overriding concerns. That, and visiting Moscow in 1956, where according to the KGB he requested that a "woman of ill repute" be sent up to his hotel room.

Max's theme: They're not making Democrats like his dad anymore.

"I think that there is a . . . uh . . . severe, a severe lack of that and . . . uh . . . you know—I continue to care deeply about the purposes and principles that have been the bedrock of the Democratic party."

It was left to the audience to ponder for themselves exactly what the "bedrock" of the Democratic party now consisted of.

Finally, mercifully, his halting, disjointed speech was coming to an end.

"I want to leave you with a message from a man who knows much more than I."

In the case of Max, that could have been almost anyone. But he was referring to the dying Joe Moakley, whose seat in Congress he presumed to inherit, as if it were his birthright.

"He said jobs are the key."

And Max needed one. A job, that is.

Even the Kennedy family's fanzine, the *Boston Globe,* was underwhelmed by Max's debut performance, quoting one family retainer (a *Globe* reporter, perhaps?) as saying, "I wanted to go up and save the kid."

The remnants of the vaunted Kennedy machine appeared rustier than ever. Writing his speeches was Robert Shrum, a veteran of every losing Democratic presidential campaign since 1980, who would go down in history a few years later by asking Sen. John Kerry on election night 2004, "May I be the first to address you as Mr. President?"

After that first bumbling speech, Teddy Kennedy summoned Max to an emergency meeting, where his campaign was dissected by, of all people, John Sasso. Sasso was another Shrum—the genius who had run then-Governor Mike Dukakis's 1988 campaign for president, managing a 17-point lead in August into a landslide 40-state defeat in November. Sasso's specialty was dirty tricks—botched dirty tricks, like getting caught peddling a video of Sen. Joe Biden plagiarizing a speech by British Labour Party leader Neil Kinnock in 1987.

Robert Shrum and John Sasso? They were the best and the brightest the Kennedys could find for one of their own? Apparently, the answer was yes. When Joe Moakley finally died on Memorial Day, it became clear that a special election would soon be held to replace him. (The primary eventually took place on September 11, 2001—9/11.)

Four days before Max's expected official announcement, the *Herald* broke the story about his earlier arrest in Cambridge with his murderous cousin Michael Skakel. Max decided to pull the plug on his campaign. The story in the *New York Times* ended with him in front of a TV set, getting ready to watch *The O'Reilly Factor* on Fox News, and the reporter telling him he could go on anytime he wanted.

"Oh, I don't want to go on," Max replied. "I just want to watch."

And that was the last most people heard of Max Kennedy for more than 15 years. Until that August Sunday morning, 2017 had been shaping up as a relatively scandal-free year for the Kennedys. No member of the family had been arrested since the day after Christmas 2016, when Max's nephew, Conor Kennedy, had been charged with assault following an after-hours brawl outside a trendy gin mill in Aspen, Colorado.

It had been a typical Cape summer for the Kennedys. A week earlier, Max had posted on his brother Bobby Jr.'s Instagram account a video of himself on his boat with country music singer Kenny Chesney, "burying the rail," or as the *New York Post* explained, "catching so much wind that the boat's deck was almost vertical, the boat's side underwater."

And naturally it wouldn't have been summer in Barnstable County without one of them trying to stiff a local or two on some bill.

"Tales of family cheapness abound," the *Post* reported. "During the recent wedding of Caroline's cousin Megan Kennedy Townsend to Billy Birdzell, a stylist had to 'chase them' for money, the family source said. The bill was about $875. 'They're very stingy,' the source said."

And now, as Labor Day neared, Max was hosting an out-of-control party at a rented home in Hyannis Port. Actually, by the time the police were called to the scene, the evening was starting to wind down. As the cops arrived, they saw a number of people walking away from the house, carrying coolers, and the yard was littered with scores of empty beer cans—the traditional detritus of a traditional Kennedy weekend on the Cape.

After Max Kennedy walked back inside the house, Feliciano tried to convince several other guests to turn down the music—"to no avail."

So he entered the house.

"Kennedy responded by now screaming incoherently and throwing himself at the wall. When he hit the wall, he grabbed a wall cabinet (filled with glass valuables) and threw it, smashing the contents. I attempted to ask Kennedy why he was acting like this."

There was no answer.

"I advised Kennedy that he was now under arrest and I attempted to place handcuffs on Kennedy due to his violent and tumultuous behavior and refusal to stop the ongoing disturbance. Kennedy attempted to pull away by stiffening both of his arms."

He was stiff all right, but not drunk. He would later demand to take a Breathalyzer, and blow a .00, after which he would be released from protective custody.

"I told him to relax his arms. He refused. Kennedy, again, pulled his arms from me—making it difficult for me to place him in custody. During our struggle with Kennedy, I observed that we were surrounded by everyone in the room."

The traditional question posed by Kennedys under duress, everywhere, but especially on their home Cape turf, is, "Do you know who I am?"

The eternal question was about to get an update, the Barnstable Police reported.

"They were yelling, 'You don't know who you're messing with,' and, 'He was a district attorney.'"

It was like Max was back on the campaign trail in West Roxbury, bragging about that brief stint as a junior prosecutor in Philadelphia.

"We eventually gained control and handcuffed Kennedy. He was escorted outside and into my cruiser. The small crowd was closing in on us and was out of control."

There's an old saying in Barnstable County: Ten-on-one is Kennedy fun.

"Once outside, we were surrounded again by a group of persons. I radioed dispatcher to send more cruisers to our location. A large number of party guests now came out of the house and into the middle of the road. I observed a female, later identified as Caroline Kennedy, grab hold of my cruiser door and open it. I recognized her as one of the party guests from in the house. As she opened the door I rushed to the cruiser as the crowd closed in."

Do they teach this at the police academy—drunken-Kennedy crowd control?

"I was able to get the door closed but this had now flared up the crowd even more. Everywhere I turned there was a cell phone camera/flashlight in my face and people were yelling and flailing their arms. The actions of both Max Kennedy and Caroline Kennedy had incited this crowd into an angry mob."

Officer Feliciano had no choice. He placed Summer under arrest for noise ordinance violation, disorderly conduct, and protective custody (PC), a Kennedy family tradition. At age 23, she had made her family bones. Caroline Rose Kennedy had a rap sheet.

At this point the narrative is picked up by Sgt. Jason Laber, the overnight watch commander, who had to book and process the two Kennedy perps. At first Caroline dummied up. Here is Laber's narrative, with his italics:

"During this time, I observed the female to slur her words and had glassy bloodshot eyes. She was unsteady on her feet and was dirty (dirt on knees and feet). During the process, I asked if she would like to have a Breathalyzer. She refused and said, '*No, I'm drunk . . . I know that.*' She continued to refuse any biographical information whatsoever."

Imagine that—a Kennedy standing up, even when she could barely stand up.

"I explained that I would have to place her in a cell and continue the process at a later time—if she continued not to cooperate. She responded by telling me her name was '*Caroline Rose Kennedy.*' She continued, '*I went to Brown and I'm a teacher—sweetheart.*'"

Brown—the new Harvard for the spoiled white-trash offspring of the Kennedys. JFK Jr., one of Kerry Kennedy's daughters by Governor Andrew Cuomo . . . and Summer.

"She stuck her tongue out and repeatedly told me to '*fuck off*' during booking. She cried and now asked if this would affect her job. I continued with booking when she continued, '*You guys arrested my father too . . . Max Kennedy . . . Yeah . . . I tried to get him out of the police car.*' She continued by saying that she did not know it was against the law to open a police car's door."

Max Kennedy, who likewise had "glassy bloodshot eyes and was sweating profusely," was cut loose after taking the Breathalyzer.

Caroline was released to begin her first job, as a teacher in Pacific Palisades. Her court appearance was set for November 22 of all days. The Barnstable Police released the reports and the mug shots Monday morning, and the story quickly went worldwide. Readers loved it. There are few things in life quite as satisfying as having one's suspicions confirmed—especially suspicions about bad behavior by people to whom much has been given, and of whom little is expected but scandal and depravity.

Some things never change. Like the Kennedys.

Barnstable Police mug shots: Max Kennedy and his daughter Caroline, aka Summer.

CHAPTER TWO

THE WOMEN

THE MOST IMPORTANT CORRESPONDENCE of the males in the Kennedy family can usually be found in research libraries or institutes bearing their names.

On the other hand, the most significant letters of the women sometimes turn up . . . in a garbage can. Rosemary Kennedy's diaries of the 1930s before she was lobotomized, Jackie's love letters to a New York lawyer after the assassination.

And of course, this undated, four-page letter from Jackie to Teddy's wife, Joan, retrieved from the trash outside Joan's house at the compound in Hyannis Port.

"This is the 20th century—not the 19th—where the little woman stayed on a pedestal with the kids and her rosary. Your life matters—as much as him—you love him—but you can't destroy yourself."

But she did, which is perhaps why Joan threw the letter away. A housemaid retrieved it, stashed it away in a storage facility, and then abandoned it without paying the bill. Some guy bought the contents of seven storage lockers at auction, went through the contents, and came up with the letter, which was sold at a much more upscale auction house in 2007.

In her distinctive handwriting on white notebook paper, Jackie was the voice of experience, although by then the former TV model Joan Bennett Kennedy had learned all too well the reality of being married to one of the boys.

Jackie with young JFK Jr.—America's ideal First Family—in public.

"Men under pressure have to let off steam sometimes—that's why even the Catholic Church has carnival and Mardi Gras. But having your own little black phone . . . so that you can talk to Mootsie or Pootsie every night—right in the house with his wife and children—and bringing them there when you're away. What kind of woman, but a sap or a slave, can stand that and still be a loving wife and work like a dog for him campaigning? It is so old-fashioned—probably got it from his father."

Or perhaps from his older brother. When Teddy was married in 1958, a film crew was hired to memorialize the nuptials. In rushes, the director heard the junior senator from Massachusetts confiding to his little brother, 15 years his junior, that being married didn't necessarily mean he had to remain faithful to one woman.

As for Joe Kennedy's role in promulgating the family's baser traditions, Jackie actually liked her father-in-law, perhaps because he supposedly gave her $1 million in the 1950s not to divorce JFK. Joe understood his son—he once told J. Edgar Hoover he should have had him gelded, to keep him out of trouble. Not that the old man didn't mind him getting

Eunice and Sargent Shriver at a wedding.

into trouble himself—when Joe gave Jackie a tour of the compound for the first time, he showed her the little "doll room" where he'd had sex with Gloria Swanson, graphically describing to his daughter-in-law just how he'd taken the Hollywood superstar, and how many orgasms she'd had . . .

"Let me tell you," Joe told Jackie, "that woman was insatiable."

Now, all these years later, Jackie was advising her younger sister-in-law.

"Forbidden fruit is what is exciting," she went on. "It takes much more of a real man to have a deep relationship with the woman he lives with. The routine of married life can become boring . . . if you married Mootsie and she had a few miscarriages—"

Joan had had three.

"—and had to go to the movies at the Cape and on the *Marlin* with the whole family every day—you'd be sneaking off from her, too, after a while."

Jackie couldn't stand the family's "star-maker machinery," to use Joni Mitchell's phrase in a different context. She called her sisters-in-law the sorority, a pack of gorillas. They called her "the Deb," as in debutante, and, after the assassination, "the Widder."

"This community living has to stop. The family that really counts is his own . . ."

Now Jackie was moving from generalities into specifics.

"He can go to all the graduations of all of Ethel's children and teach John to sail the *Victura*—but, if he botches up his own family . . . that will be a pretty sad record."

As indeed it was. For all her own faults—avarice, duplicity, her own promiscuity of sorts—Jackie could see the sad future for Joan. Now she was acting as Joan's personal advice-to-the-lovelorn columnist, a Dear Abby of Barnstable:

The Kennedys were always Hollywood perfect—at least for weddings like JFK's in Newport, Rhode Island, September 1953.

"Take vacations with your friends—not the family. Make the sisters scared to death of you so they don't walk all over your house and appropriate your husband. He's your husband (that's more important than being their brother). Tell Eunice everything and be mad when you're telling her. Say you'd like to talk to his mother about it."

As if Rose would care. Rose preferred to remain distant, above her own children's struggles, especially the boys'. A few years later, when Teddy telephoned her that he and Joan were splitting up, Rose asked sweetly, "Is there someone else?"

Someone? On another occasion, she asked her secretary where Teddy was, and she replied, "In Virginia."

"Virginia?" Rose said. "I hadn't heard of her."

But that was more than a decade in the future. As Jackie wrote her note to Joan, she was still offering advice that might help salvage her sister-in-law's disastrous marriage.

"Don't explain where you will be, don't speak of yourself as a delicate health problem—Don't ask permission . . . Be a bit mysterious . . . then he can't plan things around your absence."

In the trash, there was a second note from Jackie to Joan that would be auctioned off by Alexander Autographs of Stamford, Connecticut. Jackie offered Joan a place to stay at her house if she couldn't take it anymore.

"As you could see, we could both live here for months together and lead completely separate lives."

Like, for instance, Joe and Rose for all those decades of married life.

Rose with the president; Kennedy women were always to be treated with great respect— in public.

"I'll just be here for supper as usual—with children or you."

Joan was already at her wit's end. Jackie tried to reassure her of her own worth, telling Joan how much her own children loved their aunt the way they loved Jackie's sister, Lee Radziwill.

"John said at supper you were his favorite aunt and Caroline said you were her favorite except for Lee, and you were the prettiest!"

Indeed she was. Her brother-in-law, the president, had called her "the Dish." (See Chapter 17.) But it hadn't stopped Teddy from cheating on her. He always grumbled that it wasn't his fault that she became an alcoholic, that like himself, she carried the gene, through her mother.

True enough, but Joan was doomed, like all the women in the family. It was always all about the men. Even Rose, the family matriarch, the mayor's daughter, had her ambitions stifled from the beginning. She had been admitted to prestigious Wellesley College, but was forced to attend a Catholic convent school, so as not to cause "scandal."

Returning from an ocean cruise in 1938, JFK's grandparents, Honey Fitz and Josie Fitzgerald. Honey Fitz cheated on Josie with "Toodles" Ryan, a cigarette girl whom he met at a roadhouse.

Rose couldn't say she wasn't warned. Her own mother, Josie, who would out-live her grandson JFK, warned Rose that "all men are alike, and Joe Kennedy is no different."

Josie was right. In 1920, pregnant with her fourth child, Rose could take no more. She walked out of her home in Brookline and returned to her parents' house in Dorchester. Her father, Honey Fitz, told her she must return to Joe.

"You've made your commitment," he told her sternly, "and you must honor it now."

Or not. Joe and Rose seldom spent much time together. She bore him children, then fled to Paris on shopping sprees. They seldom had sex; after the last time they coupled, in 1931, nine months later Edward Moore Kennedy was born.

As far as Rose was con-cerned, she told friends, "Lust from men is a chore for wives."

Meanwhile, Joe went night-clubbing with his mistresses, using one or another of his henchmen as beards, while his wife went to Mass every morn-ing and played golf in the afternoons.

Even when Joe was practi-cally living with Gloria Swan-son, flaunting his affair in front

Rose was a daily communicant at Mass.

Wife and mistress, part I: Rose and Joe—sitting is Joe's "girlfriend," Janet Des Rosiers.

Wife and mistress, part II: JFK and Jackie—with his ex–gal pal, Princess Grace of Monaco, and her husband, Prince Rainier, White House, May 1961.

of Rose, even traveling together with the two of them, Rose and Gloria, on an ocean liner to Europe, Rose was serene.

"I knew I never had a thing to worry about," she recalled years later, "and I only felt sorry for poor little Gloria."

In her memoirs, Swanson wondered about her rival—if indeed they were rivals for Joe's affection, as if he had any real affection for women.

"Was she a fool?" Gloria wrote of Rose, "Or a saint? Or just a better actress than I was?"

But Rose never forgave her husband for the way he had treated her. When he was having his stroke in December 1961, she left him alone in his bedroom, tended to by her niece Ann Gargan, while she played a few holes of golf at the Palm Beach Country Club. She seemed angry when one of the help arrived on the green and told her she needed to come home.

Until his death almost eight years later, she always traveled with a black mourning dress—just in case.

As her chauffeur, Frank Saunders noted of her new relationship with Joe: "Before, he had been the Supreme Being in the Kennedy house. But after the stroke it was like a little smile came over her face as if to say, 'Gotcha now!'"

Rose's daughters understood what was expected of them. Or most of them did. One who did not was Kathleen ("Kick"), the fourth child, born in 1920. She was vivacious and short with, by her own description, "stumpy" legs.

When her father took her and the rest of the family to London, she fell in love with British high society, and with Billy Cavendish, a member of the nobility. But he couldn't marry a Roman Catholic, and she couldn't marry a Protestant. In 1944, they announced their intention to wed in a civil ceremony.

Rose cabled her: "Heartbroken."

Then Rose checked into a Boston hospital to avoid the press. When Kick was wed in May 1944 during one of Billy's leaves from the British Army, the only member of her family to attend was her older brother Joe, the Navy flier. Three months later, Joe was dead, blown up in a failed combat mission to bomb a V-2 factory in France. A month later, leading his platoon in Belgium, Billy was killed by a Nazi sniper.

Kick remained in England. She took up with another nobleman, a married bounder. In 1948, her father was in Paris, and she and her boyfriend were in Cannes. On a stormy night, they talked a reluctant pilot into flying them to Paris. The plane crashed, and Kick was dead at the age of 28.

In Paris, Joe was staying in a hotel with his pal Joe Timilty, who answered the phone and then had to tell Joe his daughter was dead. JFK, in his first term as Congressman, got the news in Washington as he was listening to a soundtrack of the new Broadway hit, *Finian's Rainbow*.

When JFK's phone rang, the song "How Are Things in Glocca Mora?" was playing. He heard the news, turned to a friend, said of the singer, "She has a beautiful voice," and then broke down in tears.

Only Joe attended Kick's funeral. Her mother Rose, according to Lem Billings, sighed and described her second daughter's death as "a matter of God pointing his finger at Kathleen and saying, 'No.'"

Kick was buried in the Cavendish family plot in Derbyshire. Her headstone said, "Joy she gave, and joy she has found."

However much joy she found, it was more than her older sister Rosemary ever enjoyed. Rosemary was a chore from birth, and as she grew older, her father feared that she would somehow embarrass his sons, for whom expectations were so great. It still seems unclear exactly what was wrong with Rosemary, whether she was "retarded," or simply dyslexic. Rose blamed her daughter's disability, such as it was, on a difficult delivery.

In the 1970s, one of Rose's secretaries, Barbara Gibson, found Rosemary's diaries from a European tour she took with Kick in the 1930s. The JFK Library did not want them; they did not fit the "narrative," as it were, because they made it clear that Rosemary was a fairly typical teenage girl living a not-so-ordinary adolescence in the Great Depression.

This was a diary entry from January 20, 1937, when she visited the White House:

"Went to luncheon in the ballroom in the White House. James Roosevelt took us in to see his father, President Roosevelt. He said, 'It's about time you came. How can I put my arm around all of you? Which is the oldest? You are all so big.'

Does this sound like someone who is "retarded?"

"Rosemary was not retarded," Gibson wrote.

In September 2018, *People* magazine printed excerpts from another, previously unknown, trove of Rosemary's letters, these to a young Irish woman hired to chaperone her during a European trip in 1938.

Pre-lobotomy: Rosemary with her grandfather Honey Fitz.

The nephew of the chaperone told the magazine that the letters "show Rosemary was filled with hope before undergoing the botched procedure."

In one letter, Rosemary proudly describes to her new Irish friend changing planes in France by herself three times and how when she landed, "As I was going off the plane they wanted to take my picture. 'Miss Kennedy, please!'"

The chaperone's family had given Rosemary's letters to Jean Kennedy Smith when she was ambassador to Ireland, hoping they would one day be exhibited at the JFK Library in Boston. All the family got in return for their generosity was a "brief and formal note" acknowledging the Kennedys' receipt of the correspondence. Until the magazine story, no one even knew the letters existed.

The various accounts—hagiographies and otherwise—differ on what led up to her father's decision to have his oldest daughter lobotomized. There are reports that she "propositioned" two waiters at Buckingham Palace, or that she attacked her elderly grandfather Honey Fitz in Hyannis Port in the summer of 1941.

Another story is that Joe read about the procedure and asked Kick, who was then living in Washington, to research it.

"It's not something we want for Rosie," Kick said, but their father was undeterred. Rose later told two different stories—that Joe acted unilaterally, and that it was a family decision.

The prefrontal lobotomy was performed in December 1941 at St. Elizabeth's Hospital in Washington, and it was instantly clear that the operation had destroyed Rosemary's mind. She was quickly packed off to St. Coletta's School in Jefferson, Wisconsin, where she lived the rest of her life.

Joe never saw her again. After his death in 1969, she was allowed to return to Hyannis Port for brief visits in the summer—always accompanied by the nuns who served as her nurses. Observers noted that post-lobotomy, she shared many of the same physical characteristics her father endured after his debilitating stroke—a paralyzed hand, a frozen expression on her face, a tendency to drool. The daughter and her father had one other thing in common: Whenever Rose entered any room they were in, both began to scream.

The family's embarrassment was clear in the various ever-changing stories they told the press for the next half century to explain her absence.

The *Saturday Evening Post* described her as "a schoolteacher in Wisconsin."

Look magazine was told she was "a victim of spinal meningitis."

Eunice Kennedy Shriver, her sister, said: "She has found peace in a new home where there is no need for 'keeping up' or brooding over why she can't join in activities as others do. This . . . makes life agreeable for her."

The *Palm Beach Post:* "It became apparent that Rosemary was different from the rest . . . Mrs. Kennedy was said to have been crushed when her oldest daughter went away."

Eunice Kennedy Shriver tosses out the first pitch at a baseball game.

In *John Kennedy: A Political Profile,* James MacGregor Burns wrote that Rosemary "helped care for mentally retarded children."

In *The Remarkable Kennedys,* author Joe McCarthy said that she "taught" retarded children.

Stanley Friedman in *Those Magnificent Kennedy Women* wrote, "After much searching of conscience, and many visits with doctors and psychologists, it was decided that she would be happier in a Catholic institution."

Perhaps the most disingenuous description of her fate came from Joe Dinneen, the family stenographer at the *Boston Globe.* In his worshipful *The Kennedy Family,* he said that Rosemary's absence was explained by her religious "vocation":

"It was inevitable, perhaps, that she should . . . devote her life to the sick and afflicted . . . She is the least publicized of all the Kennedys. She prefers it that way and her wishes are respected. An individualist who insists upon living her life as she sees it, she has always felt that too much public attention would destroy her effectiveness."

Late in life, Rose told yet another story: "Rosemary's mind is gone completely. That was due to an accident, which I don't really discuss."

In her book, *Rose Kennedy and Her Family,* Barbara Gibson recounted one afternoon after Joe's death, how she and Rose were swimming in the enclosed pool at Hyannis Port, as Rosemary watched, staring straight ahead.

"We were just paddling around, and Mrs. Kennedy, staring sadly at her daughter, said, 'Oh Rosie, what did we do to you?'"

But Rose doted on her male offspring. Her husband's chief nurse after his stroke was Rita Dallas, who wrote a fascinating book, *The Kennedy Case,* about her years at the compound. Before the assassination in 1963, she said, Rose called her "Mrs. Dallas." But after her son's murder, she could never bring herself to say "Dallas" again.

One time, Dallas complained that young Teddy was walking around the compound naked, and that she and the other nurses shouldn't have to put up with such behavior.

"You're a nurse and it shouldn't bother you," she said.

As she grew older, Rose often mused aloud about the fate of her sons. About RFK's murder, she told Gibson, "I don't know what Bobby meant by going away and leaving Ethel with all those children to raise alone."

Going away? That was one way to put it.

Rose kept up with the stories about her sons' White House days, although she couldn't accept everything she read, especially about RFK and Marilyn Monroe.

"I don't believe it could have happened," she told Gibson. "Bobby was always so *sanctimonious.*"

She read the Palm Beach papers every morning—the *Palm Beach Daily News* (the "Shiny Sheet") and the *Palm Beach Post*. One morning in the 1970s on the front page of the *Post* she saw a photo of JFK's girlfriend Judith Campbell Exner. What caught Rose's attention were her breasts.

"That woman with the large breasts," she told Gibson. "How could that have gone on in the White House with all the people and family around?"

Jacqueline Bouvier was not a virgin when she married JFK. She had been deflowered in an elevator in Paris by John P. Marquand Jr., the son of the famous North Shore novelist, the creator of Mr. Moto.

Ironically, the best-known of his father's novels, *The Late George Apley*, features a Boston Brahmin who desperately wants to marry a young Irishwoman who works for his family on Beacon Hill. Appalled at the thought of their son taking someone beneath him as his wife, they forced him to end the romance.

When Jackie told Marquand of her plans, he had the same reaction as the fictional elder Apley:

"You can't marry that mick!"

But she did, and her subsequent travails as Mrs. John F. Kennedy have been endlessly recounted.

"Did you know," she asked one friend, "that married men sometimes don't come home at night and don't tell their wives where they've been?"

For five years, until her marriage to Aristotle Onassis, she was the most admired woman in the world, and also the most sought after. She had her choice of any man in America. But it was all so complicated.

Much like Joe DiMaggio had banned a lengthy list of Rat Packers and Kennedys from Marilyn Monroe's funeral a year earlier, now Jackie had her own blackball list.

Grace Kelly, the former actress and now Princess of Monaco, wanted to attend JFK's funeral with her husband, Prince Rainier. Jackie nixed it; she suspected, with good reason, that JFK had had a fling with Grace Kelly after his marriage to Jackie. Among Grace Kelly's other pre-marital conquests in Hollywood was William Holden, with whom Jackie herself had had an affair, while married to JFK.

In a book proposal, actor Marlon Brando reported that in the mid-1960s, he had a brief affair with Jackie. Imagine what Jackie must have thought in 1967 when she saw the publicity photos in the newspaper of Brando for his newest movie—*The Chase*.

Her lover was posing with his costar Angie Dickinson, another of JFK's Hollywood conquests. The president had even brought Angie to the inauguration in 1961, using as his beard his former Navy pal, Paul "Red" Fay.

After the assassination, Fay had written a memoir of his days with the martyred president. As was the custom at the time, before publication the book had to be cleared by Jackie. And her aide who read the proposed Camelot tomes—Pamela Turnure, who had been yet another of JFK's conquests, and who had followed him from the Senate to the White House to his widow's employ in New York.

Jackie could never seem to escape the old connections. After the death of Aristotle Onassis, one of her longer-term boyfriends in the 1970s was Pete Hamill, the columnist for the old *New York Post,* when it was a liberal, afternoon tabloid.

After Rupert Murdoch bought the *Post* in 1976, Hamill defected to the rival *Daily News* and began bad-mouthing Murdoch. Hamill even got Caroline a summer job at the *Daily News*. When Elvis Presley died in 1977, she accompanied Hamill to Memphis as his assistant. It was great ink for Hamill and his new newspaper.

Never one to turn the other cheek, back at the *Post* the Austra-lian press baron decided to embarrass Hamill—and his new girlfriend,

Jackie O. Years earlier, when she first took up with Onassis, Hamill had written a particularly nasty column for the *Post* about Jackie.

Then Hamill thought better of it, and spiked it before publication. But copies still existed in the newsroom, and the *Post*'s new gossip column, Page Six, began running excerpts of Hamill's decade-old screed under the headline: "WHO WROTE THIS?"

"If it were possible to see the Aristotle Onassis–Jackie Kennedy story as a novel, instead of a rather tedious serial, we could understand Onassis's motives. But understanding Jackie Kennedy is a more complicated matter. She spent part of her adult life hidden behind the Kennedy publicity machine; she spent another crucial part, after the murder of her husband, enshrined as some national object of veneration."

As soon as the first excerpt appeared, Hamill called Jackie to apologize. But all week long it went on in the *Post*, anonymously.

"She was not, of course, the victim of that veneration; she encouraged it, indulged it, created the desire for more knowledge by cultivating the image of aloofness . . . In a world where men have most of the power and money, many women must use guile, intelligence or feigned submission to exist.

"It is outrageous to think that someone will spend $120,000 a year on clothing in a world where so few people have more than the clothes on their backs. It is obscene that a woman would have more money in a month to use on applying paste to her face and spray to her hair than the average citizen of Latin America could earn in 100 years."

On the fifth day Murdoch ran a photo of her and Hamill and printed the money paragraph—her boyfriend's contention that "no courtesan ever sold herself for more."

Jackie blamed "that loathsome Rupert Murdoch." But that was the end of her relationship with Hamill.

Ironically, before taking up with Jackie, Hamill had been running around with Shirley MacLaine, whose brother was Warren Beatty, one of JFK's favorite actors. JFK had even wanted Beatty to play himself in the unsuccessful 1963 biopic *PT 109.*

(Another contender to play JFK was Edd Byrnes from the hit TV series *77 Sunset Strip,* but the president vetoed that choice, saying he didn't want "Kookie," the goofy character Byrnes played in the detective series, portraying the war hero. Such were the pressing concerns of the leader of the Free World.)

But after JFK's death, Jackie briefly hooked up with Beatty, like so many other A-list female celebrities of that era.

By the time Jackie settled down with her final boyfriend, Maurice Tempelsman, the gossip spotlight had shifted to her son, John F. Kennedy Jr. And once again, all the old boldface names would be dredged up. One of his brief liaisons was with Princess Stephanie—the daughter of Grace Kelly, who had been in the car with her in France when she died in a fatal auto accident in 1982.

But John-John had a longer relationship with someone who infuriated Jackie much more than even Grace Kelly's younger daughter—Madonna. She was promiscuous, obviously, but even worse, she seemed to fancy herself the new Marilyn Monroe, and that was one affair of her husband's that Jackie could neither forgive nor forget.

According to Christopher Andersen in his book *These Few Precious Days: The Final Year of Jackie with Jackie,* shortly before her death in 1962, Marilyn somehow got through to Jackie and confessed her affair, adding that JFK had promised to divorce Jackie and marry her.

"Marilyn, you'll marry Jack, that's great," Anderson quoted her as saying. "And you'll move into the White House and you'll assume the responsibilities of First Lady, and I'll move out and you'll have all the problems."

Even Jackie Kennedy couldn't compare to Marilyn Monroe, especially once Marilyn was dead. It's impossible to compete with a ghost. During Jackie's unhappy marriage to Aristotle Onassis, he had complained about her lack of sexy lingerie. So Jackie called up a top New York designer and asked them to custom make her something special—as usual, the order was spare no expense.

"You mean something like," the designer innocently asked, "very Marilyn Monroe?"

"Marilyn Monroe didn't wear underwear," Jackie snapped. The designer had no idea what she was talking about, or why she seemed so angry, until years later, when the stories came out.

Eventually, JFK Jr. split from Madonna, and she went on to a new boyfriend—Warren Beatty. Jackie thought they were made for each other.

Jackie wasn't the only Kennedy woman to take up with showbiz types. They tended to be attracted to men like their brothers and fathers, and, as Truman Capote once said of the Kennedy men:

"They're like dogs. They have to piss on every fire hydrant."

Jean Kennedy found out the hard way. She married a man once described as a cross between JFK and Frank Sinatra—Steve Smith, an Irishman from New York—from a wealthy family, with deep political roots (his grandfather had been a three-term Congressman, like Honey Fitz). Smith was also, as *People* magazine described him, "a notoriously indiscreet womanizer."

At one point Smith was keeping two mistresses—one Irish, one Jewish.

Finally, Jean had had enough. She took up with the Broadway composer Alan Jay Lerner. He had his own ties to the family—he had gone to both Choate and Harvard with JFK and Joe Jr., and he was the composer of *Camelot,* which Jackie after the assassination had designated as the official musical theme of the 1,000 Days.

Jean Smith was serious about leaving her caddish husband. She and Lerner planned to meet in Paris and begin their new life together. Smith flew to Paris and waited . . . and waited. Lerner got cold feet and backed out.

Then there was Maria Shriver. As a rising TV network star, she always tried to portray herself as a good Catholic girl. Actually, she brought one boyfriend after another to Palm Beach. As the family maid Nellie McGrail once observed to another of the help, "She'll never die a-wonderin'."

Finally, she married Arnold Schwarzenegger, an actor who, like Smith, behaved very much like a Kennedy, except in one way—he was a Republican. When he was running successfully for his first term as governor of California in 2003, it was revealed that on one movie

set, he and another member
of the crew had sandwiched a
female—much like his wife's
uncle Ted had done with Sen.
Chris Dodd and the waitress at
La Brasserie in Washington.

The Terminator also
shared another habit with his
in-laws—he had sex with the
female help. He even fathered
a child by the family's married
Guatemalan-born maid, after
which the tabloids began calling him the Sperminator.

The Kennedy women often
introduced their female college
friends to the males in the family. The results were not often
positive. Joan Bennett met Ted
Kennedy through her college classmate, Jean Smith.

Maria Shriver with her husband, CA Gov. Arnold Schwarzenegger at Jackie's funeral in 1995.

A generation later, Kerry Kennedy introduced her classmate
at Brown, Mary Richardson, to her brother Robert F. Kennedy Jr.
Richardson would later hang herself after her husband's serial infidelities.

When her body was discovered hanging in the family home in Mount
Kisco, New York, Bobby Jr. flew into a rage, ordering one of his aides:

"Call her fucking family and tell them to get up here and help me
with the kids."

Violence was seldom out of the question. Teddy killed Mary Jo,
their cousin Michael Skakel was convicted of murdering his 15-year-old
blonde neighbor with a golf club. And Joe, in addition to crippling Pam
Kelley, was known to have a terrible temper.

As his cousin Christopher Lawford put it: "By the time Joe hit the
testosterone-producing years of puberty, he had developed a fairly regular addiction to punching someone over something."

The particular object of Joe's ire was his first wife, Sheila Rauch, a wispy WASP from the Main Line of Philadelphia.

She wrote a book about their marriage, if it can be called that. It was called *Shattered Faith,* and it helped shatter Joe's political career.

"By the end of the marriage," she wrote, "I had simply become afraid of him."

Joe, she wrote, was a chip off the old block, a Kennedy who "has never been exactly an advocate for equality between the sexes."

None of this came as any surprise to anyone who has observed the family for any length of time. As *The New Republic*, a totally reliable Democratic magazine, reported in 1997:

"Tell your average Boston voter that new information has cropped up suggesting that the Kennedys treat women like disposable commodities, throw their influence around to get special favors and don't win any prizes in the noggin department, and you're unlikely to provoke a look of shocked disbelief."

Like the males, the Kennedy women have always had a wandering eye. In *The Dark Side of Camelot,* Seymour Hersh reported that during the JFK administration, three different Kennedy women propositioned Secret Service agents at the White House. One of the Kennedy women was codenamed, "Rancid Ass."

Kerry Kennedy, one of RFK's daughters, married into another New York political family, the Cuomos. But she was soon cheating on her husband, the future governor Andrew, with a polo player named Bruce Colley.

Kerry also introduced the Colleys to her brother Bobby Jr. According to the *New York Post,* Bobby Jr. was soon cheating on his wife, Kerry's old college roommate, with the woman whose husband his sister was cheating with. (Both Kennedy and the woman denied it.)

In 2008, after the messy affair and the subsequent divorce from the future governor, Kerry Kennedy wrote a book, *Being Catholic Now.* It was a *New York Times* best seller, apparently because, as the wags noted, if anyone would know what it's like being Catholic now, it would be probably be a Kennedy in general, Kerry Kennedy in particular.

Years later, in 2012, Kerry crashed her Lexus SUV into a truck in northern Westchester County. She was charged with driving under the influence of drugs, and on the witness stand she admitted that she had been "overtaken" by Ambien. It was another family tradition, Ambien—the same drug her cousin Patrick claimed to have ingested before his 2006 post-midnight accident in Washington, DC.

In 2015, Kerry's youngest daughter, Michaela, age 17, was found unconscious at her family's home in Westchester County, and was transported to a hospital.

A month earlier, Michaela had been in the headlines for selling T-shirts that said, "My having a good ass does not give you the right to be one." She was apparently unaware of the old Secret Service code name for one of her female relatives on her mother's side.

Kerry Kennedy cheated on her husband Andrew Cuomo with a polo player, and then wrote a book entitled Being Catholic Now. *She now makes $352,000 a year running one of her family's "non-profit" foundations.*

A spokesman for her father, the governor, explained that she was selling the "ass" T-shirts to "raise awareness of sexual assault," as if the male members of the family hadn't already done enough to raise awareness of sexual assault over the past century.

CHAPTER THREE

KEEP YOUR FRIENDS CLOSE . . .

Eddie Moore, jack-of-all-trades first for Honey Fitz and later Joe—bagman, fixer, boon companion, procurer, babysitter, etc. Joe Kennedy sold his house at 83 Beals Street in Brookline to Moore. Joe named his youngest son after him. As Hunter S. Thompson once observed, "What can you expect of anyone named after his father's pimp?" Died at the age of 76 in 1953.

McGeorge Bundy, national security advisor. As dean of the faculty at Harvard, he had warned Sen. Kennedy to stop having sex with a Radcliffe coed. When JFK brought the Boston Brahmin to DC, he assigned him a secretary—the former Radcliffe coed with whom JFK was still having sex. Died at the age of 77 in 1996.

Francis X. Morrissey, right, longtime aide to JFK in Boston, took the bar exam 11 times before passing, became a state judge in 1958. Teddy sponsored him for a federal judgeship in 1965, but his nomination went down in flames when his résumé turned out to be totally fraudulent—one of Teddy's first major embarrassments in the Senate. His son and namesake later became a society swindler in New York. Died at the age of 97 in 2007.

U.S. Rep. Torbert MacDonald, JFK's Harvard roommate, who also became a PT boat captain during World War II, was a member of JFK's wedding party, and was elected to Congress in 1954, serving until his death at age 59 in 1976.

U.S. Rep. Nick Mavroules of Peabody, ally of Ted Kennedy in the nuclear freeze movement of the Reagan era. Convicted of extortion in 1993 and imprisoned. Died at the age of 74 in 2003.

John "Honey Fitz" Fitzgerald, former mayor of Boston and Rose's father. Elected to Congress in 1918 over incumbent Peter Tague, but was expelled from the House a year later for massive voter fraud in his campaign, which was managed by his son-in-law Joe Kennedy. At age 79, he ran for the U.S. Senate in 1942 as a straw to weaken U.S. Rep. Joe Casey. Died in 1950 at the age of 87.

W. Arthur Garrity, federal judge whose court-ordered desegregation of the public schools created decades of chaos in Boston. He was a JFK coat holder appointed to the federal bench in 1966. Garrity's order led to massive white flight and civil disorder, but the Wellesley resident was supported by the editor of the Globe, *who lived in Lincoln; the editorial-page editor, who lived in Cambridge; the governor, who lived in Brookline; and of course the senator, from Hyannis Port. Died in 1999 at the age of 79.*

U.S. House Speaker Tip O'Neill, right, who won the election to JFK's Boston-area House seat in 1952 and served until 1986, when he was succeeded by Joe Kennedy II. The old man once told Tip not to expect any appreciation or thanks from his children because "these kids have had so much done for them by other people that they just assume it's coming to them." O'Neill died at age 81 in 1994. On the left is Rep. Michael Harrington of Salem, an anti–Vietnam War ally of Ted's. In 2000, Harrington was charged with making false statements to banks, his law license was suspended, and he was fined $100,000.

Max Jacobson, aka "Dr. Feelgood," the German-born physician in New York who provided amphetamines and other drugs to a celebrity clientele that included President and Mrs. Kennedy. By May 1962 he had visited the White House 34 times to administer injections to JFK, who was so addicted he wanted Dr. Feelgood to move into the White House. In 1975, the state of New York revoked his medical license, and he died in 1979 at the age of 79.

Sen. Chris Dodd (D-CT) front left, drinking buddy of Teddy, ironic, considering that both Teddy and RFK voted to censure his senator father Tom in 1967 on corruption charges. Chris and Teddy took part in the infamous "waitress sandwich" at a French restaurant in DC, and Teddy once drunkenly asked actress Carrie Fisher to have sex with Dodd. (She declined.) In the photo, Ted is on the right, front. Back left is Ted Jr., and on the right is Patrick Kennedy.

Sen. John Tunney (D-CA), law school classmate at the University of Virginia with Ted Kennedy, later a congressman and senator, defeated in 1976 after one term in the Senate. Longtime drinking and womanizing pal of Teddy's. Was dispatched to Moscow by Teddy in 1983 as his unofficial envoy to the Kremlin. Teddy was trying to enlist the Soviets in his attempt to deny reelection to President Ronald Reagan in 1984. In return for the USSR's denunciations of the GOP, Kennedy guaranteed them positive coverage in the U.S. media that he controlled, mainly the TV networks. Teddy's espionage was revealed in KGB documents discovered after the collapse of the USSR in 1989. Tunney died in 2018 at the age of 83.

Joseph F. Timilty, Boston police commissioner and longtime companion of Joseph P. Kennedy, whom he served as bagman, fixer, and "beard," escorting Joe's girlfriends in public places. A bachelor, Timilty was indicted in 1942 and charged with conspiring to allow the operation of gambling houses. A raid on his safe deposit box resulted in the seizure of $300,000 cash. The indictment was quashed by a Democrat judge. His nephew and namesake ran for mayor three times, unsuccessfully, and went to prison for bank fraud. The elder Timilty died in 1980 at the age of 85.

CHAPTER FOUR

IN HIS OWN WORDS: EDWARD M. KENNEDY

The following quotes were transcribed verbatim from the remarks of Edward M. Kennedy, U.S. senator from Massachusetts, 1962–2009.

Is Justice Blind?—1974

"Do we operate under a system of equal justice under law? Or is there one system for the average citizen and another for the high and mighty?"

On the Horrors of Drowning—2007

"Waterboarding is a barbaric practice in which water is poured down the mouth and nose of a detainee, to simulate drowning. It's an ancient technique of tyrants. The prisoner is bound to an inclined board, feet raised and head slightly below the feet. Cellophane is wrapped over the prisoner's face and water is poured over him. Unavoidably, the gag reflex kicks in, and a terrifying fear of drowning leads to an almost instant plea to bring the treatment to a halt."

Patriots Day

"Today, more than two centuries after the embattled farmers stood and fired the "Patriots Day 'Shirt'" 'round the world, the ideals of our founders still resonate across the globe."

National Divisions

"Yet in our own time, there are those who seeks to divide us. One community against another. Urban against rural. City against surba—surba—suburb."

The Nomination of Sen. John Edwards for Vice President

Ted relaxing on the Cape in the 1980s after a dip . . . somewhere.

"I couldn't be happier. All you have to do is watch that announcement in Pittsburgh, Pennsylvania, and when that announcement that John Kerry made—that it was John Edwards, it was like a pistol crack going through the audience."

Generational Change

"Well, uh, not ur-uh really I think, uh, what is, uh, people are-are basically, uh, saying is that they want a new day and a new generation, uh, in this country, uh, at, uh, this time."

His Roman Catholic Faith

"I, uh, think that the—it's a matter of conscience. I'm very familiar with, uh, the, uh, teachings of the, uh, Church on the matters of, uh, grave sin and I have every intention of continuing to, um, to, uh-uh, live my faith in the future as I have in the past."

On His Nephew Michael Not Being Indicted for Raping a 14-Year-Old Girl

"I have nothing to, uh, add from the very beginning, not gonna make any other comment on it, just not gonna make any other c-comment, since from the very beginning, not gonna say anything more about it, still under the, uh, district attorney's, I'm not gonna say anything more."

Paul Tsongas, 1994

"He is not a flake of mine."

Synfuels

"We should expedite the synfuels program through the process of expediting."

Election Night, 2004

"It'll go, uh, John Kerry's way but, uh, you know, uh, I find in my, uh, colleagues and friends on both sides, they really wanna get about the business of addressing the challenges we're facing at home. There is a general sense, uh, among I find Republicans and Democrats alike, that we're just not dealing with the real problems and challenges that we're facing here, uh, at home and I-I think that the—John Kerry—that his great challenge will be to try and bring people together but I think, uh, with those efforts and being sincere about it, uh, he'll work hard at it and I think it can be done. It has to be done."

REPORTER: If Kerry is elected president, can he work with a Republican Congress?

"Well, uh, that's going to be, uh, certainly a challenge. I think there are, uh, members in the, uh, in the in the leadership on the in the

Republican party and among the Republicans that really want to, uh, see progress made on our domestic issues and also in foreign policies. And, uh, I know John Kerry it'll be a challenge in trying to work out, uh, you know these differences because there are a lot of, uh, raw endings, uh, from the result of this campaign. But, uh, I think he's up to the task, I think he, uh, he is ready to take that challenge on as well. It's going to be necessary, it's going to need the kind of skills that John Kerry has. But I know he's capable and will do it."

REPORTER: There is still the possibility that John Kerry might not be elected, that George W. Bush might be reelected. How disappointed will you be?

"Oh I'll be very disappointed. But I don't think I'm going to be very disappointed. Every, uh, indication is, uh, moving in, uh, John Kerry's favor. This is has been a hard, tough-fought campaign. I respect the candidates

Preparing for the inevitable Kerry presidency: left to right, John Kerry, Joe Kennedy II, Ted Kennedy.

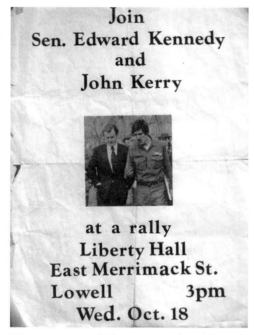

Poster promoting rally for congressional candidate John Kerry with Teddy, Lowell, 1972.

that obviously have been out there, the presidential candidates, uh, the president Bush. But I think, uh, tonight is John Kerry's night and I think we're going to see some, uh, good outcomes in, uh—for our Senate races as well. People have gone to the polls and said they want a new direction, new leadership and I think that's going to be the outcome."

On His Family's "Tusk" Funds

"We have no control over our tusks."

Public Service, 1994

"We are not in public service to make Romneys—make money."

"Working Men and Middle Women"

"People can try and divert attention, people can try as my opponent to say what he's against. But as John and as, uh, Congressman Kennedy have pointed out, at some point you have to say what you're for. And I want to tell you what I am for. I am for the working men and middle women of our great Commonwealth and I am going to fight for their interest in the United State Senate in the remaining days of this Congress and for the next six years as well."

Why Are We in Iraq?

"We didn't understand we were, uh, doing, uh-uh, in Ira-in-ah-in in Iraq, uh, we had, uh, misrepresentations about what we were able to do militarily, uh, in Vietnam. I think we are, uh, finding that out in-in Iraq, uh, as well, uh, that is basically the, uh, the-the similarity."

Winter of . . . Something

"America has heard a long winter of disconnect—disc-disc-discontempt."

Robert Bork's America, 1987

"Robert Bork's America is a land in which women would be forced into back-alley abortions, blacks would sit at segregated lunch counters, rogue police could break down citizens' doors in midnight raids, schoolchildren could not be taught about evolution, writers and artists would be censored at the whim of government, and the doors of the federal courts would be shut on the fingers of millions of citizens for whom the judiciary is often the only protector of the individual rights that are the heart of our democracy."

Facing Problems

"We must face the problems we are facing as we have always faced the problems we are facing."

Statement on 25th Anniversary of Chappaquiddick, 1994

"I bear full responsibility for the tragedy, and I always will. I have expressed my remorse to my family, the Kopechne family and the people of Massachusetts. I only wish I had the power to do more to ease the continuing pain I feel and that Mr. and Mrs. Kopechne feel for Mary Jo's loss."

The Duke Study

"Uh, that's exactly the, uh, the result of the Duke study, uh, that, uh, we, uh, have before us now, uh, what this study shows is that, people, it isn't, uh, the number of elderly people . . ."

Upsetting Budget Deliberations

"We've just passed a 2.4 billion dollar, uh, budget this next year, uh, we would have needed 8 billion dollars out of the 2.4 billion dol-uh, bil-uh trillion–2.4 trillion dollars, uh, for the, uh, funding the No Child Left Behind we got zero money in it, uh, we don't want to misrepresent, uh, this was true in terms of the Medicare system, uh, our Medicare reform and then you see the distortion mispresentation that isn't just a, uh-uh, making me upset, it's upsetting the, the students who are pulling out at a hundred percent."

Membership in the Owl Club at Harvard College

REPORTER: Are you still a member?

"I'm not a member. I've continued to pay about a hundred dollars."

REPORTER: And they do not allow women in that club?

"That's what I understand."

REPORTER: Why would you be in a club like that?

"I shouldn't be and I'm going to get out as fast as I can. It was not a co-education when I got in it 52 years ago. A lot of athletes got in it."

REPORTER: And now you'll get out?

"Yeah."

His New Book: *America Back on Track*

"Uh, people, uh, want to come together and they want to and that they want to deal with these issues but they're not being challenged. Uh, Americans do best when they're challenged . . . and they're together but that isn't what's being asked now. It's appealed to greed, it's appealed to I-can-make-it-it-doesn't-make-much-difference-the-ownership-society-I've-got-mine-it's-too-bad-if-you-don't-have-yours. We need a changed alternative otherwise we are facing these challenges around the world in, uh, India and China in terms of their math, in terms of their science, in terms of their competitiveness."

Privatizing Social Security

"I—I've, uh-uh-eh, have, uh, contacts with the, uh, with some, uh, people, uh, that are, uh, at the White House but other than just general kind of, uh, comments and statements about it, uh, I've, uh, had no, had no real interventions about trying to, to—it, it isn't really complicated. All this president has to do is drop privatization and come to the leader, uh, of the Congress and say let's work it out. I've been in the Senate 1977, 1983, that's what was done and we worked it out and we worked it out in a very, very satisfactory way. Re-Republicans and Democrats support it. That's all that is necessary for this president to do. Just give up the privatization which I think undermines and destroys Social Security and say let's try and work it out, we'll get it worked out."

On a Clear Day

"The message is going to be very kir—"

Who Loves You, Baby?

"Well I-I think it's the, uh, the American people that, uh, I'm-a most, uh, ca-care about and concerned about."

The Intelligence Committee

"And I would hope that, uh-uh, they would, uh, the Intelligence Committees, uh, of the House and Senate would be able to go through this and examine, uh, the, uh, this, uh, information, uh-uh, there was a great deal of material, additional material. I don't know whether all of it was given today—I'm not on the Intelligence Committee—but given to the, uh-uh, inspectors so, uh, we'll just have to, uh, we'll have to wait and see. I think that we oughta whatever we're gonna do has to ought be done, uh, within, uh, the United Nation . . ."

Stampede

"We're not going to let this, uh, stampede that may have gone over in the House of Representatives run roughshod here in the U.S. Senate."

Hard-Working Workers

"Workers who are hard-working whose incomes have been held down over the last period of time."

Republicans and "Scollege"

"They are undermining the scollege assistance programs."

For the Children

I NEED YOU

AND YOUR TWO VOTES

1 September 18, 1962 PRIMARY

2 November 6, 1962 GENERAL ELECTION

EDWARD M. KENNEDY
ENDORSED DEMOCRATIC CANDIDATE
U.S. SENATOR

Edward M. Kennedy Committee for U.S. Senator
Richard J. Dobbyn, 91 Claymoss Road, Brighton, Massachusetts

Ted Kennedy palm card from his first Senate campaign in 1962. He was obviously quite confident of winning the primary.

"The, uh, Congress was, uh, ready to learn, the children ought to be ready to learn when they go to school and ready to learn means, uh, giving those children the kinds of confidence building, uh, that is so essential, uh, in the very early years when their, uh, brains are in the form, uh-uh, formation. We have a million schoolchildren going to school, and that, uh, elementary-secondary education is of, uh-signif-uh, great significance and importance in terms of funding."

One Day, Er, Term at a Time

"People aaaaaaasssskkk me how long I intend to serve. Uh, I said until I get the hang of it. Uh, I'll just take, uh, one term, uh, at a, uh, time."

CHAPTER FIVE

THE RUNT OF THE LITTER'S
RUNT OF THE LITTER

TED KENNEDY WAS THE runt of the litter, and his son Patrick was the runt of his litter, which makes the boy congressman known as "Patches" the runt of the litter's runt of the litter.

"Putting it in racketeering terms," a spokesman for the Republican National Committee explained in 2000, "if the Kennedys were the Corleones, Patrick would be Fredo."

He got his nickname, Patches, from the 1970 Clarence Carter song of the same name, about a young man in the backwoods of Alabama whose father is dying. On his deathbed, Dad tells Patches what is expected of him: "Patches, I'm depending on you, son/To pull the family through/My son it's all left up to you."

It was apparently tough in Alabama back in those days. And his father's words keep going through Patches's mind.

"Patches, I'm depending on you, son/I've tried to do my best/It's up to you to do the rest."

The rest, in the case of Patches Kennedy anyway, hasn't amounted to very much.

He was born at St. Elizabeth's Hospital in Brighton, Massachusetts, in July 1967, during what his family assumed was the interregnum, that brief period between JFK's assassination and whenever RFK reclaimed the family's birthright, the presidency, from the usurper Lyndon B. Johnson, either the following year or, at the very latest, in 1972.

Patches was baptized in Hyannis at St. Francis Xavier Church where, as the *Boston Globe* reported in typical gushing fashion, "his late uncle worshiped as President of the United States."

His godfather was his grandfather Joe, "recovering from an illness," the *Globe* wrote, referring to the debilitating stroke that had totally incapacitated him in December 1961.

Young Patrick is held by his grandfather, Joe, at his baptism by Cardinal Richard Cushing, 1967.

Patches was christened, in the family tradition, by Cardinal Richard Cushing, who told the father, "You've got a beautiful baby, Ted." Outside the church, 300 Kennedy-family fans anxiously waited for a chance to see the former first lady, Jackie, as she left the church.

A few weeks later the Hearst tabloid in Boston, the *Sunday Advertiser,* checked in with its first puff piece on Patches.

"At seven weeks, he looks just like his handsome dad. The same nose. Even a matching hairline. As a bonus, he has his mother's large, dark-blue eyes . . . [and] that sunny-bright red hair—just like his grandfather, Joseph P. Kennedy, had when he was a child. He may be the 26th Kennedy grandchild, but he's going to stand out in the crowd with that Celtic thatch.

"'He's definitely a little Irishman,'" smiles his pretty blonde mother, Joan."

Yes, he was—both his parents were alcoholics. From an early age, despite the Boston papers' gushing coverage, he was a star-crossed child, always getting into accidents and trouble. His mother was soon describing her younger son as "a slow starter."

In 1975, at age 7, he skied into a tree in western Massachusetts, much as his older cousin Michael would 22 years later. Patches, however, survived. Nine months later, now 8 years old, he broke his right wrist falling off a jungle gym at the private school in Washington where he was in the second grade. He learned early on that the rules did not apply to him. A tennis coach instructed him to pick up the balls—routine, right?—and young Patches refused.

"We Kennedys," he haughtily replied, "pay people like you to pick up our balls."

As the years went by, there would be more headlines about "Ted's son"—asthma attacks, an intestinal virus, a tumor on the spine, and so forth. And then, at the age of 17, the first misadventure: "Kennedy's son Patrick robbed of $7 in Hyannis," much like another cousin, the late David, had been mugged in a Harlem hotel known for drug dealing a few years earlier.

Patches claimed to have been buying doughnuts at 12:30 a.m. at a Hyannis convenience store when he was robbed at gunpoint by a black man. But when the alleged perp was arrested a few hours later, police found no gun, and the man claimed it was not a robbery. A few months later, while a student at Phillips Andover Academy, Patches checked into his first rehab facility, for a cocaine habit. His father had been alerted to his pattern of withdrawing hundreds of dollars in cash from ATMs at 3 a.m.

There would be no Harvard College for this particular Kennedy. Nor would he remain in the Ivy League by going to Brown University, like JFK Jr. and so many of his younger kinsmen. He would, however, be matriculating at a college in Rhode Island—Providence College, not so coincidentally the alma mater of his father's best friend and DC drinking buddy, Sen. Chris Dodd of Connecticut.

But there was another reason for moving to Rhode Island. Muckraker Lincoln Steffens once described it as "a state for sale, cheap," and the old man, Joe Kennedy, a "plunger" as he was described by *The Saturday Evening Post,* had always been able to sniff out a bargain.

In the 1940s, one of Joe's best friends on the Cape was Morton Downey Sr., the famous Irish tenor. Joe even cut him in on business deals, like the Coca-Cola bottling franchise in Havana. They had a lot in common—in the 1930s, Downey was a great source of the Broadway showgirls that Joe liked to provide to Jimmy Roosevelt, the president's dodgy, promiscuous son.

Roosevelt had accompanied Joe Kennedy to Great Britain after the end of Prohibition, using his clout as the son of the new president to help Kennedy nail down the import rights to some of the biggest gins and scotches in the United Kingdom. Plus, FDR always held over Joe's head the prospect of an IRS audit—and it behooved Joe to have his own incriminating blackmail material, which was where the showgirls came in. But Downey Sr. and Kennedy had something else in common besides business and blackmail—anti-Semitism. According to Ronald Kessler's biography of Joe, *The Sins of the Father,* Kennedy and Downey used a code phrase for Jews: "Canadian geese."

Down on Cape Cod, Downey's son, Morton Jr., was always welcome to hang around the Hyannis Port compound when Joe was imparting his wisdom to the younger generation, especially the males.

One recurring theme was: Don't screw up and get married on a tipsy whim, as JFK had done with that Protestant bitch Durie down in Palm Beach in 1947. What a mess that was, cost a fortune to get JFK out from under on that one! But another subject Joe liked to expound on his boys' political future.

JFK, of course, had Massachusetts wrapped up. So RFK would have to run in New York, which was fine, because he had spent most of his boy-

Morton Downey Jr., friend of the family down on the Cape, later a controversial TV talk-show host. Died in 2001 at age 68.

hood in Bronxville after the family moved out of Brookline in the late 1920s to escape the stifling anti-Irish bigotry of the Boston aristocracy. As for Ted, Joe would say that Rhode Island would be his ultimate destination.

"Sure, it's small," Downey recalled Joe saying. "But it has two Senate seats, just like New York, or Massachusetts. And it doesn't cost nearly as much to get elected down there."

Downey was telling this story long before Patches entered Providence College. It seems Joe's plan was never totally abandoned, just postponed for a generation.

In 1988, as a 21-year-old sophomore at Providence College, Patches made his move. He would run for state representative in Providence. There was an incumbent, a funeral director named Jack Skeffington—the same last name as the fictional Curley-like mayor in the novel *The Last Hurrah*. He had been an ardent supporter of RFK's presidential run; he had campaigned for him in the Midwest.

But that sort of loyalty meant nothing to the Kennedys. Bob Crane, the state treasurer of Massachusetts, had likewise worked hard for RFK in 1968, in Indiana, not to mention for JFK in 1960. But Teddy had still demanded that he step aside for 25-year-old Joe in 1978. (Crane refused, and the Kennedys backed down.)

"I come from a well-recognized family," Patches later said. "I found a situation where I wanted to run for office, and I was told to wait my turn. That was totally repugnant to me."

Even more repugnantly, Skeffington refused to step aside for the below-average upstart. When Patches appeared on former mayor Buddy Cianci's Providence radio talk show, his future constituents were exposed for the first time to that scintillating intellect of his.

"We need to make sure the streets are sweeped." Not *swept*, but *sweeped*.

Politely asked about his plans by the ex-con host, Patches proposed a program for veterans at a local hospital, which he apparently didn't know was not in the district. Then he referred to "Mount Pleasant Parkway," a road that didn't exist. (There's a Pleasant Valley Parkway that runs through the Mount Pleasant neighborhood.)

"My mistake," Patches said, with that nervous giggle that would become a trademark of his hapless career. "It was a slip of the tongue."

A caller asked him if he could name the streets on either side of his campaign headquarters.

"Um . . ."

Like his cousin Joe in Boston a couple of years earlier, Patches had no idea of his new district's geography. But Skeffington didn't have a chance. Patches reported spending $87,000 to win a job that paid $300 a year. In the run-up to the Democratic primary, the family flooded the district with Kennedys, and only John-John, the brightest star of all, showed even a trace of embarrassment.

"He was a perfect gentleman," Skeffington later told a magazine reporter. "He said, 'I hope you realize that I don't want to be here. I don't like this, but you understand it's my cousin and I was asked to do it. I don't think it's fair.'"

In the legislature, Patches's performance recalled a line from an old Bob Dylan song: "helpless, like a rich man's child." He stumbled through his first two-year term, but in 1991 he began to try to develop a higher profile as he prepared to "move up." He decided to take on the legislative leadership, especially the House speaker, a slick Providence lawyer named Joe DeAngelis, a Rhode Island pol out of Central Casting, with a cigar, a Mercedes, and sharp suits.

Patches, on the other hand, well . . . One day in 1990 he appeared as a surrogate for his father at an event for Sen. Claiborne Pell, a patrician Yankee whose nickname was "Stillborn." Teddy figured it was a good opportunity for the boy to press the flesh with a different, non-Providence, South County crowd.

As one local told *The Weekly Standard:* "But Patrick didn't have a suit, so he showed up in one of Ted's. It was right out of the movie *Big.* It was the funniest thing you ever saw, this guy in a suit five sizes too large, trying to be Dad. That's when we started calling him 'Ted Lite.'"

He began demanding campaign-finance reform, which infuriated DeAngelis and the rest of the boys. Patches was the one who was taking in all the dark money—all by himself he was grabbing one fifth of all the money the entire legislature collected in campaign contributions. But he was putting the knock on *them,* and what was even more exasperating, Patches seemed totally oblivious to his own hypocrisy.

Pretty soon reporters in Providence and Boston were getting videotape compilations of Patches's greatest hits on the floor of the House. In one video clip he pleaded with another legislator: "What do I say?"

The now-defunct *Boston Phoenix* reported that the tape also "includes a floor speech by a confused Kennedy that is such a mishmash of sentence fragments and interrupted thoughts that it borders on the absurd."

It was, in other words, a preview of coming attractions on Capitol Hill.

Patches, however, was angry that he was being mocked. He hadn't come to the legislature to be made sport of.

"This outrages me," he said. "There are reams and reams of tape and they select a point where I am bumbling. I'm not perfect."

Those imperfections would be more evident than ever a month later, when he flew to Palm Beach to spend Easter with his family. It was, as his father would later say, a traditional Easter weekend. Much of Patches's deposition is covered in Chapter 12, and it was a treasure trove of Kennedy arcana, with Patches as usual providing more than his share of incoherence.

Asked when he and his cousin Willie, the accused rapist, had gotten to Au Bar, Patches replied, "We arove around 12:30." Not arrived, *arove*.

How was the dance floor? "Partly crowded."

As for the victim, the woman from Jupiter whose face would be covered during the trial by a blue dot, Patches described his discussion of her with cousin Willie: "In my view this was a person, like I said, sort of a *Fatal Attraction* you couldn't get rid of, and was saying all sorts of wild things and that is the way he had conveyed it to me."

Then, he said, he heard that his grandmother's urn—what his father called Rose's "yearn"—had been stolen.

"I thought, bingo, it is probably Willie's whacked-out friend."

After the alleged rape, but before the trial, his mother Joan was arrested yet again for drunk driving. Even the *Globe* was forced to mention Ted's drinking, and not in the usual way, which was to run a story every sixth year—whenever Teddy was running for reelection—about how he was "turning his life around."

Finally, Patches and his two siblings—both of whom were also drunkards—decided that an intervention was in order. It was just before their cousin Willie's rape trial in West Palm. Teddy and Patches would both be witnesses—on live national TV. The children went to the family home in McLean, Virginia. Teddy closed the sliding doors on his porch, with a scenic view of the Potomac River in the distance. Then he settled into his usual blue suede chair.

As Patches later recalled in his 2015 book, the children told their besotted father, "Dad, we're concerned, we're worried about you, and we think you're drinking too much."

Their heads, Patches recalled, were down. The three alcoholic children were weeping for their alcoholic father. It was an emotional scene—for them. For their father, it was just another betrayal, Patches told *60 Minutes*.

"What he heard was that we were abandoning him when he felt most vulnerable to the world and the judgments being made about him and his fitness as a father, a senator, and as a man. We suddenly became part of the chorus of criticism that isolated him and made his life harder."

Teddy wasn't ready to dry out. And he never did.

"Uh, he stood up, you know, opened the sliding door and walked out. And then he wrote me a letter. And he basically said, you know, 'for the time being, you know, don't think of coming by to, you know, visit.'

"That's the way it came down, He felt that we really had no place, no place whatsoever to question him. That's the defensive position of every alcoholic. Go mind your own business. Back off! That was the message."

The family code, Patches said, was to not talk about it—ever.

"And it doesn't matter whether it's in a private therapy session. That psychiatrist could go out and tell somebody."

As his mother Joan and his older brother well knew. At least one woman who attended Alcoholics Anonymous meetings with Joan later sold a story about Joan's recovery to one of the supermarket tabloids. As for Ted Jr., after the Au Bar scandal broke, he had checked himself into what the *National Enquirer* called a "booze clinic" in Hartford.

Within days, the *National Enquirer* had a full-page story about what Ted Jr. had said at the 12-step meetings: "I hate my father! He's a boozing, skirt-chasing embarrassment to me. I hate being a Kennedy. I can't take it anymore—I'd rather be dead."

In 1994, one of the two U.S. House seats in Rhode Island opened up. After the disastrous beginning of the Clinton presidency, it was shaping up as a big Republican year—in fact the GOP would soon take over the House of Representatives for the first time in 40 years. But Patches was the overwhelming favorite to reclaim the seat for the

Democrats. It didn't matter that his father was, as Ted Jr. described him at the rehab center, "a national laughingstock," or that Patches was a regional laughingstock.

As the old political saying goes, You can't beat somebody with no-body. Even if the somebody is just Patches Kennedy.

Rhode Island had, and still does have, a tradition of electing wealthy politicians not especially attuned to the realities of life in the gritty state, usually but not always patrician Yankees like "Stillborn" Pell, Sheldon Whitehouse, or the Chafees. Nonetheless, despite his family's residual popularity in the heavily Catholic state, Patches felt compelled to ex-plain his background.

"Being in the unique position that I am," he said, "in coming from the family that I've come from, not to have to worry about making mends meet . . ."

Making mends meet. It became one of his most famous quotes, er, malapropisms.

His GOP opponent was Dr. Kevin Vigilante, an articulate physi-cian, an accomplished adult—in other words, everyone Patches wasn't. He was far from a "nobody." Patches's first congressional campaign was the subject of a brilliant documentary by Josh Siftel, *Taking On the Kennedys.* Vigilante found an old lady whom Patches had stiffed on the rent for an apartment and turned it into an effective TV spot.

But the highlight of the documentary, and of the campaign, was a televised debate on Providence's Channel 6, which Patches's handlers insisted on scheduling against a New England Patriots Monday Night Football game, to ensure minimum viewership—the traditional tactic of a prohibitive favorite.

Vigilante came out swinging, comparing his real job, and real re-sponsibilities, with Patches's failure to make 850 roll-call votes in the part-time legislature.

"All you have to do is vote and you don't even do that. If you were in the private sector, in a real job, you'd have been fired."

All Patches could do was smile.

Then Vigilante asked him a question that's always applicable to a Kennedy—for someone who talks so much about the need for the rich to pay their "fair share," what exactly is your fair share?

"The big question is," Vigilante said, "do you pay any taxes at all, or is it all in tax-free municipal bonds? We need to know whether you pay taxes like the rest of us."

Again, no answer. Just a vacant smile.

The moderator asked Patches one question that he fumbled through, after which Vigilante gave an adequate, if not particularly sparkling, response. But as soon as the Republican finished, Patches piped in.

"I agree with that!" Patches said. "Dr. Vigilante said it as I would like to say it. He said it very well. That's what I was trying to get across."

A big issue at the time in Rhode Island was the situation with the supposed overfishing in Georges Bank. Patches was ready with a response.

"Any of the dollars that are coming through to help those fishermen to, uh, stay off the Georges Bank because it's being overfished, uh, we ought be very careful how those dollars are appropriated, uh, so New Bedford and Fall River fishing vessels do not capture the business that Rhode Island fishing vessels have been smart enough to anticipate because we were ahead of the curve in trying to fish for these other species of fish that were not being overfished."

At the time, his father was running for reelection against Mitt Romney, who for a while had appeared to be running at least even in some polls. As always with their backs to the wall, the Kennedys had gone down and dirty—Joe Kennedy, his uncle's nominal campaign manager, had questioned Romney's Mormon faith. Even the fawning *Boston Globe* was appalled. Joe had been forced to issue an abject apology to Romney, but the issue was still in the news, so the moderator asked Patches what he thought of his Roman Catholic family's use of the religious issue against Romney, given their own travails in the 1960 presidential campaign.

First, Patches tried to make a joke of it. When nobody laughed, he went into his now-customary deer-in-the-headlights pose, his lips moving, but no words coming forth. He looked like he was back on the witness stand in West Palm Beach. In the fetal position.

"Uh," he finally said, "I was trying to make light of something that, uh—"

The reporter asked the question again.

"Religion," Patches rotely replied, shouldn't be—play a factor in anyone's candidacy."

So have you brought up your concerns with your father?'

"Uh, no, I haven't."

He won easily, and was off to Congress, a member of the shrunken Democratic House caucus, a minority for the first time since 1955. Patches continued living *la vida loco*.

"I put vodka in Poland Spring bottles," he said later, "and I put Oxycontin in Bayer Aspirin bottles."

Patches worshipped President Bill Clinton. After all, Clinton was practically an honorary Kennedy—almost as venal as Patches's grandfather, almost as promiscuous as Uncle Jack, almost as chameleon-like in his politics as Uncle Bobby.

Early in his presidency, Clinton gave Patches a ride on Air Force One. Patches handled his opportunity the way he did most things—he got rip-roaring drunk and spent most of the flight throwing up.

The next time the Clintons were vacationing on Martha's Vineyard, the Kennedys decided to return the favor by inviting the president out for a sail. Afterward, Patches was gushing about his proximity to the leader of the free world, sounding as smitten as a certain future White House intern by the name of Monica Lewinsky.

"I'm sitting next to him, and he's talking to you, and he's asking for something for lunch, and my family is there, and I realized, 'Oh my God. It's just an incredible feeling to be that close to the president of the United States. The president of the United States!'"

The fact that Teddy was showing the president around the sight of his own greatest scandal—Chappaquiddick—did not go unnoticed. David Letterman, the CBS late-night host, did one of his trademark

Top 10 Lists: "Things Overheard During the Clinton/Kennedy Sailing Trip:"

10. "No Bill, I'm not seasick—I always throw up this time of day."

9. "Isn't there a way to catch fish that are already fried?"

7. "Who wants another Chivas and saltwater?"

4. "If you're outside U.S. waters, it's technically not adultery."

1. "Ship ahoy, Cap'n Tubby!"

Patches got along with the new Republican leadership in the House about as well as he had with the lunch-bucket Democrats in Providence. The GOP congressmen were older, they'd worked their way up, they didn't suffer fools gladly. And they tended to call Patches "son."

Rep. Gerald Solomon was an ex-Marine from upstate New York. In 1996, he was speaking about the absurdity of the proposed ban on "assault weapons."

"Shame on you!" Patches screamed at him. "Families like mine know all too well what the damage of weapons can do!"

Solomon, a combat veteran of the Korean War, couldn't believe he was being heckled by . . . Patches. He challenged him to "step outside." When Patches remained seated, Solomon angrily mentioned his wife Freda, the mother of his five grown children, living in the country by herself five nights a week.

"She has a right to defend herself when I'm not there, son," he told Patches. "And don't you ever forget it."

Another time, Bob Barr, a Republican from Georgia, quoted JFK on the floor of the House. Afterward, Patches followed Barr into the hall and began screaming at him, in front of reporters, "You quoted my uncle!"

Barr tried to calm down the obviously impaired Patches, calling him, "Son." That angered Patches even more.

"I am a duly elected member of Congress!" he screamed.

"I am duly impressed," Barr told him.

In the House, however impaired he invariably was, however wretchedly he behaved, because of his last name Patches would always be tolerated by his fellow Democrats. He was under the wing of minority leader Dick Gephardt, who wanted to run for president. With his father's connections, Patches could raise big money—he quickly became chairman of the Democratic Congressional Campaign Committee (DCCC).

The reality of the Democratic caucus was that the party was hemorrhaging "blue dog Democrats"—the kind of normal working people who had always been the base of the party.

Among the new Democrats—the Congressional Black Caucus, Massachusetts gays like Barney Frank and Gerry Studds, and professional New York leftists like Chuck Schumer and later Anthony "Carlos Danger" Weiner—Patches's utter lack of real-life experience with, among other things, employment, sobriety, marriage, or education, didn't seem nearly as much of an aberration as it would have even a decade or two earlier.

But beyond the echo chamber of the national Democratic party and its media cheerleaders, Patches became a national joke, drunkenly stumbling through hearings and speeches, mumbling incoherently about such issues as "the fundamental process of due process."

One day, he was hectoring FBI Director Louis Freeh at a hearing: "What is your answer to the fact that . . . minorities and poor people have a greater likelihood of being put to death than they have of getting cancer from smoking?"

Neither Freeh nor anyone else had any idea what he was talking about. They did, however, recall that Patches had changed his position twice on capital punishment.

He observed none of the collegial niceties either. At one point, he filed a civil racketeering lawsuit against Republican House whip Tom DeLay. DeLay was just the sort of person Patches could never figure out—a born-again Christian and former pest exterminator from Texas.

Even President Clinton's shadier operatives, understanding how many fund-raising skeletons they had in their own closets, refused to endorse the crackpot scheme to take down DeLay, especially since Patches was being directed by a lawyer from Perkins Coie, the Democratic law firm that in 2016 would act as a cutout for Hillary Clinton's campaign to funnel money to Russians for the bogus "dirty dossier" that corrupt FBI agents used to obtain a court warrant to surveil the campaign of future president Donald Trump.

In March 2000, Patches's DCCC fund-raising duties took him to Hollywood, and when he arrived—or was it *arrivé?*—at LAX for his return flight, he had a "carry-on" bag about the size of the state he represented in Congress. An elderly black woman security guard making $9.64 an hour—in other words, a likely Kennedy sympathizer—tried to stop him.

Patches shoved her, hard. Everything was caught on the surveillance cameras. First he denied anything had happened, but then, after being confronted with the video, his lawyers provided him with a new excuse.

According to Patches, the old woman "voluntarily and unreasonably proceeded to encounter a danger that was known to her"—to wit, presumably, a Kennedy. Didn't she know who he was?

Finally, Patches was in the headlines that so many Kennedy males eventually find themselves confronting: "Kennedy charged in assault on woman."

She threatened to sue—she was, after all, a member of at least three protected classes. Patches was apoplectic. After all his family's antics at airports and on commercial flights—cutting in line, demanding upgrades to first class, wandering drunkenly down the aisles—Patches was the first one ever to be sued.

He refused to settle.

"I've said I'm sorry for the last time," he said. "Enough is enough, and I'm not going to become a human ATM machine."

Then the case disappeared. Presumably because he had in fact become a human ATM machine.

That summer, Patches rented a 42-foot sloop and set off from Martha's Vineyard on a cruise with a 33-year-old woman. One evening, the Coast Guard got a mayday call from the woman's ex-boyfriend, whom she had called. The Coast Guard sent a boat out of New London to meet the sloop.

"She seemed concerned for her safety," a spokesman for the Coast Guard told reporters. "She did not feel safe on the boat, and she wanted to be removed."

This was a year after his father's yacht had run aground on Cape Cod, with a crew of two men, five much younger women, and "scores" of empty beer cans as well as assorted bottles of wine and liquor. The Coast Guardsman who handled press inquiries that time had been forced to call back reporters he'd spoken to and retract his statements— it was either that or a transfer to the Aleutians for the winter, Boston journalists suggested. But this time the woman was actually trotted out to alibi for Patches.

"Yes," she acknowledged, "Patrick had been drinking . . ."

But she wasn't concerned for her safety. In other words, it wasn't a Mary Jo Kopechne–Pam Kelley type situation. Meanwhile, a few days later, the Coast Guard came across an unmanned, unmoored yacht floating in shallow waters—it was Patches's rented sloop. He had abandoned it.

The owners had it towed back to port and were shocked by its condition. Patches had totally trashed it. His office issued a statement—the boat was a "lemon." But a few months later, his insurance company wrote a $42,000 check to the yacht owners.

Back in Washington, serving in a body where certain niceties are almost invariably observed, he blurted out more ridiculous statements, not just about Republicans, but also his fellow Democrats. In 2001, a female intern of Rep. Gary Condit (D-CA) disappeared. Her name was Chandra Levy. Condit was initially a suspect.

Back in Rhode Island for the summer recess, Patches helpfully pointed out to a reporter in Pawtucket that if Condit were convicted of murdering his intern, that "would not only force him to resign, but to go to prison."

Then Patches apparently realized what he'd said, and asked himself, aloud, "Am I saying anything out of school?"

Then he answered his own question incorrectly: "No."

Then he added of Condit: "I think he's a nice man. I have trouble believing he's the kind of person who could murder someone or who could perpetrate violence."

Blundering ahead, Patches then pointed out that perhaps the disappearance was just a coincidence unrelated to the fact "that Gary Condit happened to be having an affair with Chandra Levy."

When the story appeared in the local newspaper, the first post on the message board said, "We do not need an opinion from a Kennedy on the treatment of women!!!!!!!!"

His House mentor, Dick Gephardt, ran for president in 2004 and Patches put one of the Missouri congressman's bumper stickers on his ancient Mustang. Perpetually drunk and stoned, Patches had become a walking old-time country song.

"What Made Milwaukee Famous, Had Made a Loser Out of Him."

"Drinkin' Doubles Don't Make a Party."

The bill came due, like his income taxes, on April 15, 2006. It was 10 a.m., in Portsmouth, Rhode Island. Patches was on his way to the local CVS drugstore, where, as one local newspaper wag pointed out, "they sell many bottles that have labels pasted on them, 'Do Not Operate Heavy Machinery' after ingesting."

He was driving a 2003 Crown Vic owned by the Friends of Patrick J. Kennedy, trying to make a left turn into the pharmacy's parking lot.

Oblivious to his surroundings, he turned directly into the path of a 2000 Nissan driven by a 46-year-old man from Bristol. His Crown Vic was T-boned, demolished. The cop writing the incident report said Patches "appeared normal" but his handwritten statement indicated otherwise. It was totally illegible.

As always, the Kennedy public relations machine sputtered into action. The story didn't end up in the *Providence Journal* until six days later, when it appeared under the East Bay Sports Bulletin Board beneath a story headlined, "Two Arrested After Newport Tagging Spree."

Patches' handwritten accident report to the Portsmouth Police Dept., April 2006, with a very shaky signature.

Predictably, the story got front-page treatment in the *Boston Herald* and was totally ignored by the family's bow-tied retainers at the *Boston Globe*.

Three weeks later, Patches took the Acela from New York to DC. He sat in the club car, he recalled in his 2015 book, and drank eight straight nip bottles of vodka. Two days later he got into an even more serious traffic accident.

This time he was in Washington, DC, at 2:45 a.m., and he smashed his Mustang with the Gephardt for President bumper sticker into a barricade at the Capitol, almost hitting two police officers. He had no lights on, and after getting out of the car he began staggering around until the cops arrived. They asked him where he had been and he said, "A bar." They asked him where he was going and he said he was on his way to a "vote."

The cops drove him home. They knew who he was.

This time the headline was, "Kennedy Involved in Early-Morning Accident."

His office issued a statement saying alcohol was "not involved," but by that time, there was a new headline running on the wire stories:

"Officers Claim Brass Interfered in Investigation of Kennedy Accident."

The union for the Capitol Police said their uniformed cops had been forbidden to perform field sobriety tests and "collection of evidence" was not permitted. This kid-gloves treatment, the union said, "created the appearance of special favor for someone who is perceived to be privileged and powerful."

A few weeks later, Patches went to court, had his driver's license suspended, and was fined $300. Afterward, he spoke to reporters, accompanied by his new Alcoholics Anonymous sponsor, Rep. Jim Ramstad (R-MN). The usual questions were shouted out: "Were you drinking? Will you resign?"

He ignored those taunts, but then someone asked him, "Were you treated like everyone else?"

"I was treated fairly," he replied.

Patches tried to say all the right things.

"I'm very grateful to be on the road to recovery."

It's been a long road, the road to recovery for Patches, a long and winding road. This time it would lead to the Mayo Clinic in Rochester, Minnesota. But before he left, he darkly suggested to the *Providence Journal* that he'd been framed by a waitress—a Republican waitress—at his favorite watering hole in DC.

That night, a caller to a local radio station left this doggerel about the congressman:

"There once was a boy named Patches/Who got into a lot of car crashes./He claimed he had a condition,/Said 'twas a family tradition/ Now bad driving comes to its fruition."

In the fall, he gave an interview about his alcoholism to the *New York Times*. A few days later, his aunt, Patricia Lawford Kennedy, died at the age of 82. At the funeral, he recalled in his book, his father couldn't stop ranting about the humiliation Patches had brought upon the family.

"He called the article a disaster—the word he always used to describe the most extreme situations," Kennedy wrote in his book. "How dare I talk about the family this way? How dare I say 'these things' in public?"

Less than two years later, in May 2008, his father collapsed on Cape Cod and was airlifted to Mass General. The diagnosis: brain cancer. Teddy died in August 2009 at the age of 77. Patches's always tenuous grip on sanity snapped. Drunk, he tried to make a speech on the floor of the House, but was physically prevented from entering the chamber by his staff. He returned to Massachusetts to campaign for the Democrat running to fill his father's Senate seat. Her name was Martha Coakley. Patches called her "Marsha."

She lost, to a state senator and former male model named Scott Brown. Patches criticized him for wanting to be sworn into office immediately after the election— which was exactly how his father became a member of the Senate, the day after he was handed the seat in November 1962.

By 2010, a poll by a Providence TV station indicated that Patches's favorability rating in his district was upside down, like his

Patrick hugs his father at national convention, Charlotte, North Carolina, 2008.

father's 1967 Oldsmobile Delmont—35 percent favorable, 62 percent unfavorable. In March, seven months after his father's funeral, he delivered a slobbering, incoherent speech on the floor of the House, describing the national press corps as "despicable."

He didn't seek reelection. He couldn't. He was succeeded by the gay mayor of Providence. In January 2011, for the first time in 64 years, no member of the Kennedy family was in elective federal office. Patches went on a late-night show on ABC—the most obsequious of all the groveling broadcast TV networks—to discuss current events one final time.

As usual, everything he said seemed slightly off-kilter, or at least an unfortunate choice of words. He described the recent shooting of a Congresswoman in Arizona by a paranoid schizophrenic as "the culmination of something that was brewing." Brewing?

He talked about his new job as a visiting fellow at Brown University's Institute for Brain Science—it didn't seem like a natural fit for Patches, brain science. But he did have an interest in mental health— "the moonshot to the mind," he gushed. "We gotta do it."

Moonshot? Some more cynical viewers wondered, was Patches's moonshot anything like a Jell-O shot? And then of course he was asked about his father.

"When his light shined on me alone, there was no better feeling in the world."

As one wag asked, when his father's light shone, was Patches . . . lit?

The interviewer asked him about the infamous 2:45 a.m. crash at the Capitol in 2006.

"I don't recall much about that night."

Two months later, he announced he was getting married. This was another surprise, and of course the jokes wrote themselves. Where would the lovebirds be registered—CVS or Walgreens? Was Patches taking her for his wife, or his designated driver?

Like so many members of his family, Patches had an unfortunate fascination with nautical terms, and he said of his bride: "She has helped me navigate the uncharted waters of life."

"Abandon ship!" advised one Boston newspaper columnist. "Mayday! Mayday!"

By then, Patches had finally sobered up, or so he claimed in his 2015 book. He finally put down the bottle on what would have been his father's 79th birthday, on February 22, 2011.

"I was still reeling from his loss," he wrote. "My (future) wife expected me to go on a bender."

Four years later, his book was published. Its title: *A Common Struggle: A Personal Journey Through the Past and Future of Mental Illness and Addiction.*

It was a typical Patches mash-up. He told the *Globe* his mother "helped him with the project."

Joan responded with an email: "I had no knowledge that Patrick was writing a book and did not assist him in the project in any way."

His older brother, Ted Jr., a state senator in Connecticut, issued his own statement: "I am heartbroken that Patrick has chosen to write what is an inaccurate and unfair portrayal of our family."

Patches now lives in Delaware, with his wife and four young children of his own and one stepchild. A return to elective politics is not anticipated.

CHAPTER SIX

BROTHER-IN-LAWFORD

ETER LAWFORD WAS AS close to being a Kennedy as any in-law could be.

Patricia Kennedy's husband was an alcoholic, a drug addict, bisexual, promiscuous, fond of ménages à trois, and prostitutes. He was scandal-prone, lazy, notoriously cheap, voyeuristic, attractive in a superficial way, and easily impressed by Hollywood celebrity.

Peter Lawford's favorite photo of himself with President Kennedy, on board a Coast Guard yacht, 1961. JFK's take: "Who would believe I'm listening to you?"

As J. Edgar Hoover once scribbled in the margins of an FBI report: "Lawford is just a bum."

No wonder he was President Kennedy's favorite brother-in-law.

Steve Smith, married to Jean Kennedy, managed the family's finances from a suite of offices on Park Avenue. Sargent Shriver, married to Eunice Kennedy, worked at the family's Merchandise Mart in Chicago and later ran the Peace Corps.

But Peter Lawford served a much more important role for the leader of the free world. He was JFK's leading West Coast purveyor of what the president called "poontang."

JFK had plenty of procurers on the East Coast—Dave Powers and Kenny O'Donnell first in Boston, later in Congress and on the campaign trail and finally in the White House. Then there was Bill Thompson, the Florida East Coast Railway lobbyist, a jack-of-all-trades for JFK in both Palm Beach and Washington. And of course Bobby Baker, the Senate Democrats' bagman who operated his own little prostitution ring of sorts out of the old Carroll Arms Hotel at First and C Street.

But on the West Coast, it was up to Peter Lawford to come up with the starlets to sate the president's insatiable lust. And he delivered. His beachfront mansion, in Santa Monica, was the unofficial First Trick Pad of Camelot. Which was why it was bugged, perhaps by multiple unfriendly entities, as early as 1959.

By the summer of 1962, Lawford, like his friend Marilyn Monroe, was using pay phones to communicate with the White House. He knew everything, but unlike so many other family intimates—in-laws, girlfriends, kinsmen, staffers, even fellow members of Alcoholics Anonymous—Lawford never spilled the beans.

Several times over the final unhappy decades of his life, he began writing projects, but they always foundered when he refused to tell all.

"Jack was a wonderful person and a wonderful president," he was quoted as saying near the end of his life. "And I'm not going to blacken his name no matter how much I need the money."

No wonder James Spada called his definitive biography, *Peter Lawford: The Man Who Kept the Secrets.*

Lawford was born in London in 1923, the product of a Kennedy-like scandal. His mother was married to a junior British Army officer, but his biological father was the captain's CO, a general, a World War I hero.

His mother, May Lawford, "a dreadful snob," as she was described, said later that "Peter was an awful accident." She was 17 years younger than Peter's father, whom she married after a tawdry divorce that the Fleet Street tabloids splashed over their front pages for weeks.

Buffeted by the scandal, basically banished from polite English society, the general and May and their young son lived a nomadic existence, usually short of money. His mother dressed him as a girl until he was 11. In France, young Peter suffered a near-crippling injury to his right arm, which would render him 4-F during World War II. In 1937, he ended up in Hollywood and appeared in one film, *Lord Jeff*, with child stars Mickey Rooney and Freddie Bartholomew.

However, Lawford was unable to obtain any more film work, so the little family, more or less destitute, drifted back east, and ended up in Palm Beach. "Royalty," such as the Lawfords were, were always in short supply in Palm Beach, and it was here that Peter made his first connection with the Kennedy clan that would consume his life.

He got a job as a parking attendant at the lot around the corner from Worth Avenue, Palm Beach's premier shopping district. Now paved, the lot is still there. The owner employed three boys—two blacks and Lawford. If business was slow, the three would pass the time under a spreading shade tree in the lot, playing penny-ante poker.

One of the regulars was a "heavy cat," as they called him, because he tipped them a quarter rather than the usual dime. It was, of course, Joe Kennedy—up from the working class himself, he was always a good tipper, unlike most of his over-privileged descendants.

But Joe had one complaint about the parking lot, which he raised with the owner. It concerned the poker game.

"It doesn't look good to see the niggers sitting under the tree with the white boy."

That was the end of the Worth Avenue poker game.

As World War II began, the Lawfords found themselves back in Southern California, living in a motel. Peter supported the family with the meager wages he earned as a movie usher. But this time, Peter had more luck in Hollywood. With universal conscription, acceptable-looking young males were in short supply, especially Englishmen. Lawford soon found himself cast in the top movie of 1942, *Mrs. Miniver.*

His one line in the Academy-Award winner for Best Picture, to Greer Garson: "The Jerries are over London in the hundreds. Looks like a big show."

Soon he had a contract at Metro-Goldwyn-Mayer (MGM), the most prestigious studio in Hollywood. He got plenty of work, of course, but there was only so far a man of his limited talent could go, even in a national emergency. As Judy Garland, another MGM contract player, later told him: "You're a *lousy* actor! You were *never* a good actor! The only reason you were at MGM was that all the *good* actors were in the *war*!"

Probably the greatest success of his film career came in 1946. He starred in the sequel to *Lassie,* playing second fiddle to the collie, who was in reality an ill-tempered male named Pal. Pal, unlike Lawford, had his own dressing room. His life was insured by the studio for $1 million—$1 million more than Lawford's.

"Lassie," Lawford later recalled, "was a vicious bastard."

With Hollywood's leading men back from World War II, Lawford was quickly relegated to light comedies, one of the first Hollywood genres devastated by the postwar spread of television. Lawford later described his MGM roles in the late forties with two words: "Tennis, anyone?"

As his MGM career slowly wound down, he was linked with a number of A-list actresses: Rita Hayworth, June Allyson, Lana Turner, Judy Garland, Judy Holliday, and Ava Gardner. He was also rumored to have had homosexual liaisons with, among others, Keenan Wynn, Van Johnson, and later Sal Mineo. He frequented notorious men's rooms on public beaches.

At one point his mother May, in a fit of pique, went to MGM mogul Louis B. Mayer's office and told him that her son was in fact a homosexual. It was an act of daring recklessness—Peter was her sole support, and her octogenarian husband was dying. Mayer brought Lawford in and gently suggested the standard procedure of the day for homosexuals—a series of monkey-gland injections.

Lawford indignantly refused. He pointed out the swath he was cutting among the leading ladies of Tinseltown. Plus, he was patronizing hookers—which would become a lifelong vice. As time went on, Lawford found himself more and more attracted to black whores, the darker-skinned the better, according to Frank Sinatra's valet, George Jacobs, in his book, *Mr. S.*

All the while he was continuing to live at home with his dysfunctional parents. His greatest personal expenses were the $50 hookers that LAPD detective Fred Otash warned him to stop patronizing as early as 1948.

Lawford banked most of his MGM salary, so he was prepared when his contract wasn't renewed in 1952, as MGM cut its golden age overhead. It was nothing personal—Clark Gable and Lionel Barrymore, among many others, also got their walking papers around the same time.

So Lawford was far from the only one-time star whose career was on the ropes. Frank Sinatra, with whom Lawford had appeared in a couple of MGM musicals, had likewise fallen on hard times, but soon resurrected his career with his Oscar-winning supporting role in *From Here to Eternity.*

But even as he mounted his comeback, Sinatra was still in love with his second ex-wife, Ava Gardner, with whom he had a tempestuous relationship. In 1953, Lawford and his manager, Milt Ebbins, bumped into Ava, his old MGM studio flame, and they made a date to have a drink a few hours later. Lawford was anxious, knowing how Sinatra might react if he found out, but it wasn't really a "date date," so he went ahead.

But a gossip columnist's legman spotted them, and in the morning editions an item appeared, minus the mention of Lawford's manager at the table. Sinatra was livid. He called Lawford at 2 a.m., as soon as he read the early edition.

"Do you want your legs broken, you fucking asshole?" Sinatra bellowed. "If I ever hear you're out with Ava again, so help me, I'll kill you!"

They didn't speak again for five years. It was a harbinger of things to come.

Without a studio contract, Lawford did what he always did. He drifted. As in his early days in Palm Beach, he became a professional guest, an amusing dinner companion.

In the summer of 1952, he found himself at the Republican National Convention with an old benefactor, Henry Ford. And he was introduced to a vivacious young woman, Patricia Kennedy, daughter of "the Ambassador," doing what amounted to opposition research as her brother Jack ran for the Massachusetts Senate seat held by one of Dwight Eisenhower's most prominent supporters, Henry Cabot Lodge.

Pat Lawford worked first in radio, then TV—Catholic TV. She was eight months younger than Lawford, getting up there in 1950s marrying terms. Her likely husband was Frank Conniff, a reporter for the International News Service, the Hearst newspaper chain's wire service, a typical Red-baiter of the era. (He called big-band leader Artie Shaw "the Communist-loving clarinetist.")

Conniff would have passed muster with Joe; he had done business with William Randolph Hearst, and just after World War II JFK had worked, in a manner of speaking, as a Hearst correspondent. Conniff would eventually win a Pulitzer Prize and go on to edit the final iteration of a Hearst newspaper in New York, the doomed hybrid *World Journal Tribune*. But Lawford outmaneuvered Conniff, who at the time was posted as a foreign correspondent in Tokyo. After Pat accepted his proposal, Lawford was introduced—or, reintroduced—to the old man in New York.

"If there's anything I'd hate for a son-in-law more than an actor, it's a *British* actor."

He also couldn't keep his eyes off Peter's red socks. But he had done a background check on Lawford, courtesy of his friends in Hollywood and J. Edgar Hoover. Louis B. Mayer, the head of MGM, assured Joe that, rumors to the contrary, Lawford was not gay.

The FBI backed that up—with reports of his assignations with hookers that had turned up during a federal "investigation of white slave activities in Los Angeles, California." That impressed the old man—he and his sons enjoyed the company of hookers themselves. Lawford couldn't be all bad. Joe was also pleased by the fact that Lawford had more than $100,000 in the bank, so he wasn't another of those damnable would-be gigolos who were always buzzing around the girls.

One small note in the FBI report: his 1941 employment as a "parking lot attendant at Peruvian and Coconut, Palm Beach, Florida."

If this refreshed Joe's recollection of the white kid under the tree, he apparently never mentioned it to his future son-in-law. The Lawfords were married in Manhattan in 1954, but not at St. Patrick's Cathedral on Fifth Avenue, and not by Cardinal Francis Spellman, the notorious gay cardinal originally, like the Kennedys, from Massachusetts. The reason was that Lawford was not a Catholic, although he had agreed that the children would be raised in the Church.

The night before the wedding, the Kennedys and Lawford were partying at El Morocco, a swank Manhattan nightclub. Around 3:30 a.m., only Torbert MacDonald, JFK's Harvard classmate and future congressman, remained in the bar. He was soon in a brawl over a woman with a descendant of James G. Blaine, the 19th-century Republican Speaker of the House from Maine.

Blaine, ironically, had been about to be elected president in 1884 when one of his supporters made a speech denouncing the Democrats as the party of "rum, Romanism, and rebellion." It cost Blaine the election—he lost New York, with its large Irish-Catholic population, by fewer than 1,000 votes.

Now, ironically, one of Blaine's descendants "flattened," as the tabloids gleefully put it the next day, one of the liegemen of the family that would finally win the White House for the party of, well, in the Kennedys' case, certainly rum and Romanism, if not rebellion.

When the Lawfords returned to the West Coast, there was another small irony—the leased home they moved into turned out to be one of the love nests Joe Kennedy had used in the late 1920s during his torrid extramarital affair with Gloria Swanson, among many other Hollywood starlets.

Peter's mother, Lady May, was predictably not impressed by these typical Kennedy shenanigans. She sneered that her new in-laws were "barefoot Irish peasants."

At the time of his marriage to Pat Kennedy in April 1954, Lawford was more famous nationally than his senator brother-in-law and the rest of the family. But that was changing rapidly. On their honeymoon in Hawaii, they stopped into a movie theater and saw a newsreel headlined, "Pat Kennedy Marries Actor."

As late as the Democratic National Convention in 1956, Lawford was recognized more often in public than the senator, but their careers were headed in opposite directions. He starred in two short-lived TV series. In the later one, *The Thin Man,* he again had to risk being upstaged by a dog, this time the wire fox terrier Asta, whom he described as a "monster."

Lawford's *Thin Man* was never confused with the classic MGM series starring William Powell and Myrna Loy, and it was cancelled after two seasons.

In 1958, Lawford made the worst decision of his career—perhaps at the behest of his father-in-law, who himself never had the best taste in film even in his days as a semi-successful Hollywood producer of schlocky B movies. A small-time producer named Albert "Cubby" Broccoli had bought the rights to an increasingly popular series of British spy novels, and was looking for an experienced but youngish English actor to play the role of the secret agent.

Lawford turned down the chance to become the first James Bond 007.

Perhaps his shrewdest financial move of the decade came in 1956, when he had a chance to buy Louis B. Mayer's beachfront estate in Santa Monica for $95,000. It was a "fixer-upper" by then, but Lawford couldn't resist the location, or the fact that he'd be living in his former boss's old house.

In 1958, with JFK's political star rising, Pat Lawford met Frank Sinatra at a dinner party at Gary Cooper's house. Peter was tied up on the set of *The Thin Man*. One thing led to another and soon the two sort-of-old friends were reconciled. The fact that Pat Lawford was JFK's sister was crucial; Sinatra was desperate for political access.

Soon, Lawford was a member of "the Rat Pack," Sinatra's boozy, carousing crew of show-biz celebrities. They were all talented in one way or another—Sinatra, Dean Martin, Sammy Davis Jr., Joey Bishop—all except Peter Lawford.

Lawford did bring one asset to the table, though—a script he and Pat had bought a few years earlier that would become the basis of the hit movie(s) *Oceans 11*. While it was being shot in Las Vegas in the winter of 1960, the Rat Pack worked nights in the showroom of the Sands Hotel. It was a revolving cast of Rat Packers, and the joke in Vegas became that

Peter Lawford, center, with the Rat Pack: Dean Martin, left, Sammy Davis Jr., right. Sitting: Frank Sinatra.

the worst luck a tourist could have would be to show up on the night Peter Lawford was performing solo.

Sinatra cut Lawford in on all the Rat Pack movies; he even handed him a piece of his popular Italian restaurant in LA, Puccini's. In return, Lawford named his third child, a girl, Victoria Francis Lawford, her middle name in honor of Sinatra. More importantly, he brought around his senator brother-in-law. On a break from the primary campaign in the winter of 1960, JFK caught the show at the Sands (and met Judith Campbell, Frank's old girlfriend). Later, JFK and Lawford visited Sinatra in Palm Springs.

As Sinatra's valet George Jacobs said, "JFK was far more in awe of Mr. S. than Mr. S was of him. Because Frank Sinatra controlled the one thing JFK wanted more than anything else: Pussy!"

In his book, *Mr. S,* Jacobs recounted asking Sen. Kennedy what he wanted.

"'I want to fuck every woman in Hollywood,' he said with a leering grin."

Lawford was in with the in crowd again, but he still treaded lightly around Sinatra. One day in Palm Springs Jacobs stumbled on the two brothers-in-law snorting cocaine. The senator was nonchalant—"For my back, George," he explained.

Lawford, however, was frantic. "For God's sake, George, don't tell Frank."

The marriage of Pat and Peter had never been great. Between the hookers, the afternoons in the tearooms, and, increasingly, the drugs, it was increasingly strained. Their sex life had never been much to begin with, or so Lawford said. In later years, he would tell people his wife would make the sign of the cross before having sex.

"It was like fucking the Pope," he said.

In 1960, Lawford finally became a U.S. citizen, to vote for his brother-in-law. He was getting work—in *The Longest Day,* among others, but, as one of his friends put it, "Your pictures are getting bigger but your parts are getting smaller."

His drinking continued to get worse, as did his self-pity. He was quoted as saying, "I seem to have lost my identity."

At another point, Lawford ruefully looked back on his life in Hollywood and said defensively, "I had a career before I even met Pat Kennedy." Pause. "If you could call it a career."

But he still had the Rat Pack movies—at least until 1962. That was when JFK decided he couldn't stop over at Frank Sinatra's house in Palm Springs. JFK was in an impossible situation—J. Edgar Hoover had informed the president that he knew that his girlfriend Judith Campbell was also the girlfriend of Sam "Momo" Giancana, the boss of the Chicago Outfit.

Giancana was tight with Sinatra, had stayed at his estate in Palm Springs. The thought of the president staying in the same mansion as one of America's top mobsters (although he already had in the past, as had his father before his stroke in 1961) was unthinkable.

RFK made the decision—the trip to Palm Springs couldn't be cancelled, but instead the president would stay with another crooner—Bing Crosby. Bing Crosby! A Republican, Sinatra's musical rival from the early 1940s, when he'd knocked the older man off the top of the charts. They'd always competed with one another. Bing had an Academy Award for Best Actor; all Frank had was his Oscar for Best Supporting Actor.

Lawford had nothing to do with the decision, but as he had a decade earlier when Peter had a drink with Ava Gardner, Sinatra totally overreacted, blaming his humiliation on Lawford. The Lawfords had a guest room in the Palm Springs house, and Sinatra tore it apart, throwing all their clothes into the pool.

"Now I know how whores feel!" he told Jacobs. Sinatra cut Lawford out of the next two Rat Pack movies. In revenge, he replaced him in *Four for Texas* with Bing Crosby.

At the same time, Lawford had gotten into a serious affair with Lee Remick, a very married actress with two children under the age of 3. Hedda Hopper, the Hearst gossip columnist whose item about the drink with Ava had ruined Lawford's relationship with Sinatra in 1953, now ran an intriguing item with no names:

"I don't like blind items, but I guarantee if this one hits the papers it will curl hair from Washington to Santa Monica."

Santa Monica? Washington? Could the item have been any less "blind?"

A few days later, Hopper (whose son was at the time playing the role of detective Paul Drake in the TV hit series *Perry Mason*) ran a follow-up item about what she called "Hollywood's most hush-hush romance."

"The two parties evidently don't seem to care who knows. They dined in a popular restaurant, and if he's not careful he may lose his million-dollar baby."

A few weeks later, the Lawfords hosted a dinner party at their beach-front home. Pat stationed herself at the front door to greet the guests as they arrived. Remick arrived with her producer husband.

"Hello Pat," she said, "I'm Lee Remick."

"And I'm the million-dollar baby," Pat Lawford instantly replied.

At least, though, Lawford still had his "career." But not for long.

As the president's West Coast pimp (especially with Frank Sinatra on the outs), Lawford was tasked with arranging JFK's assignations with Marilyn Monroe, which had been going on at least since the 1950s, maybe even further back to her days as brown-haired Norma Jean Baker.

Lawford told his later wives that the president often had sex with Marilyn in the guest wing of the Lawfords' beachfront home. Lawford also said that on occasion, JFK called him in to take photos of himself nude in the bathtub with Marilyn Monroe.

In California, the president indulged in another odd habit, or so Lawford told his fourth wife, who later recounted the story in the *New York Post*. Like all the Kennedys, he never carried cash, always counting on his friends to pick up the tab. To keep up his image as a Hollywood star, Lawford carried a sizable roll. On more than one occasion, he told Patricia Lawford Stewart, he saw the president grabbing his money and pocketing it. No longer in the chips, Lawford would complain, and JFK would laugh.

"Oh Pee-tahh," JFK would say, according to the fourth Mrs. Lawford, "it doesn't matter."

In 1962, Marilyn was 36, an aging sex goddess. Never all that stable, now she was falling apart. That spring, Lawford escorted her to Palm

Springs where she spent the night with the president at Bing Crosby's house (they were seen together by reporters, who naturally filed nothing). Then, their final coupling occurred at the Carlyle Hotel in Manhattan after Marilyn sang at the president's 45th birthday party at Madison Square Garden in May 1962.

By then, though, she was basically RFK's girl. Like Marlene Dietrich and Judith Campbell before her (and most likely Mary Jo Kopechne afterward), Marilyn had been passed down.

Taking more and more drugs, she began to believe that RFK would dump Ethel to marry her. She was fired from her last movie; there have always been rumors that she had an abortion in the summer of 1962.

By late July, she was out of control, threatening to hold a press conference to reveal her affair with the brothers. Lawford, himself a drunken mess with his own career in shambles, was pressed into service.

In late July, a week before her death, he accompanied Monroe on Frank Sinatra's private plane to the Cal-Neva Lodge in Lake Tahoe, once owned in part by Joe Kennedy, now controlled by Sinatra and Chicago mobsters.

It was by all accounts a horrific weekend. A few days later, an FBI bug of Giancana's suburban Chicago headquarters picked up gangster Johnny Roselli (like Joe Kennedy a former resident of East Boston) telling his boss, "You sure get your rocks off fucking the same broad as the brothers, don't you?"

Early Monday morning, after flying back to Santa Monica, Lawford cadged a ride home with the pilot of the plane. On the way to the beach, Lawford asked him to pull over so he could use a pay phone. Logs show that he placed a 30-minute call to the White House.

That Friday, RFK, Ethel, and several of their children flew to San Francisco, ostensibly for some law-enforcement conferences. That Friday night, Marilyn got several anonymous calls at her new bungalow in Brentwood: "Leave Bobby alone, you tramp. Leave Bobby alone."

The next day, RFK and Lawford visited Marilyn. Fred Otash, the former LAPD detective who was by then a high-priced private detective, had been bugging Lawford's house since 1959. And he, or someone, had also placed listening devices in Marilyn's home. Otash later claimed he heard RFK storming through the house that afternoon, screaming at Marilyn, "Where is it? My family will pay you for it!"

Lawford invited Marilyn to join him and Pat at a small dinner party they were hosting that evening. At some point—the timing remains unclear—RFK flew back to San Francisco. But sometime around 7:30 that night, Lawford and Marilyn spoke for the last time.

"Say goodbye to Pat," she supposedly told him, "say goodbye to the president and say goodbye to yourself, because you're a nice guy."

A few hours later, she was dead. The circumstances, and who was present when she died, will never be known. But apparently sometime early Sunday morning, Lawford, even though he was drunk, called Otash.

Together they drove to Brentwood and grabbed the diary and whatever other incriminating evidence that RFK had been looking for. The next day her former husband, Joe DiMaggio, arrived, and fruitlessly searched for anything he could find. There was no diary, no suicide note, no nothing.

As the FBI, the LAPD, and local scandal-sheet reporters scrambled to get the records of Marilyn's final phone calls, DiMaggio made funeral arrangements—"no damn Kennedys!" he declared.

Lawford flew to Hyannis Port with Marilyn's assistant, who had screamed "Vultures!" at the press outside her boss' bungalow that Sunday morning. She soon embarked on an around-the-world cruise, after which RFK got her a federal job in Washington, 3,000 miles from Hollywood.

His marriage in ruins, in January 1963 Lawford flew to DC with his manager Milt Ebbins to personally inform the president that he and Pat would soon be seeking "Renovations," as gossip columnists used to call Nevada divorces. According to Spada's biography, JFK appeared unconcerned, and told Lawford a divorce from his sister shouldn't prove to be a problem.

But then Ebbins piped up, and pointed out to the president that the day after the divorce was announced, three photos would appear on the front page of the *New York Times*—Peter's, Pat's, and the president's.

JFK considered for a moment, nodded, and then asked Peter to hold off on the divorce until after his reelection in 1964.

On November 22, 1963, Peter Lawford was in Lake Tahoe, appearing in a stage act with his old friend Jimmy Durante. Knowing how much Pat now detested him, the family's original plan that Friday night was for Lem Billings, JFK's gay friend from Choate, to fly to LA and then accompany Pat to Washington for the funeral.

But Pat insisted on observing the niceties of America's premier Roman Catholic family—she would attend her brother's funeral with her husband, dissipated and broke as he now was.

Friday night, Mr. and Mrs. Lawford took a commercial flight from LA to Washington. On board, Lawford ran into a producer he knew who was also a client of "Dr. Feelgood," who provided narcotics to the stars, including JFK and Jackie.

Lawford begged some pills off his friend, and Pat arrived in DC stoned out of her mind, acting "silly," according to Spada.

At the White House, the Lawfords stayed in separate rooms. But Peter was, as always, horny, so early Monday morning, the day of JFK's funeral, he grabbed his manager, Milt Ebbins, and ordered a White House car. He arranged a quickie with a stewardess he'd been hooking up with for a while. She had worked on the press plane during JFK's campaign. Ebbins asked him if he thought that was a good idea, to take a White House vehicle to meet a girlfriend, on the morning of his brother-in-law's funeral.

Lawford didn't care. He and Ebbins got in the car and he told the driver to take them to the Shoreham Hotel. When they arrived, Lawford said he'd only be a few minutes, but then left Ebbins and the driver waiting in the car for an hour.

The day after the funeral, as the rest of the family mournfully trekked to Hyannis Port for Thanksgiving, Lawford flew back to Tahoe to resume his gig with Jimmy Durante. The decision was not well-received either by the family or the public.

The Lawfords officially split in 1965, and Pat moved back to New York with the children. Pat told him he needn't worry about providing child support, but Peter insisted. So a deal was worked out under which he would pay $400 a month for the children's upkeep. He made two payments and never made another.

His health was beginning to fail. At the Lahey Clinic in Boston, Spada reported, he was told to stop drinking, and that if he didn't, he would likely soon develop cirrhosis of the liver. He left the clinic, went directly to a bar, and ordered a martini.

In June 1966, he and Jackie Kennedy took their children on a joint vacation to Hawaii. Pat was apoplectic, even though it was apparently innocent enough—as innocent, anyway, as anything involving the Kennedys and sex can be.

Lawford's showbiz career was in tatters. Except for Sammy Davis Jr., the Rat Pack considered him persona non grata. In 1967, when Sinatra was in London filming *The Naked Runner*, he stormed out of a disco, telling his valet he wanted to throw up "because everyone talked like Peter Lawford."

In 1968, RFK was running for president. Lawford was an investor in a popular West LA disco, The Factory. In May, *Life* ran a big spread on Hollywood celebrities working in the various presidential campaigns. Paul Newman, a supporter of Sen. Eugene McCarthy, was on the cover.

And inside was a full-page photo of Lawford, in a black turtleneck, wearing a string of hippie beads. He had a shaggy haircut, was smoking a cigarette, and in front of him on a table were two glasses—one a mixed drink, the other a wine goblet. The Kennedys were not pleased.

Still, RFK was planning to hold his victory party after the California primary at The Factory. After his "on-to-Chicago" victory speech, he took a short cut through the kitchen of the Ambassador Hotel and was fatally shot in the head.

Another Kennedy funeral, another disaster for Brother-in-Lawford. He flew to New York with Ebbins for the Mass at St. Patrick's Cathedral. The invitation was for one person only, but as he was checking into his hotel, Lawford met an attractive, very young woman whom he immediately invited to accompany him to the funeral Mass.

Ebbins later told Spada: "This girl went out and bought a black miniskirt, a black hat, and black gloves. Christ, the dress was so short it was *obscene*."

In the cab to Fifth Avenue, Ebbins pleaded with Lawford not to bring the woman into the church, and finally Lawford realized he was on the verge of making a terrible mistake. He begged Ebbins to take her inside. Ebbins refused.

"She wouldn't let go of him," Ebbins recalled. "It was awful. The Kennedys were absolutely furious with him."

He lived another 16 years, but it was nothing but misery. He married three more times, each time to an ever-younger woman. Their memoirs, as well as Spada's biography, are a litany of one disaster after another.

His demands for sex became increasingly kinky. On one first date, the woman told him she had to go to the bathroom and Lawford immediately asked, "Can I watch?" When his son Chris came to visit him, Lawford set him up with one of his girlfriends and then insisted on watching them have sex. Once, he allegedly gave Chris, a drug addict at the time, cocaine as a gift. By that time, Lawford was a small-time dealer himself. On other occasions, he would invite his children out for dinner, then ask them to pick up the tab.

Before his death in 2018, Chris remembered his visits to his father in Los Angeles.

"Peter and I would stay up all night doing dope together and talking about family problems. We'd have what seemed like a breakthrough—saying we loved each other and hugging and all that. But the next morning it would be all gone. He'd snap at me and absolutely cringe if I called him 'Dad' instead of 'Peter.'"

Before he died of a drug overdose in 1984, David Kennedy told authors David Horowitz and Peter Collier about how he and Chris Lawford visited Peter in the summer of 1971.

"I knocked on the door and there's Peter Lawford. I hadn't seen him in years. The first thing he does after saying hello is offer me a pipe full of hash."

For a while he was one of Johnny Carson's top guest hosts on *The To-night Show*. But that gig ended after he attended a party in New York one night with Carson and brought along marijuana that had apparently been sprayed with some PCP-like substance. Carson ended up in a suicidal mood on a ledge. Like Sinatra, Carson blamed Lawford and cut him off.

Lawford was basically destitute. When the beachfront mansion in Santa Monica was finally sold, his cut, after taxes, liens, etc., were paid off, was a mere $14,000. Yet he continued to spurn big-money offers for his memoirs about JFK and Marilyn Monroe.

According to Spada, when one of his later wives threatened to kill herself, he told her, "Don't leave any notes."

Another time, he grew angry with one of his women and began yelling, "Who do you think you are?"

"I'm your wife," she responded.

When an old friend asked Lawford why he'd married one of them, he replied, "She gets me drugs."

His last wife's maiden name was Patricia Seaton—another Pat. Under her later married name, Patricia Lawford Stewart, she wrote a book, *The Peter Lawford Story*, in which she recounted a story about calling Ted Kennedy in 1980 during his unsuccessful campaign for president. She was 22 years old, not even married to Lawford, and she needed a favor—Richard Pryor, the comedian, had set himself on fire while freebasing cocaine. Pryor's wife had called Lawford to see if he could get the comedian an autographed photo of his former brother-in-law.

Patricia got on the phone with the senator in Boston.

"Hi kid, how are you?" Teddy said. "I hear you're the young one. You have big tits."

He began asking her when she was flying to Boston.

"The more he talked," she wrote, "the more I realized that he wanted to have sex with me. I was expected to go to Boston and service the patriarch . . . I was the new Kennedy woman. I was the young one with the big tits. I was the woman he was going to have because he had not had me yet. . . . He asked about my age and was thrilled to learn that I was 22. Apparently he liked them young."

Afterward, she called Lawford, expecting him to be outraged. Instead, he thoughtfully considered Teddy's proposition for his girlfriend.

"We haven't been getting along all that well lately," he finally said. "Maybe it would be a good idea for you to go see Teddy."

As Stewart noted, "Peter hated Teddy Kennedy the man, yet Peter felt compelled to go along with the head of the Kennedy family. It as an emotionally devastating situation that caused me to feel both pity and disgust for both men."

Lawford still followed current events. In 1976, it was revealed that Judith Campbell had been a "friend" of President Kennedy's. Lawford, who had been present at the beginning, so to speak, was fascinated when she was subpoenaed to testify before a Senate committee—and even more amazed when the lawyer assigned to represent her just happened to be picked from the law firm of Sargent Shriver, another of JFK's brothers-in-law.

Shriver insisted that it was all just a coincidence, that the fix had not been put in to silence JFK's "friend."

"If you believe that," William Safire of the *New York Times* wrote, "give my regards to the Tooth Fairy."

Lawford wasn't buying it either. He told Stewart that nothing ever changed with his erstwhile in-laws.

A couple of years later, Lawford made one final attempt to reconcile with Frank Sinatra. First, he sent him a groveling letter saying that the diminutive Sinatra appeared to have "grown about 10 feet." But Sinatra never replied, so Lawford tagged along with a friend who had rented a private jet to fly to Las Vegas. Lawford reserved a table at the Sands to see Sinatra's show. But then Sinatra found out that Lawford was in the audience.

"Two very large men came by the table," Stewart wrote, "and explained that Mr. Sinatra would not perform as long as Peter was in the room. Either we left or there would be no show for anyone. . . . It was another devastating blow to his ego."

In September 1983, his daughter Sydney married a TV editor from Boston on Cape Cod. Pat wanted to shun her ex-husband, but Sydney insisted that he be invited to attend the ceremony. After a long night drinking with some of the younger Kennedys, on the day of the wedding a reporter for the *Boston Herald* found Lawford in the hotel bar guzzling triple vodkas and looking "pale and dissipated."

"I wish I could dry out and kick this stuff," he told the reporter. "It's taking its toll, isn't it?"

As he walked his daughter down the aisle of the church to the altar, he tripped and fell down. At the reception, Lawford was totally wasted, accompanied by a young black woman with an open bottle of champagne in her hand.

The next day, the Sunday *New York Times* ran a brief story about the society wedding. The *Times* got his age wrong—he was 60, not 67, but that mistake was quite understandable. By this time Lawford actually looked like he was about 87. The *New York Times* story also included one note that seemed to sum up the new generation of Kennedys: "Sydney Lawford's cousin, Robert F. Kennedy Jr., 29, was absent. He was charged Friday with possession of heroin in South Dakota."

In December, Lawford finally checked into the Betty Ford Center in Rancho Mirage, California. He made a few bucks tipping off the *National Enquirer* to other celebrities drying out there. He also paid a drug dealer to fly cocaine in to him, landing a small private plane in the desert and leaving it for Lawford to pick up at his leisure.

As part of his recovery, one of Lawford's tasks was to write letters to people he had wronged with his addictions. He balked at the 12-step-like assignment, saying

Peter Lawford with his daughter Sydney at her wedding in Hyannis, 1983.

he'd never really hurt anyone but himself, but finally he dashed off letters to his father and his late brother-in-law, President Kennedy.

"My dear Jack," he began, "I have managed to drink myself into the B.F.C. My liver drove me down and here we are—it's a very pretty Stalag 17 which is supposed to help one back to the world of sobriety . . . You, my friend, would hate it—not a pretty girl within miles and every time you turn around, you trip over someone's ego. . . .

"How are Marilyn, Bobby? Give them my love. If you should run into Steve McQueen or Vic Morrow, give them my best. . . . Love, Peter"

He stayed at the Center for five weeks. After going home, he remained sober . . . for three days. He died on Christmas Eve 1984 at Cedars-Sinai Medical Center. His last words were to his second, younger wife by the name of Patricia: "I'm sorry."

The headline in the Hearst newspaper in Los Angeles on Christmas Day was "Peter Lawford Dead at 61," with the subhead, "Kennedy In-law Was Last to Speak to Marilyn Monroe."

The second Mrs. Patricia Lawford decided to have his body cremated, which is contrary to Roman Catholic doctrine. The Kennedys were angry, and they refused to pay for the interment of Lawford's ashes. Chris Lawford called the woman with the same name as his mother who was 35 years younger to deliver the bad news.

"We convened a meeting at Mummy's," said the young Lawford, "and we decided Daddy wasn't worth it."

The *National Enquirer* finally picked up the tab.

CHAPTER SEVEN

. . . AND YOUR ENEMIES CLOSER

Foster Furcolo, standing, longtime Democratic rival of JFK in Massachusetts. When he had the temerity to run for the Senate in 1954 against GOP incumbent Leverett Saltonstall (JFK didn't want to share the spotlight with another young ethnic Democrat), JFK called him a "goddamn guinea" and refused to endorse him. Furcolo was governor in 1960 when JFK was elected president and wanted to appoint himself to the Senate, but JFK forbade it—Joe Kennedy told Jack, "I bought that seat and it belongs to me." A placeholder was appointed until Ted could turn 30 and run in 1962. Furcolo was later indicted for conspiring to arrange bribes for members of the Governor's Council. The charges were eventually dismissed. He died in 1995 at the age of 83.

Ronald Reagan, the host of the popular TV anthology series General Electric Theater. *RFK wanted to eliminate him as a potential political rival. According to his son Michael, Reagan was fired by GE President Ralph Cordiner, who told Reagan that he "had been contacted by Bobby Kennedy, who had said, 'If you want government contracts, get Reagan off the air.'" Four years after his 1962 firing, Reagan was elected governor of California.*

J. Edgar Hoover, the FBI director, called RFK a "despicable little shit." With his longtime boyfriend Clyde Tolson, who said of RFK in 1968, "I hope he gets his ass shot off." Hoover died in 1972, Tolson three years later.

Traphes Bryant, the White House kennel keeper, author of Dog Days at the White House, *one of the first tell-all books about JFK. A sample: "I even heard him say to one of his buddies, 'I'm not through with a girl until I've had her three ways.'. . . Nowadays he would be called a 'swinger.' Then he was called just plain wild."*

Sen. Eugene McCarthy of Minnesota ran for president against LBJ on an anti–Vietnam War platform, and after he did surprisingly well in the New Hampshire primary, RFK jumped into the race. McCarthy refused to bow out for RFK. As he famously described his differences with Kennedy: "He plays touch football, I play football. He plays softball, I play baseball. He skates in Rockefeller Center. I play hockey." McCarthy died in 2005 at the age of 89.

James Michael Curley, former mayor, governor, and congressman, forced JFK's grandfather Honey Fitz out of the Boston mayor's race in 1913 by threatening to reveal his affair with cigarette girl "Toodles" Ryan. Sent to prison twice, for the last time in 1946 while mayor of Boston. Curley died in 1958 at the age of 83.

Cong. Joe Casey of Clinton, a New Deal stalwart who ran for the Senate in 1942. Joe Kennedy regarded him as a threat to his sons' political future, so he and his cousin, political fixer Joe Kane, decided to eliminate him. The Kennedys put Joe's 79-year-old father-in-law into the primary to drain votes from Casey, and they hired priests in Boston to spread the false rumor that Casey's new bride was pregnant when he married her. Casey won the primary, but the smears fatally weakened Casey and he lost the general election to incumbent Sen. Henry Cabot Lodge. Joe got his wish—Casey's career was over. He died in 1980 at the age of 81.

Ed McCormack, nephew of Speaker John McCormack. As Massachusetts attorney general, he ran for the Senate against Ted Kennedy in 1962, famously telling Teddy during this debate that if his name were Edward Moore, "your candidacy would be a joke." McCormack said election to the Senate "should be merited, not inherited." Another of his slogans: "I back Jack but Teddy ain't ready." The Kennedys started a whispering campaign that McCormack was taking a Navy disability pension. Teddy won easily. McCormack was indicted in 1993 on conflict-of-interest charges, but a judge dismissed the charges. He died in 1997 at the age of 73.

Billy Bulger, right, longtime president of the Senate and later UMass, and brother of infamous gangster and serial killer Whitey Bulger, with JFK Jr. From Southie, he was naturally a McCormack man (the Speaker had made sure Whitey was treated well while he was in federal prisons from 1956–1965). When he was solicited by the Kennedys for a Ted endorsement in 1962, then-state Representative Bulger insisted on being taken to Locke-Ober, the city's premier restaurant at the time. Bulger ordered the most expensive dish on the menu, lobster Savannah, then an astonishing $10. For decades, Bulger told the story at his annual St. Patrick's Day breakfast—how he'd taken the Kennedys for a ride.

Sen. Thomas Dodd (D-CT) father of longtime Teddy drinking buddy and future senator Christopher Dodd, seen here with LBJ, whom he supported against JFK in 1960. Unlike his son, the elder Dodd despised the Kennedys. According to his aide James Boyd, after campaigning with JFK in 1960, Dodd said of Kennedy and his supporters, "He eggs them on by reaching for their hands. You can't fool like that with crowds. Someday these monkeyshines will lead to a disaster, and remember that I foretold it." After JFK's assassination, Dodd told Boyd, "It will take us 50 years to undo the damage he did to us in three years." In 1967, he was censured by the Senate for corruption on a 92–5 vote, with both Kennedys voting against Chris's dad. He died at the age of 64 in 1971.

Sen. Howell Heflin (D-AL) with a younger, more svelte Teddy. In 1989, a paparazzi in the south of France snapped a photo of the bloated 300-pound Teddy naked on a yacht in the Mediterranean, mounting a Marymount College coed 40 years younger than himself. The prurient photo was printed in a supermarket tabloid, leading Heflin to remark, "I see Sen. Kennedy has changed his position on offshore drilling."

CHAPTER EIGHT

IN HIS OWN WORDS: JOSEPH P. KENNEDY II

The following quotes were transcribed verbatim from the remarks of Rep. Joseph P. Kennedy II, who served in the U.S. House of Representatives from Massachusetts, 1987–1997.

On Brother Michael Not Being Indicted for Raping a 14-Year-Old Babysitter

"It's, uh, basically good news I hope for, uh, for everyone concerned, I think, um, you know, obviously . . ."

On Whether Raped Babysitter's Family Sought Him Out as an "Intermediary"

"The conversation as I saw (was) very short, it was in which he had had offered to try to, uh, to be some kind of us of-of, uh, go-between and it just didn't seem to me to make any sense I, you know."

REPORTER: A go-between? On what issue?

"Well, I-I you know, uh, I'm not—look—listen this situation is one in which neither family has talked about in a public way."

On His Brother Michael's Rape of the 14-Year-Old Babysitter

"I think it would be a serious mistake on my part to be the first person to acknowledge that a relationship took place."

REPORTER: Did you ever see Michael and the underage girl together at the compound?

"No! No!"

REPORTER: You never saw the girl with Michael?

"Well, I mean I-I not in the sense of being together in the way that I think you intended it. Did I ever, uh, in the last few years . . . not in, uh, not in, uh, any incident that sticks out in my mind. But I mean I'm certain at some point I might have seen them, you know?"

Previewing His 1996 Nomination Speech for Vice President Al Gore

"First, uh, his, uh, tremendous, uh, adherence to I think the basic prin-principles of the Democratic party, the ideas that we're a party that looks out after, uh, the working men and woman of our country, that looks out after our senior citizens, that looks out after the, uh, poor and the like and-and middle class America, uh, that, uh, the, uh, that he has done that, uh-uh—"

His Uncle Ted's Honoring at the 1996 Democratic National Convention

"Well I think it's, uh, it's just a great honor that, uh-uh, that the, uh, Democratic Party and the Clinton Administration in particular has, uh, chose to, uhhhh, to recognize, uh, the contribution for-for you-you know Sen. Kennedy obviously has, uh, been probably the strongest congressional leader of, uh, this, uh, past four years."

U.S. Rep. Joseph P. Kennedy made a speech at the 1997 state Democratic convention: "I'm sorry, so very, very sorry."

Crime Wave in Lowell

"Some of the worst violent crime, uh-uh-uh-uh, criminals in the, uh-uh, city of Lowell . . ."

Reacting to the State's 1995 Proposal to Crack Down on Welfare

"—that the, that the opinions that are being, uh, laid out before us for the next couple of days are in fact the opinions of people that have a very strong ax to grind and are in fact, uh, the kinds of, uh, reputable individuals that, uh-uh, that-that, uh, have, uh, have been, uh, put forward by the official Justice Department."

On President Clinton's Nominee for Attorney General Employing an Illegal Alien

"You know, you know, I mean the thing about the woman who, uh, hired some, uh, illegal, uh-uh-uh-uh, aliens in this country, I mean the fact is I live in Brighton and, you know, uh . . . So I mean I think that there is, uh, you know, that that there is, you know, there are some, uh, you know that-that given the fact that she's going to become the attorney general of the United States there are, you, there are some ethical problems there."

On the Prospect of Him and His Uncle Being at the Top of the State Democratic Ballot, 1994

"Yeah, I mean, I listen. Obviously it's something to give some thought to and the like. I mean, uh, but I don't think I think first and foremost people recognized that there's, uh, you know, that we're two very different individuals. And, uh, you know that, uh-uh, there isn't any, uh, you know, sort of direct conflict here. I mean it's not like uh, you know that there, that there'd necessarily be any direct conflict."

Statehood for Puerto Rico

"I think that we as American citizens ought to fundamentally be wide enough in our, in our breadth of, our, uh, of our knowledge and our, uh, and our, and our, sense of other human beings to allow them their own sense of self-identification."

Parliamentary Wizard

"I reclaim the balance of my time."

PRESIDING OFFICER: The gentleman *reserves* the balance of his time.

"I yield a minute of my 30 seconds to Mr. Hansen from Utah."

Stuffing It

"This budget is a sham. Take your 15 minutes and stuff it! Stuff it in the same place you ought to stuff this tax bill. Stuff it the same place you ought to stuff these spending cuts!"

On Camelot

"Back when my family was in power . . ."

A "New Lease on Life" for William Bennett

"Over 500,000 young children in America have been cut off the rolls of our nation, the, in order to, uh, somehow or another, uh, make way for our, uh, so-called balanced budget . . . This is an individual who was hired by Ronald Reagan to dismantle the Department of Education, and be, he, he hasn't even to be ab—, been able to accomplish that. And I'm, ah, very concerned that if George Bent—, Bu—, ah if George Bush wins the nomination, and wins the, uh, presidency, that he is going to turn around and give, uh-uh, William Bennett a new lease of life."

In Which He Addresses the Problem of Mortgages for "Divorced Dads"

"I think that you know, obviously you know, when the family unit, uh, with the uh, as-as the marriage together, uh, would be called for there'd be sort of a single income, uh, that would be looked as the, as the income and that it would be based on that-that the judgement would be made whether or not, uh, a mortgage could be, uh, the level of the mortgage could be handled, uh, in terms of the, uh, the bank's, uh, position, uh, once a divorce has, uh, has-has, uh, has, uh, occurred in that, uh, you know there's gonna be a certain amount of income, uh, that the, that the individual is responsible for paying the mortgage, uh, has . . ."

Further Thoughts on the Problem of Mortgages for "Divorced Dads"

"Uh, I think, uh-uh, you know, in terms of presumption of, uh, you know, who, uh, you know the fact that so often we find that, uh, fathers, in particular, uh, are discriminated against with regard to the, uh, issue of-of-of-of, uh, whether or not you get custody and jurisdiction and that type of thing."

Pay Raises for the State Legislature

"I, uh-uh-uh, voted, uh, for my own, duh, pay raise in Congress and I, uh-uh, think that I dis-uh-uh, I mean, I agree with the Senate president from 75 State Street."

On Candidate Bill Clinton's Messy Personal Life, 1992

"Uh, the fact is that, uh, you know, I don't think anybody is, uh, going to be feeling, uh, that they ought to be knocked out, uh . . ."

REPORTER: Well's let's just get back to the point—

"No. But that is my point."

REPORTER: Do—

"I think that, uh, that was, uh, exactly my point."

Quoting His Uncle, the President

"A rising tide lefts all boats."

CHAPTER NINE

WAS YOUNG JFK A CONSERVATIVE?

DESPITE WHAT THE POLITICALLY correct textbooks now say, Cong. John F. Kennedy was not a liberal, not ever, but especially not in his early years as a member of the U.S. House of Representatives.

Could JFK be elected in Massachusetts today? Probably not, but definitely not as a Democrat. If JFK were running statewide, he couldn't even make the primary ballot, because someone with his political views would never get the 15 percent of the vote needed from delegates to the state Democratic convention.

The crew of PT 109: JFK was elected to Congress on the greatly conflated story of his heroism in the Pacific Theater, and he gleefully helped construct the myth. In William Doyle's PT 109, he is quoted as saying, "My story is getting better all the time. Now I've got a Jew and a nigger, and with me being a Catholic, it's great."

The rhetoric from his 1961 inaugural address would be enough by itself to disqualify JFK as a Democratic candidate, not just in Massachusetts but in most other states: "Ask not what your country can do for you—ask what you can do for your country . . . Long twilight struggle . . . pay any price, bear any burden . . ."

As president, he wanted to, and did, cut taxes. "A rising tide lifts all boats," he said.

Now, the top Democrat in Massachusetts, Sen. Elizabeth Warren, wants to raise income taxes back over 50, 60, 70 percent—she refused to say during her 2018 campaign just how high rates should be raised again. She has also called for the abolition of Immigration and Customs Enforcement (ICE) and basically endorsed open borders. The Democrat candidate for governor in 2018, Jay Gonzalez, took part in a demonstration at the federal courthouse in Boston in the summer of 2018 to protest the arrest of 25 illegal aliens for illegally obtaining welfare payments. Most had lengthy criminal records for heroin dealing, domestic abuse, and, in one case, murder.

Obviously, this is not JFK's Democratic party.

JFK was a conservative long before he ran for political office for the first time at the age of 29. He spent much of his young manhood in Palm Beach, Florida, where, as *National Review* noted (in italics) on April 10, 1962: *"No Negro is permitted to own a home in the President's winter town."*

As *Look* noted in a fawning piece about the winter White House: "Palm Beach is virtually free of crime . . . Every street is patrolled every 20 minutes. Strange cars are watched. Everybody employed in the city is fingerprinted and, if acceptable to the police, gets an identity card."

In the summer of 1945, JFK was making a tour of the ruins of post-war Europe as his father and his cousin Joe Kane were in Boston shopping around for an appropriate political office for him to run for. They settled on the House of Representatives, handing James Michael Curley $50,000 for his campaign for mayor of Boston, which he won, for the fourth time, after which he resigned the seat in Congress that he'd twice been elected to, in 1942 and 1944.

As the details of his anticipated debut in politics were being worked out back in Massachusetts, JFK was visiting both the Soviet Union and the ruins of Nazi Germany.

For the only time in his life, Kennedy kept a diary, 61 pages worth of observations. After visiting Der Fuhrer's Bavarian retreat, the future president wrote: "Hitler will emerge from the hatred that surrounds him now as one of the most significant figures who ever lived. He had in him the stuff of which legends are made."

While conceding that Hitler had been a "menace to world peace," JFK added, "He had a mystery about him in the way he lived and in the manner of his death that will live and grow after him."

So, in retrospect, knowing what we do now about his privately-expressed views, it is not all that surprising that JFK would run to the right of his arch-conservative, anti-Semitic father.

In October 1946, already assured of election after easily winning the Democratic primary, JFK's campaign bought time for a radio speech in which he laid out "the great issue facing the world today. The issue is Soviet Russia."

He talked about how he had recently addressed the Young Democrats of New York, a left-leaning club. In the question-and-answer session, he was asked his opinion about the USSR, one of the countries he had actually visited a year earlier.

"I told the group that I felt that Soviet Russia today is run by a small clique of ruthless, powerful, and selfish men, who have established a government which denies the Russian people personal freedom and economic security. I told them that Soviet Russia today is a slave state of the worst sort."

Then he went after "fake news" in the United States, 70 years before Donald Trump would coin the phrase.

"The complete suppression of news with respect to Russia has left the world with a totally false impression of what is going on inside Soviet Russia today. I told them that the people in the United States have been far too gullible with respect to the publicity being disseminated throughout the world by the clever and brilliant Moscow propagandists."

If JFK were alive today, would he be watching CNN and MSNBC . . . or the Fox News Channel?

"I knew that my remarks would alienate the entire group which I was addressing. And I did alienate them."

But he kept laying out the facts about Russia—this in a party whose far-left wing would defect two years later to support former FDR cabinet secretary Henry Wallace, a veritable fellow traveler of the Kremlin.

JFK pointed out that "Russia is the only country in the civilized or uncivilized world which punishes a man who has committed no crime."

He also mentioned the mass hunger, if not starvation, in the USSR, where food consumption per capita had actually fallen since Tsarist Russia, and was now 30 percent below the average for the worst-fed 10 percent of the British population.

"Is that economic security?" JFK asked. "If it is, I hope and pray that we never have Soviet economic security in the United States."

Would such a speech even be permitted today at a state Democratic convention in Massachusetts—or at a national gathering? Remember, this is a party whose delegates booed the mention of God at the 2012 national convention in Charlotte.

Just 37 years after JFK's radio speech, his brother Ted would send an envoy to Moscow to implore these same masters of the world's largest slave state to help him defeat President Ronald Reagan in his bid for reelection. According to secret KGB documents released after the fall of the Soviet Union, Teddy promised the Kremlin that he could deliver fawning coverage in the mainstream media—the same media his older brother had so devastatingly described as being fellow travelers of the Soviet Union.

What a difference a generation makes—especially for the Kennedys.

In his years in the House, from 1947–1953, and later in the Senate until his election as president in 1960, JFK compiled an utterly undistinguished record. But he won a Pulitzer Prize for a book, *Profiles in Courage,* that was written by an aide, about courageous senators of the past who had risked their careers to take a stand.

Ironically, much of *Profiles in Courage* was written in 1954, the same year that JFK didn't show up to vote on the censure of Sen. Joe McCarthy, the Republican senator from Wisconsin who was such a close friend of the Kennedys.

JFK claimed he was recovering from back surgery, and was too weak to get to Washington to take part in the roll-call vote to censure his friend McCarthy, but no one believed him. One of his highest-profile critics in the Democratic party, Eleanor Roosevelt, quipped that, "Sen. Kennedy needs to show a little less profile, and a little more courage."

In the House, JFK wasn't just a conservative, he was also a maverick. From an urban Democratic machine district, he was expected to take his cues from the House's party leadership. Especially since the number-three man in the Democrats' leadership was John McCormack of South Boston.

Until the day he died, JFK deferentially called the one-time Southie lawyer for the old Prohibition-era Gustin Gang "Mr. McCormack." But

Speaker McCormack with Massachusetts Senate President John E. Powers, two South Boston politicians. JFK tried to keep such old-time Boston pols at arm's length as he advanced in politics.

he had no intention of taking orders from Mr. McCormack or anyone else, other than his father, of course.

On JFK's first full day in office, January 3, 1947, McCormack had called a meeting of the full Democratic conference, which after the 1946 election found itself in the minority for the first time since 1930. The new speaker, Joe Martin, was also from Massachusetts—a Republican.

JFK had rolled in the previous evening from Palm Beach, well-tanned, rested. His rented house in Georgetown wasn't ready for occupancy, so JFK and his two aides—Ted Reardon and Billy Sutton—had checked into the new Statler Hilton at 16th and K Streets.

McCormack, a congressman since Calvin Coolidge had been president in 1928, wanted all his members there at the meeting on time. So his top aide, Joe Feeney, later a state judge in South Boston, was calling Reardon and Sutton. But JFK was running late—a lifetime habit. Finally, he wandered into the hotel lobby, his hair uncombed. Unlike most men in those days, he wore no hat. It had been a contentious point during the 1946 campaign between JFK and his older cousin/campaign manager, Joe Kane.

Kane thought a hat would make JFK look a bit less callow, but JFK argued that a chapeau would negate one of his greatest assets, especially with the women—his hair. JFK had been on to something. On the campaign trail, in East Boston, bobby-soxers had surrounded him, screaming, "Sinatra!"

His two aides were anxious about the time, but the new congressman was hungry, so the more they tried to hurry him, the slower he moved. Finally they all headed across the street into a drugstore for breakfast—two soft-boiled eggs and a cup of tea. Nervously, his aides kept checking their watches. JFK ate placidly.

"How long would you say McCormack's been in Washington?" he asked.

"Twenty-six years?" Sutton guessed, incorrectly.

JFK smiled. "Then I don't think he'd mind waiting another 15 minutes."

JFK was under no illusions about his status as low man on the political totem pole. He was the youngest of the 14 congressmen from

Massachusetts. (The state is now down to 10, and may well lose yet another after the 2020 census.) About to turn 30, JFK still looked so youthful that in the years ahead, he would occasionally be mistaken for a page by older members.

Even though JFK was now in Congress, he'd never lost his prep-school nonchalance about clothes. He had money; he didn't need to dress well to impress anyone.

"He didn't care," Billy Sutton recalled years later for one of the many post-assassination tomes. "He'd go on the floor of the House in khaki pants and sneakers! He had this old suit he had made in London about 1939. It was worn out and much too small. I told him he had to get rid of it. It fit me pretty well, so he said he'd sell it to me for $11."

In that era, Congress was all about seniority. It didn't matter how well-groomed JFK was, or how articulate. It was all about serving one's time, and following leadership's orders. And JFK knew exactly where he stood.

"We were just worms over there in the House," JFK said later. "Nobody paid any attention to us nationally."

So JFK was often a no-show on Capitol Hill. One morning, McCormack called a meeting to discuss a housing bill. He looked around the chambers for his freshman colleague from the Bay State. Then he started waving a newspaper, with a headline listing Kennedy's demands for immediate action on the bill.

"Where's Johnny?" McCormack yelled. "Where's Johnny?"

That was a recurring question in those days, and later in his Senate career. Especially in January every year, JFK was a no-show. If you had a problem, or a question, you called his aide Ted Reardon.

"What's the point in hanging around Washington at the beginning of the session when I can be in Florida?" he asked. "Nothing important is going on anyway. Besides, Ted can handle things in the office."

When he arrived in DC in 1947, he had only one specific goal in mind. He wanted to get the FBI tapes J. Edgar Hoover had ordered made of him and Inga Arvad in bed in that Charleston hotel back in 1942.

"That bastard," he told his aide Langdon Marvin, "I'm going to force Hoover to give me those files."

Cooler heads prevailed. No such demands were made.

In the summer of 1947, having just turned 30, the young congressman had to make his first tough decision. Back in Boston, the usual turmoil was roiling the political scene. Mayor James Michael Curley, age 72, was about to be sentenced to federal prison, but the president of the Boston City Council, who under normal circumstances would succeed him, had just been indicted for soliciting bribes. No one wanted him to become mayor, even temporarily.

The legislature had been forced to change the city's mayoral succession laws, and Curley's sentencing had been postponed as wrangling continued at the State House. But finally the continuances were over—the city clerk would become acting mayor. It was time for Curley to begin his second prison term, 43 years after his first, state incarceration. Curley pleaded ill health, but the judge refused to suspend the sentence.

"You are imposing a death sentence on me," Curley told the unsympathetic judge.

Curley was sent to Danbury, Connecticut, to begin serving a minimum of six months in durance vile. Within a few weeks, over 100,000 people had signed a petition urging President Truman to grant "executive clemency." John McCormack, from the Curley stronghold of South Boston, spearheaded the effort. He got more than 100 congressmen to sign on, including a number of Republicans who remembered the old reprobate, who had served in the House as recently as two years earlier, with a certain fondness.

Ten of the 11 Democrats in the Massachusetts delegation signed, everyone except JFK.

This would be one of the rare occasions where he defied his father. His cousin Joe Kane also pleaded with him to sign. John McCormack personally brought the petition to him. But JFK wouldn't be cowed. Curley had driven his beloved grandfather from politics, using the Toodles Ryan sex scandal to humiliate Honey Fitz . . . not to mention his daughter Rose, JFK's mother.

Curley knew the old axiom of politics as well as the Kennedys.

"Don't get mad, get even."

JFK's rented house in Georgetown became a social hotspot. A friend from Choate recalled going there for dinner, and then going out to a movie with JFK and an attractive blonde from West Palm. After the movie, JFK whispered to his prep-school friend, "Well, I want to shake this one. She has ideas."

Then another young woman walked in.

"I went to bed figuring this was the girl for the night," the friend later told JFK biographer Nigel Hamilton, "The next morning, a completely different girl came wandering down for breakfast. They were a dime a dozen."

Also hanging around the Kennedy house was a freshman Republican senator from Wisconsin, Joseph McCarthy. He was dating Eunice, and occasionally Pat. But the man who would become known as "Tailgunner Joe" was closer to young RFK, who idolized him, and to old Joe, who appreciated his amiable disposition—"he was never a crab," Joe recalled after McCarthy's death, when it was not fashionable for anyone, especially Democrats, to say anything positive about McCarthy.

But McCarthy was extremely popular in Massachusetts, especially among Irish-Catholic voters. In those days, it was said that McCarthy could have beaten then Archbishop Richard Cushing in a one-on-one political race in South Boston, which happened to be Cushing's hometown. Of course, Boston had been one of the strongholds of prewar isolationist radio priest Charles Coughlin, not to mention the anti-interventionist America First movement. Many of those erstwhile Coughlinites and America Firsters now gravitated toward McCarthy.

In 1952, Congressman Kennedy was at a dinner in Cambridge at his alma mater, Harvard College, preparing to run for the U.S. Senate. One of the speakers attacked McCarthy, saying he was glad he hadn't gone to Harvard. JFK stood up and angrily denounced the McCarthy critic, then walked out of the hall. It was good theater, and good politics.

JFK wedding, Newport, Rhode Island, 1953: Sen. George Smathers, standing, third from left, was one of two Protestants in the wedding party. (The other was Lem Billings, fourth from left.)

JFK and McCarthy may have been tight, but Kennedy's closest friend in Congress was a fellow freshman House Democrat, George Smathers of Miami.

As an undergraduate at the University of Florida, Smathers' nickname had been "Smooch." In Gainesville, he had been in the same fraternity as Phil Graham, who as publisher of the *Washington Post* would later become another of JFK's best friends in Georgetown (and, at the end of his life, a tremendous political liability, as will be seen in Chapter 22).

"We had a natural chemical reaction," Smathers said after JFK's death. "I liked him and he liked me. Our offices were close by. We had a lot in common."

Namely, Florida and women. Joe Kennedy came to appreciate Smathers as well. Smooch was a lot like JFK, but he came from a middle-class family. Unlike JFK, he understood money. One day Joe appeared in Smathers's office at the Capitol with his son in tow.

"I want you to tell him it's damn hard to make a buck these days and money needs to be kept track of," the old man told Smathers. "Jack doesn't know or understand why he should even keep records of his expenditures."

Smathers said he was always surprised, first in the House and later in the Senate, how conservatively JFK voted.

"Sometimes the positions he'd take," Smathers recalled, "would be much more conservative than the position I'd take."

Like another one of their House friends, Republican Richard Nixon of California, Smathers was elected to the Senate in 1950, two years ahead of JFK. He decided to take on his political mentor, Sen. Claude Pepper, in the Democratic primary. Even by Smathers's hardnosed standards, it was a cynical play.

When Smathers had graduated from law school in 1938, Pepper got him a job as a prosecutor in the U.S. attorney's office in Miami. After military service in World War II, Smathers decided to run for Congress against an entrenched incumbent in Dade County. Pepper wrote some of Smathers's stump speeches for him. But by 1950, the good-old-boy oligarchy that had controlled Florida forever had tired of "Red" Pepper. He was too independent, too liberal. He wouldn't do what he was told.

So they looked around for a challenger. And they came up with Smathers. Suddenly Smathers's old patron was a stooge of Stalin.

"The leader of the radicals and extremists is now on trial in Florida," Smathers said of Pepper. "Arrayed against him will be loyal Americans . . . Florida will not allow herself to become entangled in the spiraling spider web of the Red network."

Congressman Kennedy, a winter resident of Palm Beach, endorsed Smathers.

Smathers's most memorable speech of the campaign was quoted in *Time*, although he later denied ever making it.

"Are you aware that Claude Pepper is known as a shameless extrovert? Not only that, but this man is reliably reported to practice nepotism with his sister-in-law, and he has a sister who was once a thespian in wicked New York. Worst of all, it is an established fact that Mr. Pepper, before his marriage, practiced celibacy."

On the campaign trail in north Florida and the Panhandle, Smathers carried in his coat pocket a newspaper clipping from 1946 in which Sen. Pepper was quoted as imploring Americans to pray for Stalin.

Smathers would pull the article out of his pocket, read it aloud, and then ask the crowd, "Did you pray for Stalin this morning?"

A CIO union drive to register black voters in Florida was denounced by Smathers as "the most dangerous invasion of carpetbaggers since the Civil War." He offered to defend, pro bono, any policeman in Florida indicted for civil-rights violations.

Smathers was relentless. Just in case the carpetbaggers and thespians and nepotism practitioners tried to swarm the polls in the Sunshine State on primary day, the young congressman set up an "Order of Smathers Sergeants," an anti-Red, Bund-style organization of "red-blooded Americans . . . to keep order on Election Day."

Pepper was saddened by his protégé's cynical transformation, as he wrote in a letter to a friend in May 1949: "Interests who hate me and what I stand for have made it so alluring to him financially to oppose me that he couldn't resist . . . By the time he has wallowed through a campaign with such as will be around him in major places, I am afraid he will be a very much transformed person."

Pepper was proven correct. The moderate congressman became an arch-conservative senator. In 1964, the same year he offered to pay Dr. Martin Luther King Jr.'s bail to get out of jail in Saint Augustine if he would leave Florida forever, Smathers gave an oral interview to the new John F. Kennedy Presidential Library. Reminiscing about his early years in Congress, he mentioned a number of JFK's best friends, including Reps. Richard Nixon of California and John Rankin of Mississippi.

Rankin was known as an arch-segregationist. He called Jews "kikes" and often used the word "nigger" on the House floor. After the Port of Chicago munitions disaster in 1944, the U.S. Navy asked Congress for a special budgetary appropriation to pay $5,000 to all of the victims' families.

Rankin discovered that most of the 320 dead were black sailors, and demanded that the payments be cut to $2,000 per survivor. The Navy compromised at $3,000.

Rankin also opposed statehood for Hawaii, because he said it would mean "two Jap senators" in Congress. In 1950, Smathers asked Sen. Joe McCarthy to investigate Communist infiltration in the islands. Smathers voted against statehood for Hawaii, and so did JFK.

In his oral history for the John F. Kennedy Presidential Library, Smathers also provided background about the Kennedys' relationship with Joe McCarthy. He said it was only natural for young RFK to work for him as a committee staffer when he graduated from law school, although he didn't last long. The problem, of course, was that McCarthy's top staffer was Roy Cohn—a flamboyantly gay Jew, everything, in short, that RFK despised.

Yet McCarthy remained close to the Kennedys until his death at age 49 in 1957.

"I always had the feeling," Smathers recalled in his oral history, "that Jack Kennedy was very sympathetic to Joe—not with what Joe was saying—but sympathetic to Joe as a person. . . . Jack liked him personally."

In those early years, it was important for JFK to have Joe McCarthy on his side, or at least not denouncing him on the Senate floor, or in South Boston. And sure enough, in 1952, when JFK was waging his uphill struggle for the Senate against Republican incumbent Henry Cabot Lodge, McCarthy stayed out of the fight, despite Lodge's pleas to McCarthy to campaign for him in Massachusetts.

In the House, before his Senate campaign, JFK had made quite a name for himself as an anti-Communist crusader. In June 1948, addressing a Polish club in Roxbury, he delivered an address that the *Herald* headlined: "Kennedy Says Roosevelt Sold Out Poland to Reds."

After the Communist takeover of China in 1949, during the prolonged "Who Lost China?" finger-pointing, Kennedy denounced the Truman administration, saying, "The responsibility for the failure of our foreign policy in the Far East rests squarely with the White House and the Department of State."

Like his father, JFK never had much use for Harry S. Truman. And Truman reciprocated—in spades. He once called Joe "the biggest crook in the country." And when he balked at endorsing JFK in 1960, favoring instead his fellow Missourian Stuart Symington, Truman was asked about rumors that he opposed Kennedy because of his religion.

"It's not the Pope," Truman would reply. "It's the Pop."

But that was a decade in the future. In 1950, young JFK was still establishing his bona fides as a conservative, what 30 years later would be called a "Reagan Democrat."

In a speech to an Italian charitable organization in Massachusetts in 1950, he called the government "the all-absorbing Leviathan— the State."

Elaborating, he told the businessmen, "Every time that we try to lift a problem from our own shoulders and shift that problem to the government, to the same extent are we sacrificing the liberties of the people."

In November 1951, Cong. John F. Kennedy addressed the Boston Chamber of Commerce, basically coming out in opposition to the War on Poverty more than a dozen years before the term was even coined.

"We cannot abolish the poverty and want . . . There is just not enough money in the world to relieve the poverty of all the millions of this world . . . The vision of a bottle of milk for every Hottentot is a nice one, but it is not only beyond our grasp, but is beyond our reach."

When was the last time any American politician of either party referred to blacks as "Hottentots?"

JFK's most telling summation of his political philosophy in those days came on November 10, 1950, during a speech at, of all places, Harvard University.

Two years later, during his Senate campaign against Henry Cabot Lodge, the *New Republic* would print an account of his remarks as transcribed by a young Harvard teaching fellow, John Mallan. As late as 1959, JFK would be disputing the facts in Mallan's story, unsuccessfully trying to renounce or at least downplay what he said.

The McCarran Act to which he refers was the "anti-subversive" legislation that Congress passed over President Truman's veto earlier in the year. It was one of the premier legislative accomplishments of JFK's allies like McCarthy, Rankin, Smathers, and the rest of their colleagues on the House Un-American Affairs Committee.

In his lead, Mallan simply listed what JFK had said at his alma mater: "(a) that he could see no reason why we were fighting in Korea; (b) he thought that sooner or later we would 'have to get all these foreigners off our backs' in Europe; (c) he supported the McCarran Act and felt that not enough had been done about Communists in government; (d) that he rather respected Joe McCarthy and thought he 'knew Joe pretty well, and he may have something'; (e) that he had no great respect for Dean Acheson or indeed almost any member of the Fair Deal Administration; (f) that he personally was very happy that Helen Gahagan Douglas had just been defeated in California by Richard Nixon."

On the subject of (f), however, he did not tell the "eggheads," as Ivy League academics were then called, that he had personally contributed $1,000 to Nixon's campaign.

This was the young JFK, the one schoolchildren never read about in their history books.

CHAPTER TEN

FUNDAMENTAL TRANSFORMATION

S EN. TED KENNEDY, AGE 32, was adamant about what his immigration bill would not do to the United States.

"First, our cities will not be flooded with a million immigrants annually," he said in February 1965, 15 months after his brother's assassination, 3 months after the Democrats' landslide victory in the presidential election of 1964.

"Under the proposed bill, the present level of immigration remains substantially the same."

There were no longer enough Republicans, or conservative Democrats, to successfully object to the fantastic lies Kennedy was spewing out one after another to the Senate Judiciary Subcommittee.

"Secondly, the ethnic mix of this country will not be upset," he continued, reading from his prepared text. "Contrary to the charges in some quarters, (the bill) will not inundate America with immigrants from any one country or area, or the most populated and deprived nations of Africa and Asia . . . In the final analysis, the ethnic pattern of immigration under the proposed measure is not expected to change as sharply as the critics seem to think."

Teddy concluded by repeating his opening remarks—falsehood after prevarication after lie.

"The bill will not flood our cities with immigrants. It will not upset the ethnic mix of our society. It will not relax the standards of admission. It will not cause American workers to lose their jobs."

Legend has it that JFK's 1958 book, *A Nation of Immigrants*, helped inspire his brother Ted's obsession with the "fundamental transformation" of America, as Barack Obama openly put it more than 50 years later.

Like so much of the Kennedy mythology, that version of the story is apocryphal. First, it's an exaggeration to refer to *A Nation of Immigrants* as a book. At best, it's a pamphlet, coming in at fewer than one hundred pages.

And second, like most everything else ever "authored" by JFK, from *Why England Slept* to *Profiles in Courage*, *A Nation of Immigrants* was actually the work of others (in this case, the Anti-Defamation League [ADL]). As president, JFK was just starting on a plan to revise and lengthen it into a book. That project ended with his assassination.

The pamphlet was part of a series from the ADL titled the One Nation Library, and one can only wonder if the group's leadership cared that the two men arguably closest to the president—his father Joe and his brother Bobby—were themselves virulent anti-Semites. RFK did, however, hold his nose long enough to write an introduction for the ADL to a posthumously published edition that was stretched into a book.

Perhaps JFK's concern was spawned by a combination of the "No Irish Need Apply" bigotry of his youth and the experience he had gained earlier as a young congressman representing a district heavily populated by newly arrived immigrants from Southern Europe. It was the support of Irish American and Italian American voters—in other words, Roman Catholics—that helped elect JFK to the Senate.

These groups had been the target of the Quota Acts of 1921 and 1924, both of which were carefully crafted to deliberately and drastically limit the entry of Southern and Eastern European immigrants into the United States. Caught in the crosshairs of the legislation were Catholics from Italy and Poland, as well as Jews from the Russian Pale of Settlement, all of whom were considered unable to assimilate into American culture. Both acts also included quotas that basically banned the entry of Asians and Africans.

JFK's interest in immigration seemed to begin during his time in the Senate in the 1950s. He had won his Senate seat by beating Henry

Cabot Lodge Jr., whose grandfather had supported the prominent Immigration Restriction League, a group that lobbied to favor immigrants from Northern Europe. Years before, the elder Lodge had battled JFK's grandfather Honey Fitz over literacy tests for immigrants. Lodge had later also narrowly defeated JFK's grandfather in the 1916 Senate race—the first popular election for the Senate in Massachusetts after the ratification of the 17th Amendment to the U.S. Constitution in 1913.

Kennedy hagiographers like plagiarist Doris Kearns Goodwin often include in their worshipful tomes a reference to Honey Fitz's brief career as a congressman, and how in 1895 Sen. Lodge called him "an impudent young man" for opposing his legislation to restrict immigration. To which Honey Fitz supposedly replied that the only difference between Lodge's and his ancestors and the current immigrants flooding Massachusetts were "a few boats."

Immigration had already drastically changed the Massachusetts of the older Lodge's youth. (He was born in 1850.) Since the 1880s, when the Irish took over the city government of Boston, the retreating Yankees had created political firewalls, allowing the governor, presumably always a Yankee, to appoint both the police commissioner and the board that controlled liquor licenses in the city. The state also created an independent finance board that oversaw the city's finances, the better to keep the Fenians in line.

But the Yankees' control over the state grew ever shakier, as wave after wave of immigrants arrived. In 1916, in his first popular election as senator, Henry Cabot Lodge had nearly lost to the "impudent young man," Honey Fitz. The future was obvious; it belonged to the new immigrants.

And so the Irish were an obsession of the Yankees. T. Jefferson Coolidge, one-time U.S. ambassador to France who was born in 1831, once wrote of a visit to Jamaica: "The Negroes vexed us and spoke with Irish accents."

The Irish would never be accepted by the Brahmins of Boston. Rose Kennedy once mused to one of her son JFK's blue-blooded Harvard classmates: "When will the nice people of Boston accept us?"

According to family lore as imparted by Ted almost a century later, Honey Fitz's later conversations with young JFK about these and other issues faced by immigrants in Boston had an effect on "the President," as Ted called his brother.

But in the 1960s, immigration was not in the forefront of most Americans' minds. Instead, the issues that dominated the news were civil rights, the Vietnam War, and riots in the streets.

As Ann Coulter put it, "At the precise moment in history when the United States abandoned any attempt to transmit American values to its own citizens, never mind immigrants, the 1965 immigration act began dumping the poorest of the poor from around the world on our country."

Nevertheless, in the summer of 1963, JFK would send Congress a recommendation to write a new immigration law that "reflects in every detail the principles of equality and human dignity to which our nation subscribes." Of course, he would not survive to see it become law.

A year and a half later, during his State of the Union Address, Kennedy's successor, President Lyndon B. Johnson, told Congress that he intended to pass "an immigration law based on the work a man can do and not where he was born or how he spells his name." And so, in the wake of the Civil Rights Act of 1964 and the Voting Rights Act of 1965, came the Immigration and Nationality Act of 1965.

It would prove to be the most calamitous legislation ever passed during the Great Society, inflicting far greater lasting damage on American society than even the War on Poverty. It opened the floodgates to hordes of indigent third worlders at the very moment that the Democrats' created welfare state was making it possible for the newcomers to neither work nor assimilate, and as "affirmative action" programs gave those who chose to actually earn a living an edge in the workplace over most American citizens.

To navigate the bill through Congress, the ever-shrewd LBJ picked the late president's youngest brother, Ted, now a first-term senator serving on the immigration subcommittee. As the overwrought national mourning over the slain president continued into its second year, LBJ knew that whatever the Kennedys wanted, the Kennedys would get—in this case, what would turn out to be in effect open borders and the subsequent fundamental transformation of America.

Unsurprisingly, it was Teddy's ability to throw back tumblers of Scotch rather than his vast knowledge of demographic trends that landed him a seat on the immigration subcommittee. As he told the story in a 2007 interview, Kennedy met with Sen. James Eastland of Mississippi to discuss his subcommittee assignments. Eastland was ready for the president's slower-witted kid brother. "Now Ted, I've been thinking about what subcommittees you might want. I bet you want the immigration subcommittee."

Surprised at Eastland's perception, Kennedy asked him how he knew.

"Well," Eastland said, "you have a lot of Italians up there, a lot of Italians, a lot of immigrants."

Kennedy replied, "Well, that's very interesting. Do you think there's some opportunity for me to get on that immigration subcommittee?"

Fortunately for Teddy, Eastland decided to test his boozing prowess rather than his intellect. Eastland reached over and picked up a bottle of Chivas, poured a couple of fingers over ice, and handed it to Kennedy.

"Half the glass was amber," Kennedy recalled, with the precision of one who had imbibed far more than his fair share of blended Scotch whiskey.

"If you drink that drink down," Eastland told him, "you're going to find yourself on that immigration committee."

Naturally, Kennedy chugged the glass down, as he would so often throughout his life. Eastland repeated the challenge for two more subcommittee assignments, and each time, Kennedy eagerly guzzled the Scotch.

Impressed, Eastland called to an aide and informed him, "I just told Sen. Kennedy he's on immigration, civil rights, and constitutional rights."

A couple of years later, it would be left to a handful of Southern Democrats and a few fiscal watchdogs to point out the chaos of open borders.

"The people of Ethiopia have the same right to come to the United States under this bill as the people from England, the people of France, the people of Germany, [and] the people of Holland," grumbled Sen. Sam Ervin, a Democrat from North Carolina. "With all due respect to Ethiopia, I don't know of any contributions that Ethiopia has made to the making of America."

Sen. Spessard Holland, a Florida Democrat, pointed out that "this is a complete and radical departure from what has always heretofore been regarded as sound principles of immigration."

But the dystopian future of the United States was most unerringly predicted by a woman named Myra C. Hacker, from a group called the New Jersey Coalition. In February 1965 she testified before Kennedy's Senate subcommittee:

"Are we prepared to embrace so great a horde of the world's unfortunates?"

She asked if the American people should be asked "how they feel about providing jobs, schools, homes, security against want, citizen education, and a brotherly welcome . . . for an indeterminately enormous number of aliens from underprivileged lands . . . to hoard our bounteous minimum wages and our humanitarian welfare handouts . . . lower our wage and living standards, disrupt our cultural patterns. . . .

"Whatever may be our benevolent intent toward many people, [Kennedy's bill] fails to give due consideration to the economic needs, the cultural traditions and the public sentiment of the citizens of the United States."

Or, as economist Milton Friedman would put it more than 30 years later, "It's just obvious that you can't have free immigration and a welfare state."

Secretary of State Dean Rusk, who served under both JFK and LBJ, told Congress that he did not see "a world situation where everybody is just straining to move to the United States."

In reality, the foreign-born population has risen from 9.6 million in 1965 to a record high of 45 million in 2015 as estimated by a study from the Pew Research Center Hispanic Trends Project. Immigrants accounted for just 5 percent of the U.S. population in 1965 and now comprise 14 percent.

In 1964, while still attorney general, Robert Kennedy told a House subcommittee that under the legislation, no more than 5,000 Indians would immigrate to the United States, "after which immigration from that source would virtually disappear; 5,000 immigrants would come the first year, but we do not expect that there would be any great influx after that."

A year later, as a freshman senator, RFK again urged passage of the bill in a letter to the *New York Times*.

"The time has come for us to insist that the quota system be replaced by the merit system."

What exactly he meant by "merit" remains unclear, since the cornerstone of the bill was "family reunification," rather than ability, technical skill, or education level.

Meanwhile, Congressional Democrats insisted that the bill should prioritize this new imperative of "family reunification." It was a concept which would come to include even the most distant of kinsmen, or alleged kinsmen, as the major factor in determining eligibility, while minimizing every traditional measure of a would-be newcomer's worth—namely, their potential to contribute to, rather than leech off, the host American society.

What might have seemed like a minor shift to an unwitting public at the time has had enormous consequences for the county more than a half-century later. Hart-Celler's new citizens would in turn send for their families, creating an endlessly repeated cycle today referred to as chain migration.

Republican Sen. Hiram Fong of Hawaii reassured his colleagues that "the people from [Asia] will never reach 1 percent of the population."

The namesake of the legislation, Democrat Rep. Emanuel Celler of New York, argued, "There will not be, comparatively speaking, many Asians or Africans entering this country." In reality, by 2002, the number of Asians and Africans entering the United States each year exceeded the annual average total number of all immigrants entering the country during the 1960s.

But the greatest ethnic shift that resulted from the Kennedy-backed legislation involved the massive increase in the number of His-panic immigrants. Despite Robert Kennedy's promise, "Immigration from any single country would be limited to 10 percent of the total," Mexico alone accounts for more than 20 percent of all immigrants to the United States, and Hispanics account for nearly half of all immigrants since 1968.

As a result of these shifts, and despite assurances to the contrary made in 1965, the racial and cultural makeup of the country has changed drastically. The ethnic origin of the nation's immigrants has shifted from 95 percent European to 95 percent third-world origin. And immigra-tion levels have skyrocketed, with at least 40 million immigrants enter-ing the country since the bill was passed. That's a far cry from RFK's false statements in support of the bill: "It would increase the amount of authorized immigration by only a fraction."

Two important loopholes in the 1965 Act led to the enormous increase in immigration. Neither immediate family members of U.S. citizens nor political refugees were subject to quotas. Refugee provisions that Teddy Kennedy fought for so ardently over the decades have led to some of the most egregious abuses, including the admission of a number of welfare-dependent Muslim terrorists who have perpetrated horrific attacks on the United States homeland.

As *FrontPage Magazine* reported, "In 1965, Ted Kennedy confi-dently predicted, 'No immigrant visa will be issued to a person who is likely to become a public charge.' However, political refugees qualify for public assistance upon setting foot on U.S. soil. For example, the explod-ing Somali refugee population of Lewiston, Maine (population 36,000), is largely welfare-dependent. Likewise, 2,900 of Wausau, Wisconsin's 4,200 Hmong refugees receive public assistance. In all, 21 percent of im-migrants receive public assistance, whereas 14 percent of natives do so. Immigrants are 50 percent more likely than natives to live in poverty."

The deceit involved in the selling of the 1965 Act was neatly summed up by President Johnson at the time of its signing, held at the Statue of Liberty.

"The bill that we sign today is not a revolutionary bill," LBJ intoned. "It does not affect the lives of millions. It will not reshape the structure of our daily lives."

Has any U.S. president ever made a more perniciously false statement?

Bob Dane, executive director of the Federation for American Immigration Reform (FAIR), put it bluntly: "No legislation of the 20th century was more deceptively packaged, nor imposed more adverse consequence and non-consensual change on the country than the Hart-Celler Act of 1965. Skeptics at the time were patted on the head by pitchman Ted Kennedy who assured them nothing would change. Now we see everything has changed. But today's skeptics aren't patted, they're clubbed any time they voice concern about constant changes that further expand a flawed immigration system perpetually premised on lies and special interests."

In his dotage, Ted Kennedy had a hard time accounting for the difference between his assurances and reality. During a 2006 interview with NPR (of all places), he was confronted with what he said in 1965 and what eventually happened. In a series of incoherent, stumbling attempts at explanation, he was unable to explain even the most basic failures of his landmark legislation. He oddly blamed illegal immigration for the increased number of legal immigrants, and when pressed inexplicably spoke of the birthrate among immigrants once in the United States.

Q: What's striking about the debate in 1965 is how so many people did not expect a huge increase in immigration, or a change in the demographics of the nation. You told Congress that immigration levels would remain "substantially the same," and that "the ethnic mix of this country will not be upset." Why weren't these changes foreseen?

KENNEDY: There were enormous changes as a result of illegal immigration. A lot of the antagonism, frustration, and anger is better focused at the illegality and the illegals that came here in very significant numbers. [People] are certainly frustrated by the illegality and the explosion of illegals who come here that have impact in terms of the economy, depressing wages, and taking jobs.

Q: But the level of even legal immigration has increased dramatically since 1965, even though many supporters of the legislation then said it would not.

KENNEDY: Everybody obviously wants to come, because this is the land of opportunity, but we've seen a rather dramatic shift as well in terms of the birthrate here. That was not really foreseen.

One provision of the bill for which the liberal icon never had to answer for during his lifetime was its prohibition of homosexual immigration to the United States. Kennedy's act added "sexual deviation" as a medical ground for denying prospective immigrants entry into the United States.

Honey Fitz's stories to JFK aside, the Kennedys' greatest motive for bringing the third world to the United States was simple: it allowed their Democrat party to import a new underclass, voters who would be dependent not on the sweat of their own brows, but on government handouts. The term for such immigrants, usually but not always illegal, but almost always on welfare in one form or another: "undocumented Democrats."

If you couldn't convince Americans that you should be in political office—and the Democrats obviously could not—then immigration from the third world might be the solution. It would create a replacement population for those taxpaying, law-abiding Americans that coastal elitist Democrats dismissed as "bitter clingers" or, later, "deplorables." Between illegal immigration and the "War on Poverty," the traditional party of the American working class became in short order the party of the non-American, nonworking classes.

As the 20th century wound down, the only problem for the Democrats was that it was taking much too long to overwhelm the native population with their unskilled, non-English-speaking indigents from the third world.

So Ted Kennedy went back to work. By the late 1970s, he was working to massively expand "refugee" programs, thus encouraging a taxpayer-funded domestic resettlement industry that would go on to lobby for even more overall immigration, at ever greater costs—both financially and culturally—to the American population.

In 1986, Kennedy had another trick up his sleeve. This time, Congress was working on the Immigration Reform and Control Act (IRCA), the aim of which was the legalization of millions of illegal aliens and, ostensibly, enhanced enforcement at the border.

Twenty years after the fantastic lies of Hart-Celler, Kennedy was back with his utterly false estimates, lobbying heavily for the bill and proclaiming it would only lead to the legalization of 1.3 million immigrants. When all was said and done, the actual number of illegal aliens who received amnesty was closer to 3 million—more than double his estimate. As for border security, Kennedy assured the public, "We will secure the borders henceforth. We will never again bring forward another amnesty bill like this."

Four years later, the IRCA of 1986 still hadn't accomplished all he had hoped. So Ted took on a major role in drafting the Immigration Act of 1990, which increased overall immigration by another whopping 35 percent. Kennedy's unabashed view of the American immigration system as his own personal plaything was no more evident than in this law's provision for a green card lottery. In order to be fair, the green cards were meant to be awarded randomly, with a preference to Middle Eastern and African, and, of course, Irish migrants.

Despite the deleterious effects of illegal immigration on both the Republican party and the nation, the Bush family eagerly embraced Kennedy's ruinous policies. As president, George W. Bush would say that illegals were "only doing the jobs that Americans wouldn't do."

What jobs was he talking about? Selling heroin? Driving drunk? Organizing gangs like MS-13 to murder their rivals with machetes?

Bush's younger brother, Jeb, who would mount a hapless campaign for president in 2016, described the gangbangers and Muslim terrorists swarming into the homeland as "valedictorians." According to Jeb, their crimes, no matter how gruesome, were "acts of love."

Even Teddy faced blowback in Massachusetts as the evidence of his unprecedented folly mounted. In the early 1990s, in Lawrence, a gritty mill city on the Merrimack River where the traditional blue-collar working classes had been mostly scattered since 1965, a flood displaced a large number of illegal aliens.

Teddy naturally went to the scene, to offer solace to his new amigos. At an impromptu press conference, a reporter asked him if he thought the fact that most of the affected population were illegal aliens, as a GOP spokesman from the Bush 41 White House had apparently described them, would affect the federal relief effort.

Teddy immediately challenged the reporter's use of the term "illegal aliens."

"No," Teddy said, "uh, the question is, if there are some 'undocumented' living in his area—"

The reporter interrupted him. "No, he said 'illegal aliens.'"

"Well," Kennedy snapped, "that is what I call them. You call them what you want, I'll call them what I want. He said there are undocumented people living in this, uh, community and will that have any adverse impact in terms of the application? Absolutely not, nor should it and we are very hopeful of, ah, of, ah, having a good legislation."

By the mid-1990s, using the immigration pipeline to secure votes had become the standard modus operandi for Democratic politicians. Teddy had schooled them well. In 1995, with President Bill Clinton facing reelection, Immigration and Naturalization Service (INS) Commissioner Doris Meissner, a presidential nominee, instituted the Citizenship USA program. Keenly aware of the need for more Democratic voters for the incumbent's reelection bid, the INS put forth a major effort to grant citizenship to nearly 1 million applicants in time to vote . . . for Clinton, of course.

In order to complete this massive effort, the INS let some things slide—like background checks for at least 180,000 applicants. A post-election audit found that 71,000 applicants were granted citizenship despite having criminal records on file with the FBI, and of those, 10,800 were convicted felons.

Just to make sure these new citizens would vote the right way, the Clinton Administration pushed the INS to abandon its age-old form letter to new citizens and substitute it with a personalized greeting from the president. The agency demurred, but the intent was clear: The immigration system was once again being used to ensure electoral victories for the left.

Even at the age of 75 in 2007, Teddy was still carrying the Democrats' torch on immigration, and, more specifically, amnesty. Despite his boasts after the 1986 bill that "We will never again bring forward another amnesty bill like this," he was now proposing yet another amnesty, this time for 12 million illegal aliens.

His 2007 "Secure America and Orderly Immigration Act," coauthored with GOP Sen. John McCain, would have granted a proposed "Z Visa" for everyone living in the United States without a valid visa on January 1, 2010. It was obviously an incentive that would have encouraged all illegals residing in the country at the time to stay, as well as not so tacitly enticing even more indigent foreigners to illegally swarm into the nation before the deadline. Such a provision would have ballooned the number of illegal aliens eligible for the Z Visa.

The Z Visa would have been like a golden ticket—the recipient would have the legal right to remain in the United States for the rest of their lives, receive a Social Security number, and, after eight years, be eligible for a green card that would put them on a path to citizenship (i.e., welfare). All this for just a $2,000 fine and a convoluted ploy to collect payment of back taxes for only some of the time they might have worked illegally.

The Kennedy-McCain bill would have also established a guest worker program that granted a "Y Visa" allowing 400,000 temporary workers to stay in the United States for two years—more than enough time to drop an "anchor baby" who would automatically be a U.S. citizen, and thus eligible for welfare.

Finally, the bill included provisions of the infamous DREAM Act to allow for a path to citizenship for illegal aliens brought into the United States before turning 16. Dreamers would have supposedly been required to attend college or serve in the military.

(After Teddy's death, Barack Obama approved the Dreamer program through executive order—after saying publicly 22 times that such a decree would be unconstitutional without congressional approval. A subsequent Harvard University survey showed that 74 percent of the so-called Dreamers, supposedly the most productive of the tens of millions of illegal aliens in the United States, were on at least one form of welfare or another. Thousands were convicted felons.)

In a televised interview, Teddy seemed unable to find the right words to defend his legislation.

"I think our leader Sen. (Harry) Reid has outlined hope that the opportunities and challenges that still remain will send a very clear message to a very important group of citi—" He caught himself; even Teddy couldn't bring himself to describe illegal aliens, er, undocumented, as citizens.

"Si se puede! Si se puede!"—one of Teddy's late-in-life applause lines.

"—of individuals who are here and that is if you work hard, you're devoted to your family, you play by the rules, you pay your taxes, uh, and you are working towards the American dream that you can be included too as our great, uh, grandparents and great parents have in the past. Americans admire those qualities. Those qualities of hard work, playing by the rules, devoted to your children and devoted to the, uh, community. Those people who are out there today, the 11 million we are sending a message and that is you're going to be welcomed and you won't have to live in, uh, fear in the, uh, in the future."

Playing by the rules? As many times as he kept saying it, did Teddy truly believe that his undocumented Democrats were "playing by the rules?" As Kennedy continued, he seemed ever more befuddled.

"Wh-what is it about the bill that the Republicans find so offensive? Is it the fact that we're for strong national security, is that what it's unfair about? Is it unfair because it's going to help meet, uh, important needs in terms of taking jobs that other Americans that won't take? Or that they just feel that other people that work hard, play by the rules, pay their taxes, want to become part of America and will work for 11 years should be a part of our nation? What is that they want us to, uh, change in that particular agenda?"

For once, Kennedy lost an immigration fight. Even with the support of Republican President George W. Bush, the advocates for the fundamental transformation of America couldn't garner the necessary votes. Surprisingly, Democrats were the key to the bill's demise. Labor unions were miffed at the guest worker program and were displeased with the fact that the bill limited chain migration only to nuclear family members.

Still, that explanation seems too pat. As Sean Higgins wrote in the *Washington Examiner*, the alternate explanation is that the Democrats preferred to use the defeat as a way to drive voter turnout among illegals, who aren't legally allowed to cast ballots, but do, obviously, in ever-growing numbers, and almost always for Democrats.

"A less charitable interpretation," Higgins wrote, "is that Democrats cared far less about immigration reform than they did about using the issue to improve their margins with Hispanic voters."

Kennedy's shrewd yet cynical grasp for power was in its 42nd year. He was still trying to wield his clout in the Senate to ensure such a torrent of indigent illegal immigrants into the country that the future electoral dominance of the Democrat party would be forever secure, whatever the catastrophic cost to the nation.

Roy Beck, CEO and founder of NumbersUSA, an immigration education and research foundation, put forth some interesting theories about what else might have inspired Ted Kennedy's obsession with illegal immigration.

As Beck sees it, those with a kindlier view of the "Lion of the Senate" believe that Teddy—cossetted by his political power, his eight-figure trust funds, not to mention a lifetime of privilege and immunity from every normal restraint, including even prosecution for the most horrendous of crimes—never had to personally experience the destruction and despair that his ruinous policies were inflicting on his fellow countrymen. And once the damage had been done, this theory continues, it was simply too late for him, or the United States, to change course.

The cancer had metastasized.

Plus, Kennedy relished the accolades from certain politically correct communities too much to hit the brakes. That he might have been intentionally trying to radically change America seems implausible to some, especially given the fact that Kennedy was never regarded as a great intellect. Alcoholics seldom are. One longtime acquaintance of Ted's confided to Beck, "He's not smart enough for that."

Others believe that Teddy harbored a fundamental grudge against the American people.

"Perhaps there was a sub-conscious hatred for the overall American people because of the assassinations . . . ," Beck wrote. "Perhaps he had some Irish immigrant chips on his shoulder about WASPs disrespecting his family. If he disliked the balance of power among the citizens of this country, wildly increasing immigration levels could largely shift the balance of political power and ideology in the country."

The continuing aftershocks of Kennedy's 40 years of reckless legislation are no longer devastating only what used to be called the border states, like California and Texas. Even Massachusetts has suffered grievously from illegal and legal immigration.

In April 2013, two Muslim Chechens who had come to the United States with visas as children and were granted asylum as political refugees apparently didn't think that was a sufficient sign of decency on the part of their new homeland. Nor were the education, housing, and myriad welfare programs they and their parents and siblings subsisted on for years, while never working, at the expense of the American taxpayers.

So, Tamerlan and Dzhokhar Tsarnaev purchased pressure cookers and learned how to construct deadly nail-packed bombs from an online Al-Qaeda magazine called *Inspire*. The pair placed their bombs in backpacks and planted them near the finish line of the Boston Marathon. The explosions ripped through the gathered crowd of spectators, killing three and injuring hundreds; 16 people would lose at least one limb in the Muslim terror attack.

In 2011, Matthew Denice of Milford was only 23 when he was struck on his motorcycle by a drunken Ecuadorean illegal alien, Nicolas Guaman, who had run a stop sign. Attempting to flee the scene, Guaman ran over Denice, who became trapped in the wheel well of the Ecuadorean's pickup truck and died a grisly death.

Arrested, Guaman claimed he spoke neither English nor Spanish. A translator for his obscure Indian dialect had to be found. He of course had a public defender, who used more taxpayer funds to hire a psychologist who said that Guaman could not be held responsible for his drunk driving because as a "Mongoloid" from South America, he "lacked the enzyme" to metabolize the alcohol.

Not even a Kennedy had ever used that defense—that as Irish Americans, they "lacked the enzyme" to not drive drunk.

Schools throughout Massachusetts now struggle with maintaining reasonable classroom sizes and students who don't understand English and are, in some cases, illiterate in their own language. The needs—and costs—of limited English proficiency students are skyrocketing out of control, far beyond the means of most municipalities. According to FAIR, the cost to Massachusetts for LEP education is $1.4 billion.

In 2013, Republican legislators forced the state's liberal Democrat governor to admit that his administration was spending $1.8 billion a year in state funds alone on welfare for illegal aliens.

Criminal aliens have been involved in a disproportionate share of mayhem in Massachusetts, and not just drunk driving among those who "lack the enzyme." In 2017, a homeless African slit the throats of two anesthesiologists—immigrants themselves—in Andrew Square in South Boston. The alien had robbed two banks in downtown Boston, but the Democrat district attorney of Suffolk County—the office in which young Ted Kennedy had worked 60 years earlier—had reduced the charges to larceny from a person, so that the African would not be deported. He wasn't, and after serving just seven months for the two bank robberies, he was released to murder the two physicians—a 49-year-old Englishman and a 38-year-old Colombian woman—in cold blood. They had recently gotten engaged.

Horrific crimes were now being committed by foreigners on an almost daily basis in Ted Kennedy's hometown. The Supreme Judicial Court (SJC) decreed that state law enforcement must no longer cooperate with federal authorities trying to detain illegal aliens suspected even of violent crimes.

The SJC made its ruling in the case of an illegal alien drug-addicted career criminal from Cambodia, whose return the Cambodian government refused to accept. Days after being cut loose by the SJC, he was arrested again, charged with savagely beating an elderly wheelchair-bound American woman in the West End of Boston while robbing her of $2,500.

In the spring of 2018, a Superior Court judge in Essex County refused to impose a prison sentence on an illegal alien heroin dealer from the Dominican Republic, whose brother was a convicted cocaine dealer. The judge admitted that he would have sentenced an American convicted of a similar crime to prison, but that he couldn't send the illegal to prison because it would mean that it would result in his deportation—and his separation from his girlfriend and their child, the anchor baby that made them all eligible for every form of American welfare.

Gresham's law in economics—that bad money drives out good—also applies to the justice system. Bad law drives out good. If the criminal justice system devolves into a two-tier system—with one set of laws for citizens, and another with next to no laws or penalties for illegal aliens—it won't be long before no laws are enforced for anyone.

Which is just what has been happening, and not just in Massachusetts either. In Essex County, the same judge who released the illegal-alien heroin dealer soon had an American career criminal in front of him, on charges of reckless driving and illegal possession of multiple firearms.

After the same judge cut the American's bond from $50,000 to $5,000, the tattooed criminal made bail, drove to Maine, and murdered a sheriff's deputy.

This is Ted Kennedy's home state of Massachusetts, 53 years after he assured the nation that nothing like this chaos could ever happen, would never happen, period.

But now it has, with no happy resolution, no end in sight.

Today, everyone agrees that the immigration laws in the United States are broken, with one side preaching open borders and the other a wall to stem the tidal wave of crime and dependency. The Department of Homeland Security's ICE arm struggles to stem the flow, with a recent report stating that they had investigated only .05 percent of visa overstays in 2016. At least half a million foreign nationals annually overstay their visas after entering the United States through an airport or seaport.

The importation of millions of unskilled, uneducated, non-English speaking, welfare-dependent foreigners has been an incredible boon for the Democratic party. Promoting an agenda of ethnic grievances and identity politics, the party of Ted Kennedy has flourished as the nation has suffered through the fundamental transformation envisioned by Barack Obama.

In 1998, in an article for a Cornell University publication, Democrat pollster Patrick Reddy summed up the immigration act of 1965 as "the Kennedy family's greatest gift to the Democratic Party."

A gift for the Democrats, a disaster for America.

"The costs Americans pay," a *Breitbart* writer noted in 2015, "in lowered wages, strained social safety nets, their children's blood, their declining quality of life, the chaos of sharing space with an ever-swelling criminal population aided and abetted by the nation's elite, the berating Americans of every stripe endure when they dare ask their country merely be preserved—that's the real legacy of Ted Kennedy."

"Power to the people right on!"

CHAPTER ELEVEN

"NAMES" IN THE NEWS

The Kennedys have always had problems remembering the names of lesser mortals—up to and including the president of the United States. Here are some of the people whose names various members of the family have mangled over the years.

2010: Massachusetts Attorney General Martha Coakley campaigning for the Senate with President Obama. In his endorsement of her to fill his late father's seat, Patches Kennedy called Coakley "Marsha." And in 2008, asked a question by a reporter about the Democratic nominee for president, Ted Kennedy responded, "Why don't we just ask Osama bin Laden—, uh, Osama Obama, uh, Obama, what the, what his sense is—"

1992: A contested Democratic primary for Congress in the Merrimack Valley, pitting Marty Meehan, left, against incumbent Rep. Chester Atkins, right. When Meehan won, Teddy went to Lowell for a unity breakfast and heartily congratulated "Andy Meehan." Earlier, when Atkins won a seat on an important House committee over his nephew Joe, Teddy issued a press release lauding "Rep. Chuck Atkins."

Teddy and his wife Joan, who is being eyed by Boston Mayor Kevin White. On election eve 1960, at a rally at the Boston Garden, JFK had endorsed the statewide Democratic slate, including White, who was running for secretary of state. JFK called him "Calvin White"—an unusual first name for an Irish Catholic from West Roxbury.

Rupert Murdoch, longtime foe of Teddy, then owner of the Boston Herald *and the* New York Post. *On a Boston talk-radio show in 1988, Teddy called him "Rudolph Murdoch," and said he was tired of listening to Rudolph's "dribble" (as opposed to* drivel?*).*

Now Sen. Ed Markey, from one of the families known in Massachusetts as "K-Mart Kennedys"—because they fancied themselves emerging political dynasties. One day in the 1970s as CBS News was filming a day-in-the-life piece about Teddy, he took a phone call from Markey, then promptly forgot his name. As recounted in Richard Burke's book, The Senator, *Teddy put his hand over the mouthpiece and hissed, "Ricky, Ricky, what's his name?" Burke replied, "Markey," and Ted said, "No, no, no, what's his first name?" Burke told him and Teddy then resumed the conversation, Burke wrote, in a "syrupy tone": "Oh, Ed, how are you?" The next night the entire exchange aired on the CBS Evening News.*

Baseball sluggers Sammy Sosa and Mark McGwire. Or, to quote Teddy: "It is a special pleasure for me to introduce our two home run kings for working families of America, Mike McGuire and Sammy Sooser of the White House." (Sosa played for the White Sox.)

CHAPTER TWELVE

COMFORTABLY NUMB BY THE SEA

B Y 1991 ANYONE WHO had been paying attention knew that the Kennedy family no longer had much in common with those dashing, well-tailored, immaculately coiffed Cold Warriors who had prowled the New Frontier 30 years earlier.

The only male Kennedy of that generation who survived was Teddy—obese, disheveled, dissipated. The new generation of Kennedys were mostly ne'er-do-wells, shuffling back and forth between court appearances and rehab facilities, occasionally appearing at airports to cut in line and yell, "Do you know who I am?"

But any lingering doubts about the family's utter ruination were put to rest by the 1991 rape trial of William Kennedy Smith in West Palm Beach. In thousands of pages of court documents, the family's fall was laid bare.

It was the first Easter since the death of Willie's father, Steve Smith, who was married to the former Jean Kennedy. Before his death of lung cancer at the age of 66 the previous summer, Smith had run the Kennedy enterprises, and basically acted as the family fixer for close to 40 years.

"There wouldn't have been a Camelot without Steve Smith," Ted Kennedy said in his eulogy, probably more truthfully than he meant to be. "Steve was the shoulder we all leaned on in any of our endeavors . . ."

Indeed, he hired some of the local lawyers for Teddy during Chappaquiddick. After the assassination of JFK, when Bobby and Jackie needed a place in New York to shack up in out of sight of the Secret

Service, it was Smith who gave them the keys to his Fifth Avenue apartment. He negotiated the settlement with Pam Kelley after Joe Kennedy II put her in a wheelchair for life on Nantucket in 1973.

When Ethel was sued for stiffing a caterer in Aspen, it was Smith who showed up in small-claims court with a check. Ditto, when Chris Lawford was busted for buying Valium with a forged prescription. It was Steve Smith who, after bailing out David Kennedy after one of his many drug arrests, told the press with a straight face that his wife's nephew was "suffering an affliction similar to drug addiction."

"Steve," Teddy said, "was like a brother in our family."

Yes, he was. He treated their sister abysmally—what could have been any more Kennedy than that? And his son, like so many of the family's male offspring, was nothing but trouble. Willie Smith's treatment of women was worse than that of any other Kennedy in his generation. His predatory ways were a throwback to those of his grandfather, Joe Kennedy.

And yet, the oddest thing was, he was one of the very few in his generation who in the beginning actually seemed to have amounted to something—he had become a physician. He had flown into West Palm

Brother-in-law Steve Smith was a real member of the family. Here, he marches in the November 1963 funeral procession, just behind the surviving brothers and Jackie.

Beach for Easter weekend with his newly widowed mother, along with Ted and Patches and a few family retainers, like former RFK bodyguard William Barry, an ex-FBI agent.

After a Good Friday of epic drinking, the Kennedy men had driven to Au Bar, a trendy new bar off Royal Poinciana Way. Following last call early Saturday morning, Patches and Willie brought young women back to North Ocean Boulevard. As was so often the case, Patches couldn't close the deal. In his own inimitable way, Willie did—he raped his date. Or so she said.

In the Kennedy tradition, the 29-year-old Smith claimed his sex with the single mother from nearby Jupiter was consensual. The initial police report, written a few hours after her escape from the ramshackle mansion, indicated otherwise.

"[She] was sitting on a couch with her legs drawn up to her chest, in a fetal position, and she would panic at any quick movement in the room. She appeared to be emotionally frightened, distraught and in shock—she was physically shaking. The victim was also exhibiting pain when she would change position on the couch and, when walking, could only manage to walk at a very slow pace."

All this on the holiest weekend of the year on the Christian calendar. Even by Kennedy standards, it was shocking, at least to the most loyal Kennedy voters, who after all these years, and all these scandals, were still mostly ethnic Roman Catholics from the Northeast and the Midwest.

JFK had been elected president in 1960 in large measure because of his Catholicism. His candidacy had represented a no-win situation for Republicans—Catholics were expected to vote for JFK because he was a Catholic. And Protestants were likewise expected to vote for JFK because he was a Catholic—to prove they weren't prejudiced.

It was the same catch-22 that Barack Obama would exploit against the GOP 48 years later. Blacks would vote for him in racial solidarity because he was black, and whites would vote for him because he was black—to show they weren't bigots.

Of course, beyond Rose, and to a lesser degree Ethel, none of the family were religious. But they still observed their faith's shibboleths—

"Catholic gobbledy-gook," as Congressman Joe Kennedy called the dogma of Holy Mother the Church.

And so, on Easter Sunday, Teddy and his son Patrick drove to St. Edward Church for the 10:30 High Mass. The pews were all filled, it was standing room only, so the two Kennedys quickly fled around the corner to Royal Poinciana Way. They pulled up a couple of barstools at Chuck & Harold's, then a popular island gin mill.

A witness later reported that he heard fragments of their conversation, including one of the Kennedys saying, "And she will say it was rape . . ."

Their bar tab was later introduced in court as evidence. It was opened at 10:48. Ted started with a bullshot—vodka and beef consommé, with a splash of Worcestershire sauce. A little hair of the dog . . .

At the time, Patches was just a few years out of his cocaine rehabilitation. Usually, a recovering addict shuns other intoxicants, or is at least encouraged to by everyone around him. Abstinence is the sine qua non. But this was the Kennedy family. Patches ordered a Long Island Iced Tea. Under oath, the bartender would later recall the ingredients of a Long Island Iced Tea—"vodka, gin, rum, tequila, triple sec, sour mix and a splash of Coke."

Finishing the bullshot, Ted switched to a screwdriver—vodka and orange juice. The Kennedys settled their tab at 11:40. Suitably fortified, Teddy was feeling no pain when he arrived back at 1095 North Ocean Boulevard, carrying a foreign load, as they say in Boston.

The 80-year-old housekeeper, Nellie McGrail, would recall this and so much more when she was deposed under oath a few weeks later by the state's attorney.

"The senator was laughing with me and joking about all of the fancy dresses the ladies had on and the fancy hats."

Easter dinner was to be leg of lamb, which Nellie had bought at the Publix supermarket down the street from St. Edward the day before. It would be served with, what else, champagne—another family tradition, apparently. But before dinner could be served, the Palm Beach police arrived, asking to speak to the senator and his nephew, who were sitting outside on the ocean side of the estate.

Suddenly a retired FBI agent and weekend guest of the family named William Barry appeared at the door. This was the "Mr. Barry" to whom Teddy would refer at his MIT press conference a few weeks later. A former bodyguard for the late Sen. Robert Kennedy, Barry well understood what Kennedy family protocol required when confronted by unfriendly—or at least skeptical—local law enforcement.

Mr. Barry lied. He told the Palm Beach police that Kennedy was "out at the moment." He also said he "believed William Smith had flown out yesterday but he did not know for sure."

Barry assured the female police officer at the front door that he would have the senator call her as soon as he returned. But when he hadn't called an hour later, the police again telephoned the mansion and spoke to an unnamed employee "who stated that Mr. Barry had taken Sen. Kennedy and William Kennedy Smith to the airport for a 3 p.m. flight."

Another lie: only Smith had gone on the lam. Teddy didn't fly back to Washington until the next morning. But the story about the alleged rape broke in the media that evening, right around dinnertime at the mansion. Jean Saba recalled the menu.

"That was the night they opened some champagne. And it was a little celebration because it was Easter and—"

Nobody had been accused of rape in about 36 hours.

Early Monday morning, the houseman Dennis Spear saw Teddy in the kitchen, after all the police visits and the bullshots and the screwdrivers and the champagne. He was eating . . . cornflakes.

A couple of hours earlier, around 11 Sunday night, Bobby Kennedy Jr. called asking for an update. One of the male servants held up the phone to a TV set carrying the local newscast from West Palm Beach. Perhaps Bobby Jr. was relieved that for once, he wasn't the Kennedy cousin under suspicion by the police.

As soon as the charges were officially filed, the Kennedy family lawyers unveiled what the Clintons a few years later would call the "nuts and sluts defense"—sliming the victim, a 29-year-old single mother named Patty Bowman.

Again, the court filings would tell the story. The Kennedys put on the public record the most salacious details of the woman's background—unwed mother; two or three abortions and a miscarriage; sexual abuse at age 8; a "heavy drinker" for a stepfather; prescriptions for tranquilizers, muscle relaxants, and painkillers; a terrible driving record. It was positively Kennedy-esque, the way she was described. The Kennedy investigators even mentioned her "promiscuity." One defense motion demanded that she take an AIDS test.

The Palm Beach County Office of the State's Attorney was likewise working the court of public opinion. In July, the prosecution released depositions from three other young women who claimed they had been attacked by Willie Smith. One victim, now a physician, said Smith tried to rape her in Georgetown after the two went skinny-dipping while they were both in medical school. She said he suddenly grabbed her by the wrists, "threw me over the couch and I landed on the floor on my back, ummmm, pinned to the floor by his wrist with him on top of me."

He eventually let her go, and she never reported the incident to the police, she said in her deposition, "because I know how powerful his family is."

But, she said, she had read in the Palm Beach police report how Willie had told Bowman the same thing he had told her—that no one would believe her anyway. The doctor said she wanted to "lend a hand" to her fellow victim.

A second woman said she had actually been raped by the Kennedy cousin in 1988, after getting "incredibly drunk" at a medical school party. He got her back to his apartment and attacked her.

"I could see it in his face . . . ferocious . . . [there was an] almost animal-like look to him . . . it was just horrible and I got scared."

The next morning, she said, he took a phone call from another woman, and denied that he had anyone with him in bed. His victim described herself as "hung over" and unsure what to do.

"Should I slap him in the face and walk out? . . . What should I do? . . . You know, I remember at the time thinking about pressing charges and, you know . . . My God, I don't want to do this."

After Smith was charged, the Kennedys began putting the full-court press on this second victim. They knew how damaging her testimony to a jury from the witness stand might be. A female friend of hers called saying, "Please don't testify." An ex-boyfriend was next, and she asked him if the Kennedys had put him up to it.

"He said, 'Well, Willie called me, and then Willie's lawyer calls me . . . Willie wants to talk you.' And I said, 'I don't want to talk to Willie,' and he said, 'But he really wants to talk to you . . . He can't understand why you're . . . going out on this, and, you know, would you talk to him?' And I said no . . . I think I would have gotten sick if I had spoken to him."

A third woman was the former girlfriend of Max Kennedy, Willie's younger cousin. She said she was attacked in 1983, when she was 19 and Smith was 23. He had offered her a place to sleep in his parents' home on Fifth Avenue in Manhattan.

It was 3 a.m. Smith was "kind of slurring his words and his eyes were somewhat glazed." Once he got her into the guest bedroom, she said, it was the same type of attack as the others—"tackled onto the bed . . . his body completely over mine and (he) had me pinned to the bed." She escaped and he apologized. But then he jumped her again, tackling her, throwing her back onto the bed, "almost as if it were a repeat performance."

She fled out onto Fifth Avenue and the next day called Max, telling him his cousin was a "sick-o." She said she "expected some sympathy," but Max told her, "Oh, hey, it's no big deal, he just made a pass at you."

Eight years later, after the latest attack in Palm Beach, she said, she telephoned Max, and this time he apologized for not taking her seriously in 1983.

"He said, 'Sounds like Willie has a really big problem. He needs some help.'"

Max told her the scandal was proving to be very difficult for the family—"it was hard for his family at that particular moment because people were perceiving them as 'you sick rapists.'"

During their conversation, Willie mentioned yet another of the women who'd accused him of assault. But, he told his ex-girlfriend, "she was dumb, she spoke to the [*National*] *Enquirer*, and the implication there was that it was going to affect her credibility that she had spoken to this disreputable newspaper."

That woman may have been Nancy Narleski, a one-time fiancée of David Kennedy, who had died of a drug overdose during an earlier traditional Easter weekend for the family in Palm Beach, in 1984. She had been interviewed not by the *Enquirer*, but by another supermarket tabloid, the *Star*. She later ended up on a syndicated TV gossip show owned, like the *Star*, by Teddy Kennedy's arch-nemesis, Rupert Murdoch.

She was attacked, she said, in April 1980, when she and Willie were both working as volunteers in Teddy's doomed presidential campaign. They discovered that they had been born on the same day in 1960, which Willie told her was a significant connection. Even though he knew she was committed to his junkie cousin David, he invited her up to his hotel room. Again, the same modus operandi—he threw her on the bed and "started straddling me and I was screaming . . . and yelling at him to get off me and he just looked at me with these eyes and I'll never forget them . . . and he said, 'Shut up bitch!'"

In other words, a variation on what he allegedly said to Patty Bowman 11 years later—"Stop it, bitch!"

She escaped when her screams brought other campaign workers to the door of the hotel room. The next day she called David Kennedy and got much the same response that his younger brother Max had offered his girlfriend when she was assaulted by Willie.

"He told me I should have known better than to be alone with Willie," she was quoted as saying in the *Star*. Later he bought her a dog tag that read, "Property of David A. Kennedy. Hands Off!" Giving it to her, he said, "Maybe this will make you feel a little more comfortable around some of my family."

Narleski was not amused.

A few months later, she was invited to Hyannis Port for a reunion of campaign workers—a sort of updated version of the boiler-room girls of Chappaquiddick. Sen. Kennedy, she said, took her for a walk along the rocks on the beach, consoling her, "comforting me and telling me how much he understood . . . Then he lifted my head and tried to kiss me. At that point I lost it. I just lost it."

After fleeing back to her parents' home in New Jersey, she called David in Sacramento, where he was once again trying to kick his drug habit.

"Whereas with Willie he seemed really upset," she told the *Star,* "he just laughed this one off. He said, 'Nancy, you're not the first person this has happened to, you're not going to be the last. Look at it as an initiation.'"

After the 1991 alleged rape, she got a phone call from Willie's cousin, U.S. Rep. Joe Kennedy, advising her to stay out of the Palm Beach case. She at first agreed, she said, but "my conscience never would have left me alone."

The story that ran in the *Star* was headlined, "I Had to Fight Off Willie—and Sen. Ted/Now I've Been Warned to Keep My Mouth Shut."

As damaging as all these stories were to the family image, most of them only peripherally involved Teddy. But then the prosecutors started taking depositions from "the help," and his alcoholism and sheer degeneracy were exposed once and for all, and it was much worse than anything that had ever appeared in the gossip columns.

On Good Friday, for instance, the drinking began around noon, 15 hours before the alleged rape, at least according to Jean Saba, one of the housekeepers put under oath. She was not a willing witness.

"See," she said, "I kind of mind my own business. I don't ask too many questions."

Always a good policy when associating with the Kennedys. But now Saba was under oath, and she had to tell the truth about Good Friday at the mansion, which the wags in Boston were now calling "Comfortably Numb by the Sea," after the old Led Zeppelin song "Comfortably Numb." The Kennedys started the day with daiquiris.

"Always," she said. "Always at lunch. It's a family tradition."

The daiquiris were followed by wine, she continued, "which is very, very normal and very typical."

How much wine, she was asked.

"I would say quite a bit."

Remember, Good Friday is the holiest day on the Christian calendar. So after lunch, Saba said, "A few of the men had a few drinks."

Who had the drinks?

"I don't know. They would just—I don't really want to—I really don't want to say. I don't know—I didn't pay that much attention. I do my work. I don't ask questions."

Predinner, the Kennedys switched back to daiquiris. Then it was time for the evening meal—pompano with red potatoes and zucchini au gratin. And of course "three or four" bottles of wine. And how was the senator by that point in the evening?

"Very talkative."

Ted Kennedy was deposed in New York, at the offices of Joseph P. Kennedy Enterprises on East 42nd Street. He himself was asked whether he continued drinking after dinner.

"I may have. I don't have a clear recollection." Which was understandable, under the circumstances. "But I may have had one at dinner."

After dinner, Willie and Patches headed out to an island bar, but quickly returned home. They were in their room, asleep, when Teddy knocked on their door around midnight and asked them if they wanted to return downtown to Au Bar for "a couple of beers"—actually, in the senator's case, Chivases and sodas.

Patches Kennedy later testified that despite the fact that he and Willie had been asleep, they immediately agreed to accompany Teddy back into town. They wanted to share a little quality time with the family patriarch. Apparently the 10 or 12 hours of drinking earlier in the day hadn't been sufficient.

"We wanted to spend time with him . . . I wanted to be out with my father . . . We shared some conversation about how he was feeling . . . and it was very personal conversation and one that meant a lot to me."

They set off in the family's white convertible—a traditional Kennedy vehicle. Once they arrived at Au Bar, Teddy began guzzling more Scotch—"maybe a couple." Suitably refortified, the Kennedys then chatted up several women, including Anne Mercer, who hours later would arrive at the mansion to pick up her friend Patty Bowman after the alleged rape.

At Au Bar, Patches later recalled, Mercer had words with Sen. Kennedy.

"She, I think she could have said, 'You have been drinking too much.'"

Patches was asked for his take on the victim, Patty Bowman. The state representative from Providence responded, characteristically, incoherently.

"It was a quiet, it wasn't like, hi, hey, hello. She sort of put out her hand, and didn't, you know, give any sort of way recognize that you versus in terms of, you know, greeting someone when you meet them."

Later, as they were about to leave, Patches picked up another woman, Michelle Cassone, 27, either a waitress or an heiress, depending on which newspaper you read.

"She started walking out with us," Patches said. "And at which point I said, 'Are you leaving?' She said, something to the effect, 'Are you leaving?' She said, 'Yes, I am leaving.' Would you like to join us for a quiet drink back at the house? Or, you know, and she said, 'yes.'"

Back at the mansion, Patches found a bottle and poured some wine for Michelle and they settled down inside the study. Patches was trying to get a little, as he would put it, "you know." Teddy vanished for a while, but when he returned, the blazer and the shirt he had been wearing at Au Bar were gone. So were his trousers. All he was wearing was a button-down Oxford shirt.

"Ted had a really weird look on his face," Cassone told the *Boston Herald* on April 6. "I saw his bare knees and freaked out. I said, 'I gotta go. This is getting weird. It's getting late. I should go home.'"

Patches insisted on one final walk down to the beach, and as they returned, she saw another disconcerting sight—"the senator strolling across the lawn, still in his shirt."

Cassone was soon all over television and newspapers. Rumors spread that she was going to pose nude for one of the girlie magazines.

The Murdoch organization obtained photographs of Cassone in a compromising position and then invited her onto *A Current Affair* for yet another interview. The host, an Australian hack named Steve Dunleavy, asked her three times whether she was planning to, or had ever posed nude. Three times the heiress, or waitress, answered no.

Then he showed her copies of the photographs. She jumped up and began pounding the host with her fists. She bit him at least twice, down to the bone, or so Dunleavy would later claim. The video can still be seen on *YouTube*.

The avalanche of negative publicity continued unabated. The menus for the weekend were released, and it became clear that women's liberation wasn't the only movement the Kennedy family had missed over the past two decades. Nouvelle cuisine appeared to have totally passed them by. The Kennedys seemed to be in a culinary time warp—on Easter Saturday, for instance, Ted Kennedy breakfasted on eggs à la Lee.

"It's an English muffin with a piece of ham, a poached egg, and mushroom sauce. It's supposed to be General Lee's favorite."

That tidbit of information came from Nellie McGrail, whose name Teddy had mentioned at his disastrous press conference at MIT in May. Nellie, who turned 80 that summer, had kidney dialysis three times a week. But the Kennedys still worked her like a coal-mine pony.

She got up at 6:30 every morning "to say my prayers." Then she'd start in on her daily chores. She squeezed the oranges by hand—"You squeeze oranges for 14 people, it takes you a little while."

Before turning in for the evening, she had one more cooking chore—"they order a chicken every night so they can come in and cut it and eat it and have a little bit of salad."

Then there was Patches. While in Palm Beach, he customarily got up at the crack of noon.

Jean Saba explained Patches's MO in Palm Beach.

"He will sleep longer . . . So many times everybody is up and in the ocean or somewhere and Patrick is still sleeping."

When he finally woke up, he would stumble out of the bedroom, appear at the kitchen door, and bellow, "Nellie, my usual!"

His usual: three scrambled eggs, a half pound of bacon, and three English muffins.

"You'd think he never ate a meal in his life," Nellie reported.

He was also a bit of a slob, according to Jean Saba. She was asked about the room he shared with Willie Smith. Did they make their beds, Jean?

"Well, they're young men."

"What does that mean?" asked the prosecutor.

"A mess. But no—I mean, their clothes would be thrown. Especially Patrick. He's always like that."

Following the early-morning alleged rape, Ted had worked up quite an appetite. On Easter Saturday, Nellie testified, after Ted's breakfast of eggs à la Lee, for lunch he feasted on chicken salad and crabmeat thermidor, with a sauce made of, among other things, mushroom, white wine (yes!), flour, whipping cream, butter, and grated Swiss cheese.

And for dinner, broccoli hollandaise—yet another egg-and-butter-based sauce, the third of the day. The meat that evening was filet mignon—"I had to cut a couple thinner to make them go 'round."

The family fortune just wasn't what it used to be, apparently.

Nellie had worked for the family for 20 years, but she would tell prosecutor Moira Lasch that Easter Weekend 1991 was the first time she ever left the kitchen.

"I never did, never in my life. If you did, you'd be fired."

Nellie's magic moment came when the Palm Beach police arrived looking for Teddy and Willie. William Barry, the ex-FBI agent, met the cops in the kitchen and began speaking for the family. And that was the cue for Nellie. With her was Bridie Sullivan. For 27 years, she'd been employed by Jean Kennedy Smith, Willie's mother.

"He started to speak. Well, we don't stay in a room when people are speaking . . . We disappear. We never stay when people are speaking. You don't eavesdrop."

Lasch was fascinated. She was getting a glimpse into a world long vanished everywhere else, except at Comfortably Numb by the Sea.

"Are you talking about with your employers?" Lasch asked Nellie.

"With anybody. You never stay when two people are speaking. At least, that's how we're brought up. We stood in the dining room because we knew it wasn't our business."

Nobody came out of the depositions looking good. Jean Kennedy Smith, Willie's mother, had come down to Palm Beach with her own servant, Bridie Sullivan, the Irish, one-time governess who was now Jean's cook and companion. Asked if she was a maid, Bridie bristled: "I never wear a uniform."

Bridie, in the words of Nellie, "came, yes, with the baggage and stuff."

Some of the stuff was Willie Smith's dirty laundry. He brought it with him to Palm Beach, for the help to clean.

Jean Smith was asked under oath if she'd ever gone to Au Bar.

"No," she replied. "Thank God."

Then Lasch asked Smith if she had ever discussed the evening at Au Bar with her son.

"No. But—no, that is not unusual. I mean, he doesn't usually talk about—they never discuss—none of them ever discuss what they do in the evening with me."

In other words, don't ask, don't tell. That was the Kennedy family motto, at least for the men.

Still, even with all the commotion on Saturday, and the visit from the police on Easter Sunday, the events were apparently nothing out of the ordinary for the Kennedys in Palm Beach.

"Do you know," Nellie said, "it was one of the quietest weekends we ever had in our life."

Dennis Spear, the male houseman, was also deposed. He reported that he had another job—at the Sailfish Club, then one of few remaining gentile-only "restricted" bastions on the island. He was asked about the first night the Kennedys were in town, when Teddy and Patches picked up the two women at Au Bar on Holy Thursday.

No word on how Teddy made out with his date, but Patches apparently had less luck with the "you know," as he would put it. Once again, he couldn't close the deal.

So around 3:30 Friday morning Patches asked Spear to drive his date back to the Ocean Grand Hotel in her rented car. The Ocean Grand was 10 miles from the mansion. So how did Spear get home? He threw a bicycle into the trunk, and after getting the woman back to her hotel, pedaled home at dawn—10 miles.

It might not have been as arduous as squeezing orange juice by hand for 14, but it couldn't have been much fun. But, like Nellie, Spear dummied up. The Kennedy help still observed the old Mafia tradition of omertà—silence. Lasch asked him about his conversation with the woman on the 10-mile drive back to her hotel.

PROSECUTOR: "And did you meet the woman at that time?"

SPEAR: "No."

PROSECUTOR: "Where was the guest?"

SPEAR: "I don't know."

"Surely," the prosecutor asked, "you must have talked to her about something during the ride."

"Never asked her name," Spear said. "Never saw her again."

In early June, Teddy's loyal liegemen at the Sunday *Boston Globe* tried to run interference. But unlike the 1962 revelations about his undergraduate Harvard cheating scandal, this apologia would not run below the fold on the front page. The headline, though, would be familiar to any longtime *Globe* reader, especially in election years:

"Kennedy Says Lifestyle Will Change"

It wasn't until the third paragraph that Kennedy was allowed to "reject the notion" that he had a drinking problem. Later he "bristled" at the notion that he needed to seek help for his addictions.

"I've gone 37 days without," he said. "Three years ago: 55 days or something."

Next came the traditional anonymous "loyal friend," who was quoted as saying, "Ninety-five percent of the time he's working hard. The other 5 percent of the time, he has a need to anesthetize the pain."

The pain? Well, the *Globe* noted, he did "hold some responsibility" for the death of a young woman, who the *Globe* didn't name, in an accident at some unknown time in a location the newspaper also neglected to mention.

For Teddy, the timing was particularly inopportune. A new Supreme Court justice had just been nominated to replace Thurgood Marshall—a conservative black federal appellate court judge named Clarence Thomas. Given his race, and the fact that he'd already been confirmed once by the Senate, he would be much harder to "bork."

Plus, Thomas and Teddy already had a history. Prior to his judgeship, he'd been commissioner of the Equal Employment Opportunities Commission (EEOC), and during one Senate hearing, Thomas had been on the receiving end of a drunken Teddy rant. Thomas was so enraged at his shabby treatment that he finally slammed his fist on the hearing desk.

"Senator," he told Teddy, "I was born in poverty. I was raised by my grandparents. It was a tough time, but they taught me values. And in our living room were pictures of three people: Jesus Christ, Martin Luther King, and John F. Kennedy. Senator, I think if President Kennedy is watching these proceedings now, he can't be very well pleased."

The Democrats put off the confirmation hearings, to give themselves more time to dig up dirt on Thomas. Finally, they found what they'd been looking for. One of his female aides, Anita Hill, who had followed him from job to job, now claimed that he had sexually harassed her.

The charges represented a good career move for Hill. Forever after, she would be a feminist martyr. But it was a he said–she said case—not the sort of thing Teddy had any business meddling in during the run-up to his nephew's trial in Florida. As the confirmation hearings neared, conservative groups bought TV spots, stressing the checkered pasts of Thomas's Democratic inquisitors—Joe Biden's recidivist plagiarism, Alan Cranston's "Keating Five" savings-and-loan scandal, and, of course, "Teddy's Sexy Romp," as the *New York Post* headline that ran in the spots put it.

Teddy was not a factor in the Senate hearings, and Thomas eked through on a 52–48 vote. But down in Palm Beach, things were beginning to look up for Willie Smith. The Kennedys had hired the best defense lawyer in south Florida, Roy Black, from Fort Lauderdale, and he and his team were working on the case full-time.

The prosecutor, Moira Lasch, was described in the press as a real hard charger, "Maximum Moira," a vegetarian from Vassar with a dentist for a husband. She was supposed to be very good, but as discovery continued, she was stuck with her regular trial caseload.

Compared to the defense, the prosecution turned out to be unprepared. The Palm Beach police had interviewed the victim five times, in addition to taking her formal deposition, so at trial Black would have plenty of story variations to pummel her with.

As jury selection began in December, JFK Jr. was sitting in the courtroom. Later, a Democratic congressman would read into the public record a sworn affidavit from a friend of JFK Jr., James Ridgway de Szigethy.

The affidavit was made part of the public record of Ohio Rep. James Traficant who, in one of the many ironies of the case, would eventually be convicted of bribery and tax evasion and sent to federal prison for seven years, while Smith of course would not serve a day.

In the affidavit, de Szigethy said, "John told me that when the trial took place, he would have to put in an appearance in the courtroom. He told me he did not want to do this and his mother did not want him to either."

JFK Jr. had also been pressured to have his photograph taken with Smith, which was then given to the wire services and distributed to hundreds of newspapers.

De Szigethy said JFK Jr. told him sadly, "You just don't understand the pressure I'm under." Later, the friend sent Traficant another letter, saying JFK Jr. was a victim of "blackmail." But, he said, "It was not his uncle," who coerced him into appearing in the courtroom. In a recent book about Robert F. Kennedy Jr., Jerry Oppenheimer wrote, "If Kennedy didn't cooperate in making a public show of support for Smith, he faced the release of personal information about his private life."

In other words, the Kennedys were now blackmailing one another. This was a long, long way from Camelot.

On October 25, after Thomas's confirmation, Teddy went over to Harvard to deliver yet another groveling, *Globe*-like apology, saying he was "painfully aware" of the criticism, not just from his political foes, but also "the disappointment of friends and many others who rely on me to fight the good fight."

He continued: "To them I say, I recognize my own shortcomings—the faults in the conduct of my private life. I realize that I alone am responsible for them, and I am the one who must confront them."

The trial of William Kennedy Smith was actually a bit of an anticlimax after the first day, when the female judge refused to allow the prosecution to introduce the statements of the three women who claimed they, too, had been sexually assaulted by Smith.

Prosecutor Lasch argued that the similarities in all four cases proved a pattern, a "signature" as it was known in Florida law. But increasingly she seemed in over her head. She didn't manage her time well, at one point putting her star witness, the victim Bowman, on the stand late in the day. That allowed Black all evening to pick her testimony apart before cross-examination began the next morning.

Perhaps as importantly, Lasch was up against the entire Kennedy family. Once voir dire was completed, JFK Jr. had flown back to New

Willie Smith at the John F. Kennedy Presidential Library in 1994 with two politicians who'd also been accused of abusing women, President Bill Clinton and Uncle Ted Kennedy.

York, but every day different family members were photographed walking into the courthouse in West Palm Beach, and on Sundays into Mass at St. Edward on the island.

Smith took the stand in his own defense. During cross-examination, when he said he had ejaculated twice inside Bowman, Lasch sneered back at him, "So what are you, a sex machine?"

In his closing statement to the jury, Roy Black said of the sex, "This is right out of a romance novel." Lasch choked up and began sobbing as she told the six-person jury: "She said 'No' and he didn't care."

It took the jury only 77 minutes to return a verdict of not guilty. Afterward, outside the courthouse, a crowd of hundreds chanted, "Willie! Willie! Willie!"

Addressing the crowd, Willie said, "I have an enormous debt to the system and to God. And I have a terrific faith in both of them."

Six blocks away, Bowman's lawyer read his own statement to the press: "The jury has spoken. However, 'not guilty' does not equate to 'innocent.'"

Two years later, Willie was arrested after a barroom brawl in Alexandria, Virginia. He claimed that he only punched his victim after he was "hassled, baited and insulted." The charges were dropped.

Like so many Kennedys of his generation, he started a nonprofit foundation, in Chicago, to provide assistance to victims of land mines. In 2004, he was sued by his former assistant who claimed he had lured her to his apartment and sexually assaulted her after a night of heavy drinking to celebrate her 23rd birthday in 1999.

Her case was dismissed, but not before it was reported in open court that he had recently quietly settled two other sexual-harassment lawsuits filed by young female employees. Speaking to reporters after the decision, the attorney for the female plaintiff said of Smith, "He's got seven women under gag orders right now."

Two marriages came out of the Palm Beach trial. Roy Black married one of the jurors. And Ted Kennedy knew he needed a new wife as well. He would be 60 in two months. He was much too old to have to keep making all these abject apologies.

After the traditional Easter weekend, Palm Beach was never the same for the Kennedys. The 15,347-square-foot mansion, which Joe Kennedy had bought from one of the Wanamakers of Philadelphia for $120,000 in 1933, was sold in 1995 to a merchant banker for $4.9 million. Arthur Schlesinger Jr. was trotted out to say the usual kinds of things he could always be counted upon to say on such occasions.

"Palm Beach is not a place where the youngest generation of Kennedys finds sustenance. They're all off involved in good works of sorts, and Palm Beach is dedicated to frivolity."

In 2015, Comfortably Numb by the Sea was sold again, to a New York real estate heiress, for $31 million.

Nellie died at the age of 84 in 1995, the same year the Kennedys sold the mansion. The obituary in the *Palm Beach Post* did not mention if she ever got out of the Kennedy's kitchen again after that memorable afternoon on Easter Sunday 1991.

After the verdict: Willie Smith and his mother Jean meet the press. In the background, defense lawyer Roy Black, who later represented Rush Limbaugh.

CHAPTER THIRTEEN

GAYS

Sen. Joseph McCarthy (R-WI) and his chief aide Roy Cohn. McCarthy was a friend of the Kennedy family. He was the godfather of RFK's first child, Kathleen. RFK went to work as a staffer for McCarthy, but clashed with Cohn, who was both gay and Jewish. After being outed as homosexual by the Las Vegas Sun *in October 1952, at the age of 44 McCarthy married his secretary, and they adopted a child. He drank himself to death in 1957 at the age of 48; RFK flew to Wisconsin for his funeral. Cohn moved back to his native New York, where he represented, among many others, Rupert Murdoch and Donald Trump. In his later life, Cohn was indicted on various federal charges including perjury and witness tampering, but was acquitted. He was finally disbarred by the state of New York in 1986, shortly before he died of AIDS at the age of 59.*

Lem Billings with RFK after his best friend's assassination. He met JFK in 1933, when they both entered the Choate School in Connecticut. He bragged later about how they both lost their virginity together at a Harlem whorehouse. They paid the hookers $3 each. But Lem was the proverbial "confirmed bachelor," a closeted gay from an old-line Brahmin family left penniless by the Depression. Billings was Princeton Class of 1939, but he was always around JFK. When JFK announced to the family that he was marrying Jackie, RFK quipped, "You mean, you're taking a second wife?" Billings had his own room at the White House.

After JFK's death, Billings's own life spiraled downhill. Seen here with Ethel, he attached himself to the younger Kennedys, eventually doing large amounts of drugs with Bobby Jr., to whom he left his Manhattan co-op when he died in 1981. Jackie cut him off from JFK Jr. after she discovered Lem was surreptitiously taking photos of "the Hunk" jogging shirtless through Central Park. Near the end of his life, Billings claimed he'd actually had sex with JFK, and described himself as "the last of the Kennedys." In the Princeton alumni magazine in 2017, Billings was quoted as saying, "Jack made a big difference in my life. Because of him, I was never lonely."

Cardinal Francis Spellman of New York. Joe Kennedy dismissed the clergy as "silly little men running around in black suits." Spellman married most of the Kennedys. He was originally from Whitman, Massachusetts. During his life he had two hobbies—collecting stamps and Broadway chorus boys. The former can still be viewed in a museum at Regis College in Weston, Massachusetts.

U.S. Rep. Gerry Studds represented Hyannis Port. In 1983, was censured by the House on a 420–3 vote for plying a young male page with vodka and then sodomizing him. He was reelected six times after the scandal. Before his election, Studds was a teacher at St. Paul's School in Concord, New Hampshire, alma mater of John Kerry and Robert Mueller. According to reports and lawsuits in 2017–2018, before he was fired in 1969 for his inappropriate behavior with male students, he once asked a student, "Can I beat you off?" and another, "May I hug you out of desperation?" Another student reported Studds gave him marijuana that had apparently been laced with a stronger substance, which caused him to pass out, and when he awoke Studds was rubbing his chest. Studds required the male students in his dorm to take part in dorm meetings nude. He died in 2009; he has a national marine sanctuary named after him.

Bayard Rustin, top aide to Martin Luther King Jr., who organized the March on Washington civil-rights rally in 1963. One of the attendees was Marietta Tree, a socialite who was a U.S. delegate to the United Nations. RFK ran into her at a party and said, "So you're down here for that old black fairy's anti-Kennedy demonstration."

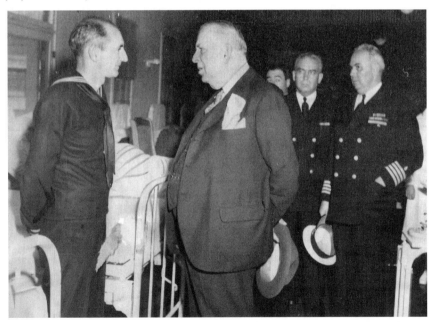

Sen. David I. Walsh, center, first Irish-Catholic governor of Massachusetts, later senator, made many visits to Navy bases. Defeated for reelection in 1946 by Henry Cabot Lodge after he was anonymously identified by the FBI in 1942 as the U.S. senator who had been patronizing a gay male brothel on the Brooklyn waterfront run by a Nazi spy. Boston papers refused to cover the story, much as they later shied away from Kennedy family sex scandals.

Rep. Barney Frank, with Joe Kennedy II. In 1990 Frank was reprimanded by the House on a 408–18 vote for his conduct with a male prostitute named Steve Gobie, to whom he had paid $80 for anal sex. Gobie, who was known as "Hot Bottom," moved in with Frank, continuing to run a brothel out of the Newton congressman's apartment. Frank fixed hundreds of dollars of parking tickets for Hot Bottom, and was reelected 11 times after the scandal. When he retired after the 2012 election, he was succeeded by Joe Kennedy III.

CHAPTER FOURTEEN

NIXON ON THE KENNEDYS

RICHARD NIXON AND JFK were both first elected to the House of Representatives in 1946. Both had been Navy officers in the Pacific Theater during World War II. Nixon beat Kennedy to the Senate by two years, defeating Helen Gahagan Douglas in 1950.

The Kennedys did not care for Douglas; JFK personally delivered $1,000 to Nixon's office on Capitol Hill, and Joe gave him a much larger donation—estimates are as high as $100,000.

Their relationship changed in 1960, when the Kennedys basically stole the presidential election from Nixon, in Cook County, Illinois, and, likely, in South Texas.

Nixon wandered in the political wilderness for years, but in 1968, he was finally elected president. In 1969, he moved into the Oval Office with its voice-activated system of taping conversations. It was that technology, initially installed at the direction of JFK, that eventually brought Nixon down, by recording his discussions with top aides about the botched burglary of Democratic National Committee headquarters at the Watergate in June 1972.

In a 2014 book, *The Nixon Tapes 1971–1972,* authors Douglas Brinkley and Luke A. Nichter transcribed more than 700 pages of the tapes, including repeated references to the Kennedys, mostly Teddy, but also Nixon's old "frenemy," as the authors described JFK.

On April 15, 1971, Nixon offered this stark appraisal of JFK to aides Bob Haldeman and Henry Kissinger: "Kennedy was cold, impersonal, he treated his staff like dogs, particularly the secretaries and the others.

He was not a beat man, he didn't read, all these other things. His staff created the impression of warm, sweet and nice to people, reads lots of books, a philosopher, and all that sort of thing. That was a pure creation of mythology. We have created no mythology."

A week earlier, the president had spoken by telephone to the Rev. Billy Graham, who was in Vero Beach, Florida. Graham told Nixon about an op-ed piece he had just written for the *New York Times* about the origins of the Vietnam War.

GRAHAM: "I'm putting all the whole thing on Kennedy."

NIXON: "That's right! He started the whole damn thing! . . . He killed [Ngô Đình] Diem!"

GRAHAM: "Right."

NIXON: "And he sent the first 16,000 combat people there himself!"

GRAHAM: "Well, I'm saying that the first time I heard about involvement was four days before he was inaugurated, playing golf with him. He said, I quote, 'We cannot allow Laos and South Vietnam to fall to the Communists. And then I—'"

NIXON: (laughs).

Graham continues to lay out the points he'd made in his upcoming *New York Times* piece, but Nixon interrupts him, to return to the subject of the overthrow and murder of Diem and his brother, exactly three weeks before JFK's own assassination in Dallas.

"And Diem had been murdered," he said. "You see, Billy, the key thing here was Kennedy's, and I must say our friend Lodge's, agreement to the murder of Diem. Diem, that's what killed the, opened the whole thing."

These conversations in *The Nixon Tapes* began less than two years after Chappaquiddick, a subject that naturally fascinated the president, considering that he had believed Teddy was the front-runner for the Democratic nomination for president in 1972. In the fall of 1969, he had asked J. Edgar Hoover to investigate rumors that Mary Jo Kopechne had accompanied Ted on his trip to Europe in 1968 to negotiate the financial terms of his sister-in-law Jackie's marriage to Aristotle Onassis.

The rumors proved to be untrue, but Nixon still believed he might end up running against Teddy. In a conversation in April 1971, he and his aides discussed how to keep an eye on the senior senator from Massachusetts.

NIXON: "Well goddamn it, there ought to be a way to get him covered, I wouldn't bother with McGovern. Certainly I think with Teddy, the reason I would cover him is from a personal standpoint. You're likely to find something on that."

He meant Chappaquiddick.

"You watch," Nixon said. "I predict something more is going to happen . . . I mean, it's a matter of judgment. I mean, he's just gonna . . ."

Then they began discussing a recent visit to the White House by Joan Kennedy for a luncheon of Senate wives. Joan was clad in what Haldeman described as "some crazy outfit" including what Ron Ziegler called "a bare midriff" and a "body stocking, which is flesh tone."

NIXON: "Weird."

HALDEMAN: "She was going to wear hot pants but Teddy told her she couldn't."

NIXON: "It's crude. What the hell's the matter with them? What's she trying to prove?"

HALDEMAN: "Whatever it is, she ain't gaining many votes, because they've got the super-swinger jet-set types are going to be for them and not for you no matter what happens."

Nixon then listens as his aides discuss whether even "the super-swingin' jet-set types," as Ziegler describes the core Kennedy constituency, could relate to Teddy's depraved lifestyle. Joan's behavior they find particularly odd.

ZIEGLER: "She has to have some sort of hang-up herself personally. She knows what Teddy was doing out there with that girl (Mary Jo), running her into the water, you know, and what he's been doing."

HALDEMAN: "But the family's used to that."

NIXON: "They do it all the time."

HALDEMAN: "That's the price you pay when you join that club. They all know that. Ethel, Jackie, and all the rest of them."

NIXON: "They gotta expect that."

The use of the Internal Revenue Service (IRS) to harass political opponents would not become official government policy until the presidency of Barack Obama, when Democrat operatives basically weaponized the IRS in a crude, attempt to put pro-Republican Tea Party groups out of business.

A Democrat dirty trickster on the IRS payroll named Lois Lerner ended up taking the Fifth Amendment when asked at a congressional hearing about how she organized her agency's harassment of the GOP groups during the Obama regime. In the summer of 2018, the IRS agreed to pay $3.5 million in damages to the aggrieved Tea Party groups as part of a lawsuit against the Obama Administration. (Later that summer, Lerner spent $1.9 million to buy a house on the island of Nantucket, where Joe Kennedy II crippled Pam Kelley in a Jeep accident in 1973.)

During Nixon's presidency, use of the IRS was for political persecution remained mainly an Oval Office fantasy, not the official, if unspoken government policy it would later become under Obama. In September 1971, Nixon told aide John Ehrlichman, "I could only hope that we are, frankly, doing a little persecuting."

He mentions Democratic senator Edmund Muskie, and former vice president Hubert Humphrey. But then Nixon gets to his real concern.

NIXON: "Teddy? Who knows about the Kennedys? Shouldn't they be investigated?"

EHRLICHMAN: "IRS-wise, I don't know the answer. Teddy, we are covering—"

Then he mentions how Teddy had gone to Pakistan, and on his way back home, had stopped off in Hawaii for a vacation, and he'd been put under surveillance by some parties Ehrlichman does not identify.

NIXON: "Be careful now."

ERLICHMAN: "Affirmative. He was in Hawaii on his own. He was staying at some guy's villa and we had a guy on him. He was just as nice as he could be the whole time."

NIXON: "The thing to do is watch him, because what happens to fellows like that, who have that kind of problem, is that they go for a quite a while . . . and they'll break open."

That same month, in September 1971, Nixon mentions a recent statement by Teddy about seeking peace in Vietnam. The president tells Kissinger, "Speaking of whimpering, that goddamn Teddy overstepped when he said he would crawl on his hands and knees—"

On April 17, 1972, Nixon says, "Teddy is a, well, unbelievable . . ."

From reading the transcripts about the Kennedys, Brinkley and Nichter point out, "It remains unclear whether Nixon admired or detested them more."

Actually, while his feelings about JFK and RFK do appear mixed, Nixon's take on Teddy seems consistent, as in this conversation with Kissinger in August 1972.

NIXON: "What the hell is the matter with Teddy? It isn't a question, I mean, I don't think it's a sex business. I think his problem, meaning his lack of discretion, don't you think it's the booze? He can't resist the booze?"

KISSINGER: "Well, these can't—first of all, he drinks."

NIXON: "No, no. But Bobby and Teddy—Bobby and Jack, everybody knows it, had their own way. But they were a hell of a lot more discreet."

Then Kissinger recounts how he was told by Cristina Ford, the wife of auto magnate Henry Ford II, about Teddy's drunken advances toward her. The first incident occurred at his own house in Virginia, at a party during the opening of the Kennedy Center in Washington. There were two dinner tables, one on the first floor and the second upstairs.

KISSINGER: "He took her upstairs. All during the dinner, she had to fight him off because under the table he was grabbing her by the legs, and—"

NIXON: "Oh Christ! And there were other people present?"

KISSINGER: "That's right, at his own house. With his wife heading the table downstairs."

Not long after, Teddy resumed his stalking of the married woman at the Kennedys' favorite love shack in Manhattan, the Carlyle Hotel. The Fords had an apartment there, Kissinger told the president, so Teddy rented his own room "ten floors down. Walked up the stairs, practically beat her door down."

All Nixon said was, "Uh-huh."

KISSINGER: "And she said she's been pursued by many men in her life, but Teddy, just, is impossible! She finally told him, 'What if the newspapers get this?' He said, 'No newspapers are going to print anything about me. I've got that covered.'"

NIXON: "Jesus Christ! That's pretty arrogant."

Later in September, Nixon is talking with his top chief aides, Haldeman and Ehrlichman, about whether or not Teddy should be given Secret Service protection until the election. None of them want to give him protection other lawmakers aren't afforded, but the reality is, Teddy is in more danger. Nixon ponders whether he can somehow get some return on investment, by installing more sets of eyes and ears on Teddy as he continues his drunken, misogynistic escapades.

NIXON: "You understand what the problem is. If the son of a bitch gets shot they'll say we didn't furnish it. So you just buy his insurance. Then after the election, he doesn't get a goddamn thing. If he gets shot, it's too damn bad."

EHRLICHMAN: "All right."

NIXON: "Do it on that basis, though, that we pick the Secret Service men. Not that son of a bitch (James) Rowley (then head of the Secret Service). Understand what I'm talking about? Do you have anybody in the Secret Service that you can get to?"

EHRLICHMAN: "Yeah."

NIXON: "Do you have anybody that we can rely on?"

EHRLICHMAN: "Yeah, we've got several."

NIXON: "Plant one, plant two guys on him. That would be very useful."

CHAPTER FIFTEEN

IN HER OWN WORDS:
CAROLINE KENNEDY

ALL DIALOGUE GUARANTEED VERBATIM from New York newspaper interviews in December 2008 of Caroline Kennedy—she ditched her husband's last name of Schlossberg—on the occasion of her possible appointment to the U.S. Senate to finish the term of Sen. Hillary

Caroline Kennedy waved goodbye to her chances of being appointed to the U.S. Senate when she gave interviews to the New York newspapers.

Clinton, who was about to become Secretary of State in Barack Obama's new administration.

One of the papers to which she gave an interview was the *Daily News,* where she had worked as an intern in the 1970s. As the *Daily News* noted, "Her speech was often punctuated with extra 'you knows' and 'ums.'"

The *New York Times* reported that Caroline used the phrase "you know" 138 times in her interview with their reporters at a Manhattan coffee shop.

After these interviews, Caroline was not appointed to the Senate seat once occupied by her uncle Robert.

Not Beholden to Mayor Bloomberg

"I'm really coming into this as somebody who isn't, you know, part of the system, who obviously, you know, stands for the values of the Democratic party. I know how important it is to, you know, be my own person. And, you know, and that would be obviously true with my relationship with the mayor."

Relationship with Andrew Cuomo After His Divorce from Her Cousin Kerry Kennedy

"Andrew is, you know, highly qualified for the job. He's doing a, you know, a great job as (state) attorney general, and we've spoken throughout this process. You know, I think, you know, we're sort of, uh, sharing some of this experience. And um, as I've said, he was a friend, a family member, and, um, so, and, uh, obviously, he's, you know, he's also had an impressive career in public office."

What It's About

"It's really, you know, it's not about just the Kennedy name. It's about my own work and what I've done with those values."

De Rigeuer Question About Drug Use

REPORTER: Have you ever done illegal drugs?

"Well, you know, I grew up in the '70s, so I'd say I was a typical member of that generation."

REPORTER: How typical?

"Not that typical. Atypically typical."

State of Her Marriage

"In terms of my marriage, you know, falling in love with my husband was by far the best thing that's ever happened to me. And we've been together for, what, almost 28 years. So you know, he is, you know, an incredible person, and the more time I spend with him, the happier I am."

Her Husband's Reaction to Her Possibly Becoming a Senator

"He's, you know, really excited for me also, and feels like, you know, it would be—I think both of us understand that this is one way of serving. And so, you know, he himself has always worked hard on education and other issues, and so he feels like if I have an opportunity and a chance to bring attention to issues that, you know, I should really pursue that, and that it's important. I've been kind of, you know, working from home most of the time that my kids were young, and so this would be obviously a big change for me."

More on Her Husband's Reaction

"I think he believes strongly that, you know, that I would be great, and that I, this is, you know, an unbelievable privilege that I have, and he's as concerned as I am about, you know, what we see here in this city and state that we both grew up in, and, you know, and that we both care about."

Her Kids' Reaction to Her Potential Appointment

"I think they were really—obviously, they were supportive of me and think this would be an incredible opportunity. And, you know, then we talked about whether their life was going to change, and whether our family life was going to change and, you know, they understand that there will be adjustments, but I think they feel, like we all do, that if you have an opportunity to make a difference and help people and contribute in a positive way that that's a great thing to have, so, you know, they're very excited."

Appointment to the Senate

"Well I knew it would be a big change in my life, and I have really a wonderful life, and but, I feel like, you know, it's, you know, it's not really complete if there are things you could be doing that would benefit others and you're not taking, you know, the time and making the effort to do that. So, um, so I think it's really the, you know, it would be a big change, and change can be, you know, traumatic."

Review of *Slumdog Millionaire*

"It was, you know, on many levels a terrific movie."

What Would Jackie Think About Your New Career?

"She would just think it was, you know, funny that things had come full circle in a way. But she's one of those people that once she made a decision, you made a decision, she was totally in your corner and would get so excited and, you know, do anything she could."

Relationship with Her Uncle Ted

"So, you know, I do talk to him. I try to call him every few days, see how he's doing. You know, he loves to hear what's going on, what the kids are doing, what my different cousins are doing, so there's lots to talk about, this included obviously."

Does Uncle Ted Want Her in the Senate?

"I mean, he loves the Senate, it's been, you know, the most, you know, rewarding life for him, you know, I'm sure he would love it to feel like somebody that he cared about had that same kind of opportunity, and I think he really—and so do I, think the impact he's had on, you know, working people, you know, the minimum wage fights that he's led, health care . . . Whether it's voting, civil rights, you know, across the board . . . I mean, I think for those reasons he would love to have somebody that he cares about following, you know, that tradition. But I think in terms of me, you know, he doesn't care, you know, he's happy if I'm happy."

9/11 as a "Defining Moment"

"I think that was really a defining moment for me, like a lot of people in New York. You know, thinking about, you know, how to become more involved on a civic level in this community. And I think over the last year, you know, during the Obama campaign, was really probably the most important thing that led me to this, because when I did travel much more extensively than I did in 2004, and, um, you know, talked to people across the country . . . This is, you know—nobody can sit out this one anymore. So I am volunteering to pitch in, if I'm, you know, if there's something I can contribute . . ."

Different Voices

"So I think in many ways, you know, we want to have all kinds of different voices, you know, representing us, and I think what I bring to it is, you know, my experience as a mother, as a woman, as a lawyer, you know, I've been an education activist for the last six years here, and, you know, I've written seven books . . . So obviously, you know, we have different strengths and weaknesses."

Bringing Attention to New York

"I think it's to New York's advantage to have somebody who can, you know, bring attention to New York, you know . . . and really put that to work for average people. This is not, you know, about me, it's about what I can do to, you know, help New York get its fair share."

An Economic Crisis

"I think this is about the future, and, um, you know, that's what I want to talk about, which is, what's going on in our state, you know, why I would be the best person to help deliver for New York. We're facing, you know, an economic crisis, the paper this morning said there's, you know, five billion dollars of construction projects which just stopped, you know, that's, you know—"

Topics to Discuss

"Um, you know, if you want to talk about, sort of, the economy or the issues, or me, that's, you know—I'd be happy to do that. But—"

A Proud Democrat

"And you know, I am a proud Democrat, those are the values, you know—middle class tax relief, helping working families, fixing the health care system—those are the national priorities you know—I am trying to become a Democratic senator, so I don't, um—I mean, there are issues along the way, that I'm sure that people have differences of opinion."

On Governor David Patterson

"I think he's done a great job as a leadership, yeah, absolutely."

CHAPTER SIXTEEN

FOREWORD TO LEO DAMORE'S *CHAPPAQUIDDICK*

(This chapter is adapted from the foreword to the 2018 reissue of *Senatorial Privilege: The Chappaquiddick Cover-Up* by Regnery Publishing. Damore's book has been retitled *Chappaquiddick: Power, Privilege and the Ted Kennedy Cover-Up*. The chapter has been expanded to include more material about the nature of the Kennedy family's century-long influence over the mass media.)

If anyone ever truly deserved a Profiles in Courage Award, it was the late Leo Damore, the author of this book.

Of course, the awards are handed out by the Kennedy family, and they are all about, not courage, but Political Correctness. But no one can dispute the fact that Damore put himself and his career on the line to write this book, and that one way or another, he paid the ultimate price—as a suicide, in 1995, at the age of 66.

Senatorial Privilege: The Chappaquiddick Cover-Up was a *New York Times* best seller in 1988. It sold more than a million copies. Damore's volume established a little-known publishing house, Regnery, as a major force in the book trade. Its success also disproved what New York publishers had long believed, or perhaps just hoped, that there was no real market out there for books that spoke, really spoke, truth to liberal power.

Hyannis Port 1944: In the front row, the two cousins, Teddy Kennedy and Joe Gargan. Standing, far left, is Paul "Red" Fay, who would be the "beard" who accompanied JFK's girlfriend Angie Dickinson to the presidential inauguration in 1961.

If you are just now discovering *Senatorial Privilege,* you may not be aware of the controversy that surrounded its initial publication. Damore seemed a most unlikely person to blow the lid off the Chappaquiddick cover-up. Born in Ontario, he was a reporter for the *Cape Cod Times.* His first book, in 1967, had been a standard post-JFK assassination hagiography, *The Cape Cod Years of John Fitzgerald Kennedy.*

In the final scene of *Cape Cod Years,* JFK returns to Boston for the final time, in October 1963, for a major black-tie fundraiser with the Democratic governors of New England. As Damore told the story, after the dinner a Hyannis housepainter named Fred Caouette approached the president and was "brusquely challenged" by a Secret Service agent.

Then JFK spots his humble Cape neighbor and yells to the agent, "Let the little guy through!" Shaking Cauoette's hand, the president says, "Freddy, it's awfully nice to see you," and finally tells him, "I'll see you next year."

That's the way all Kennedy books were written back then, even by Leo Damore. Little did Damore or anyone else know that earlier that

JFK's final trip to Boston, October 1963, as described in Leo Damore's first book.

evening, the tuxedoed president had summoned Mimi Alford, the intern whom he had deflowered in the White House a year earlier at the age of 19, to his suite at the Sheraton Plaza, where he ordered her to fellate his younger brother Teddy.

"You've got to be kidding, Mr. President," she recalled herself replying in her 2012 memoir.

Damore got a $150,000 advance from Random House, and he spent years digging up the truth. His most important source would be Joe Gargan, Teddy's first cousin who rented the cottage that evening. Like Michael Skakel, the convicted murderer in the next generation, Gargan was a kinsman, but not really a Kennedy. And like Skakel, in his fury against his mistreatment by the family, Gargan would eventually spill the beans.

The most explosive charge in *Senatorial Privilege* came from Gargan. After the accident, and the repeated rescue attempts of Mary Jo by

Teddy, Gargan and former U.S. attorney Paul Markham, Teddy floated an alternative story:

"Why couldn't Mary Jo have been driving the car? Why couldn't she have left me off, and driven to the ferry herself and made a wrong turn?"

To which Gargan eventually responded: "You told me you were driving."

When Damore handed in his manuscript to Random House, all hell broke loose. This was the home, after all, of William Faulkner, Andre Malraux, and Robert Penn Warren, not to mention Babar the Elephant. Imagine the reaction of the Random House editors as they read Damore's account of the court hearing in Pennsylvania on the exhumation of Kopechne's body, as the state medical examiner of Maryland blurted out a very inconvenient truth:

"It was apparent to me from the record that she lived for a certain time underwater . . . So she breathed, that girl. She *breathed!*"

You just couldn't write things like that about the Kennedys back then. Seldom was heard a discouraging word about America's First

A photo of the death car, taken in Edgartown Saturday morning by a crew member on one of the other boats in the Edgartown Regatta. The 1967 Delmont Oldsmobile was quickly removed from the island and compacted before any evidence could be collected.

Family. Even the biggest names in journalism were muzzled, like James "Scotty" Reston, the Washington columnist for the *New York Times* who owned a little weekly paper on Martha's Vineyard. Reston was there at the police station in Edgartown that Saturday morning as Teddy shakily wrote out the accident report. Damore quoted Scotty in his manuscript:

"I'd love to tell the story but they won't let me."

If it came down to a fight with the Kennedys, Random House couldn't win. In 1967, Jackie Kennedy had tried to stop publication of another, much more innocuous book, *The Death of a President.*

Jackie famously told the author, "Anybody who is against me will look like a rat unless I run off with Eddie Fisher."

In retrospect, Damore was lucky to have found any publisher willing to stand up to the wrath of the Kennedys. When it was finally published by Regnery, *Senatorial Privilege* was ignored by the critics, but Damore's expose was so thorough and so damning that even with no publicity, it still skyrocketed to the top of the best-seller lists.

But then, Chappaquiddick was a scandal for the ages, even by Kennedy standards.

Mary Joe Kopechne, for instance—everything about her screamed Kennedy girlfriend. She wasn't wearing underwear when she died, and she was drunk—her blood-alcohol level was .09. Her first boss in Washington was Sen. George Smathers of Florida, JFK's best friend in Congress, who used to travel with the future president to Havana in those pre-Castro days, where they were treated to the finest prostitutes in Cuba compliments of gangsters Meyer Lansky and Santo Trafficante.

In Washington, Kopechne's landlord was Bobby Baker, the longtime bagman for, among others, LBJ. Baker also ran a private DC "club", which offered the services of high-priced hookers, among them Ellen Rometsch, a suspected East German spy who was being investigated by a Senate committee for her relationship with JFK when she was suddenly deported in 1963.

The Kennedys may not have been able to stop publication of *Senatorial Privilege,* but revenge, as they say, is a dish best served cold. And after those first few big royalty checks, nothing was ever the same for Damore.

As his wife divorced him, he fell into a deep depression and began threatening suicide. At the same time, Damore also started research on a new book about Mary Pinchot Meyer, one of JFK's last blue-blooded girlfriends.

Meyer was the drop-dead gorgeous sister-in-law of Ben Bradlee, later the editor of the *Washington Post*. Bradlee was so close to JFK that in 1962 he was given the assignment of using his magazine, *Newsweek,* to spike the scandalous true story of JFK's first marriage, to a twice-divorced Protestant socialite in Palm Beach in 1947.

Meyer was another fascinating subject—during her affair with JFK, she got into drugs, and had begun visiting LSD guru Dr. Timothy Leary in Boston just before the assassination. Less than a year after Dallas, she was mysteriously shot to death while jogging on a canal path in Georgetown.

An obviously innocent young black man was arrested and charged, and then acquitted. The evening of the murder, Meyer's brother-in-law Bradlee went to her house to retrieve her secret diary about the affair with JFK. Inside, in the dark, Bradlee discovered that another intruder had gotten there first—James Jesus Angleton, the legendary CIA spook, who had his own sneaky eyes-only reasons for wanting the diary of the late president's paramour.

In short, Leo Damore had emerged from one Kennedy rabbit hole only to tumble into another, perhaps even deeper one. One of Meyer's biographers quoted Damore as telling him:

"What do you think it would do to the beatification of Kennedy if this woman said, 'It wasn't Camelot, it was Caligula's court.'"

I met Damore in 1994, on the 25th anniversary of Chappaquiddick. I was doing my radio show from the cottage on Chappaquiddick, and I booked some of the surviving principals. Only Damore asked for money—$100. Every time I spoke to him, he seemed nervous, agitated. The day after the show he telephoned again, begging me to send him the money ASAP, which I did.

Fifteen months later, Damore was depressed and broke, about to be evicted from his rented house in Essex, Connecticut. As a visiting nurse and a constable (who was there to serve the eviction notice) looked on in horror, Damore pulled out a gun and shot himself in the head.

Ted Kennedy died of brain cancer in 2009, at the age of 77. In his later years, it was considered bad form to even mention Chappaquiddick in polite company. Teddy himself seemed oblivious to the scandal—he named his last dog Splash.

The Kennedys' official fanzine has always been the *Boston Globe.* Every sixth year, when he was running for reelection, the *Globe* would run stories about how Teddy was "turning his life around," and how in an amazing feat of self-discipline, he had totally sworn off alcohol until his birthday—February 22. On the day after Chappaquiddick, the *Globe* ran a front-page headline that read, "Senator Wandered in Daze for Hours."

In 2003 the *Globe* perfectly summed up the mainstream media's revisionist take on Chappaquiddick:

"If she had lived, Mary Jo Kopechne would be 62 years old. Through his tireless work as a legislator, Edward Kennedy would have brought comfort to her in her old age."

Obviously, even by the shameful standards of the *Globe,* that was an extreme example of press obsequiousness. But until *Senatorial Privilege,* the predominant theme of all Kennedy coverage was . . . adulation. There were occasional negative stories or books, like Victor Lasky's cut-and-paste hatchet jobs on JFK and RFK, but they were few and far between.

From the beginning, Joe Kennedy cultivated the media. As a working-class kid from East Boston who went to Harvard, the old man could operate at every level of society, unlike his sons. Joe hobnobbed with the ink-stained wretches—one of his first friends in the press was Walter Howey, the Hearst editor in Boston who became the model for the fictional Walter Burns of the Broadway play and movie, *The Front Page.* In the early 1920s, Kennedy and Howey exchanged tips—on both stocks and news stories.

Joe Kennedy loved seeing his name in the newspapers. Even more, he loved seeing his children's names in the press. It was an investment in the future, as he saw it. Richard Whalen, one of Joe's early biographers, quoted a *Boston Post* editor as saying that the Boston newspapers covered the Kennedys "almost the way we covered City Hospital and the courts."

Joe wined and dined New York gossip columnists and Washington bureau chiefs, and when he went to Palm Beach in the winters he hung around with newspaper and magazine publishers like Henry Luce of *Time*. Col. Robert McCormick, the publisher of the *Chicago Tribune,* was his neighbor in Florida. He advised William Randolph Hearst when "the Chief" was in dire financial straits during the Depression.

The Kennedys always understood that journalists, like so many cops, were for sale. In the 1930s, the White House correspondents covering FDR each received a case of Joe's Haig & Haig Scotch every Christmas—the same as J. Edgar Hoover and Clyde Tolson of the FBI. Plus, Kennedy also sent along to each reporter a selection of fine Sulka ties. For the really important journalists, Joe could deliver other perks. Arthur Krock, the *New York Times* columnist who acted as Joe's unofficial lobbyist/promoter in Washington, was provided with prostitutes and showgirls, and in return promoted Joe in whatever office he was serving in, or seeking, that year.

When Joe arrived in the United Kingdom to become ambassador to the Court of St. James, Krock accompanied him, filing one breathless dispatch after another, the kind of coverage Joe sought, and came to expect, first for himself and then for his children:

"Here is Kennedy back again," Krock began, "the rage of London, the best copy in the British press, his counsel steadily sought by statesmen of the country to which he is accredited, his influence manifest and powerful in all matters in which the United States has an interest in Great Britain . . . Here he is back again, undazzled by such a taking up socially and officially as no American perhaps has known abroad since Franklin's day."

Krock was comparing Joe Kennedy to Benjamin Franklin! It was just another day at the office.

Nothing was too good for Krock, but the *Times*man finally put his foot down when Kennedy sent him a new automobile for Christmas. Krock appreciated the gesture, but accepting it might have . . . raised eyebrows.

Krock, not Damore, was the kind of reporter the Kennedys were used to dealing with. He handled the rewrites of JFK's first book, *Why England Slept,* and two decades later he heavily lobbied the Pulitzer Board to get the coveted nonfiction prize for JFK's best seller, *Profiles in Courage,* which was actually written by Ted Sorensen, although Joe threatened to sue columnist Drew Pearson for pointing that out on television.

It was important for his sons to have those books on the résumé—whoever actually wrote them, what really mattered was the name on the title page, and the dust jacket, and the spine.

As Joe Kennedy once wrote to Jack: "You would be surprised how a book that really makes the grade with high-class people stands you in good stead for years to come."

Conversely, the same could be true of a bad book—a negative book, like *Senatorial Privilege*. Which was why the Kennedys tried so hard to kill it. And of course after all those years of . . . doing the right thing . . . by their media sycophants, the Kennedys never had any problems finding "journalists" to do their bidding. And it was no secret in Washington how easy it was to buy good coverage, even in the supposedly reputable newspapers.

One of Joe Kennedy's greatest detractors in the Roosevelt Administration was Secretary of the Interior Harold Ickes, who watched with both fascination and disdain as Kennedy paid off the press.

"He is a grand hand at cultivating the correspondents," Ickes wrote. "He is a very rich man who is always doing favors for newspapermen. For instance, when he is to be away from his large and luxurious Washington house, he will turn it over to some newspaperman who can entertain lavishly, leaving all the bills to Kennedy when he returns."

Naturally, the Kennedys liked to get a good return on their investments in the care and feeding of the Fourth Estate. In 1953, Sen. John F. Kennedy was planning to marry Jacqueline Bouvier. Obviously, the best time for a wedding is the midsummer, especially if it's to be a high-society affair in Newport. But there was a problem—the *Saturday Evening Post,* one of the largest weekly magazines in America, was planning a lengthy piece on the freshman lawmaker for June.

The proposed headline, to run on the cover: "The Senate's Gay Young Bachelor."

Jack and Jackie had no choice. They waited to announce their nuptials until 12 days after the magazine arrived on the newsstands. They were married in September.

But it was worth it—even by the hagiographic standards that the family routinely expected, the *Post* story was about the Senate's gay young bachelor was over the top. It began with his arrival in the Senate the previous January.

"Kennedy appeared to be a walking fountain of youth," the author gushed in the first paragraph. "He is six feet tall, with a lean, straight, hard physique and the innocently respectful face of an altar boy at High Mass."

Joe's investment in the Senate seat was beginning to pay off. A year earlier, he'd spent millions to win the Senate seat for his son in an up-hill fight against incumbent Republican Sen. Henry Cabot Lodge. The largest single line item in Joe's budget was $500,000 to the publisher of the *Boston Post,* then the largest circulation newspaper in New England.

Despite its immense influence and huge readership, the nominally Democratic-but-rabidly-pro-Joe-McCarthy *Post* was on shaky ground financially. So Joe sought out the publisher, the hard-drinking John J. Fox, and offered him a "loan" of $500,000. A few weeks later, after weeks of adoring front-page coverage, the *Post* endorsed Eisenhower—and JFK.

Five years later, the *Post* was out of business, but the Kennedys were gearing up for JFK's run for the presidency in 1960. In those days, the cover of *Time* magazine meant something. A cover story in *Time* was worth . . . well, in November 1957 Joe had lunch with Cardinal Francis Spellman in New York.

According to Joe's biographer Ron Kessler, in his book *Sins of the Father,* Joe bragged, "I just bought a horse for $75,000. And for another $75,000, I put Jack on the cover of *Time.*"

On December 2, 1957, just as Joe had predicted to the cardinal, Sen. Kennedy was featured on the cover of *Time.*

At least JFK was an appealing, albeit superficial, figure. Teddy, on the other hand, would always be a harder sell. Especially since he was continually getting into trouble.

On May 2, 1958, after reports of Teddy's carousing at law school in Charlottesville got out, Joe wrote "the gay illiterate," as JFK called Teddy, a brief note.

"Dear Teddy," it read, "If you're going to make the political columns, let's stay out of the gossip columns."

But Teddy had another skeleton in his closet, much more significant than his traffic citations in Virginia. In 1952, he'd been expelled from Harvard College for hiring another student to take a Spanish exam for him.

"What a fool he was!" Joe exclaimed to his young mistress, Janet Des Rosiers.

Ten years later, with Joe paralyzed and unable to speak after his stroke, it fell to the next generation to bail out Teddy. The cheating story had to be gotten out . . . but in the proper, respectful way. It was an assignment that could only be handled by . . . the *Globe*. One of the editors, Bob Healy, was summoned to the White House, and he huddled with the president three times as they negotiated how the story would be played.

Healy said the story had to go on the front page, but the president insisted it be laid out "below the fold," so that the headline couldn't be seen on newsstands. The president argued that the revelation of Teddy's expulsion should be buried deep inside the story, which would be a sort of soft feature on the youngest Kennedy. Healy countered that the cheating had to be the lead, but he was willing to compromise on the headline:

"Ted Kennedy Tells About Harvard Examination Incident."

An "incident." As Bill Clinton said of his perjury and obstruction of justice, "Mistakes were made."

It was such an egregious example of journalistic malpractice that when Healey died in 2008, it was prominently mentioned in an otherwise fawning obituary as an event that "some would say (was) inglorious."

Healy, of course, was a typical "journalist" of the day. He had no regrets. The Harvard-cheating story, he said, a "once-in-a-lifetime" opportunity—to kiss Ted Kennedy's ass.

That was the world that Leo Damore lived in—and died trying to expose.

In 2015, the Edward M. Kennedy Institute for the Senate opened in Dorchester. One of its exhibits is entitled the "Senate Immersion Module." Immersion—you can't make this stuff up.

Near the end of his life, in 2009, Teddy wrote a sorrowful letter to Pope Benedict XVI:

"I have always tried to be a faithful Catholic, Your Holiness, though I have fallen short through human failings . . . I know that I have been an imperfect human being but with the help of my faith, I have tried to right my path."

Then he added, in a somewhat incongruous attempt at penance, "I have worked to welcome the immigrant."

Somehow I don't think Teddy was referring to Leo Damore.

Few of the principals ever talked about what happened that weekend on Chappaquiddick. The prosecutor, Walter Steele, was quickly appointed to a state judgeship—another nationwide search, as we say in Massachusetts. As a judge, his most famous case involved allowing a convicted child predator to leave the state without restriction, after which the offender moved to Montana and then murdered and cannibalized a 7-year-old boy.

When Steele reached the mandatory retirement age of 70 in 1996, the local New Bedford paper ran a story about him without a single mention of Chappaquiddick. But Judge Steele did obliquely mention the difficulty of explaining to victims and their survivors how sometimes an obviously guilty party gets off scot-free:

"It's awful hard to explain to them that you think you're doing justice."

Do you think the Kopechnes would have understood what Judge Steele was getting at?

As for Gargan, Damore paid him $15,000 for "legal and editing work" on *Senatorial Privilege.* Gargan eventually ended up with a hack job in Boston as chairman of a state board that essentially returned licenses to convicted drunk drivers.

Ironically, despite his intimate knowledge of what happened at Chappaquiddick, Gargan became the leading proponent on the board for allowing convicted drunkards back on the road. When Republicans regained control of state government in 1991, Gargan was summarily fired.

Gargan died in Virginia at the age of 87 in December 2017. By then he was such a forgotten figure that when his paid death notice appeared in the *Globe*, no Boston reporters even noticed it for three weeks.

According to the paid obituary, "Joe was dedicated to helping those who suffer from alcohol addiction."

The boiler-room girls you will soon be reading about have maintained omertà—silence—for almost half a century. But as Damore notes in Chapter 54, on the fifth anniversary of Mary Jo's death in 1974, Rosemary "Cricket" Keough did issue the following terse statement:

"My friend Mary Jo just happened to be in the wrong car at the wrong time with the wrong people."

In a strange way, Damore's life turned out like Mary Jo's—*Senatorial Privilege,* now retitled as *Chappaquiddick: Power, Privilege and the Ted Kennedy Cover-Up,* is an unforgettable book, muckraking in the best sense of the word. But for Damore personally, it was the wrong book at the wrong time about the wrong people, and it cost him his life.

But at least we still have his book—and the truth.

Ted Kennedy was so wracked with remorse about Chappaquiddick that he named his last dog, a Portuguese water spaniel, Splash.

CHAPTER SEVENTEEN

JOAN KENNEDY: "THE DISH" IN PHOTOS

S EN. JOHN F. KENNEDY called his future sister-in-law Joan Bennett "the Dish." Both her parents were alcoholics, as was her husband-to-be, Edward Moore Kennedy—in other words, it would probably not end well, and it hasn't.

All three of her children were alcoholics. Her daughter Kara died young, her elder son lost a leg to cancer, her younger son became a national laughingstock, the next generation's face of the Kennedy family's dissolution. Both sons' political careers ended prematurely.

This is a photo album of Joan Bennett Kennedy.

Joan and Ted, in happier times.

Sharing a laugh together: a photo from very
early in their marriage, obviously.

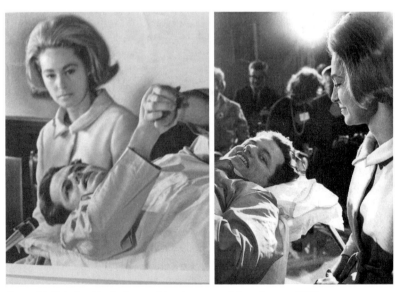

Joan with Ted after his airplane accident in western Massachusetts, 1964.

Joan, Ted, and Rose: the glamour days.

Joan with a hairdo that was not ozone layer–friendly.

Joan and Ted with a young Edward M. Kennedy Jr., future alcoholic and state senator from Connecticut.

Another day, another crowd, another stylish outfit.

Sometimes the same outfit that Joan wore when, say, taking her youngest son Patrick home from the hospital in 1967 . . .

. . . could be repurposed two summers later when she accompanied her husband to the courthouse in Edgartown where he pleaded guilty to reduced charges in the death of Mary Jo Kopechne.

Looking older: Was it the high cost of living or the cost of living high?

Joan on a boat with her sister-in-law Eunice Shriver: "Surely, Joan, you knew what you were getting into when you married into this family?"

Divorced, Joan spent more and more time *Joan Kennedy today: What a long strange*
alone . . . drinking. *trip it's been.*

Drunk again: Joan in court in Quincy, turning over her driver's license 1991.

CHAPTER EIGHTEEN

JOE KENNEDY AND "THE PANTS PRESSERS"

Joe Kennedy did not like Jews. He may have had some Jewish friends, as his apologists sometimes point out. But by and large he had no use for "kikes" or "sheenies," as he often called them, sometimes even to their faces.

Even when he spoke least disparagingly of the Jews, Joe would often simultaneously slur them. For instance, according to Seymour Hersh in *The Dark Side of Camelot,* during his time as ambassador to the Court of St. James, Kennedy confided to Harvey Klemmer, one of his closest aides: "Individual Jews are all right, Harvey," he said, "but as a race they stink. They spoil everything they touch. Look what they did to the movies."

Ironic, considering Kennedy's record in Hollywood as a purveyor of forgettable, if mostly profitable schlock. When he finally met superstar actress Gloria Swanson in 1927, she hadn't heard of a single film that Kennedy had produced. His top grosser at the time was *The Gorilla Hunt.* The top original star developed by any of his minor studios was Red Grange, the one-time college football star, signed to churn out three-reelers at the behest of his older sons, Joe Jr. and JFK. Yet Joe felt superior to the "furriers, pants pressers and other merchants of drivel," as he called them.

Even after he sold off his Hollywood interests, Joe still considered himself a cut above the "sterling patriots," as he referred to Harry Cohn of Columbia Pictures. In December 1940, he wrote to his old friend Arthur Houghton about how he had snubbed Cohn.

"I am glad that Mr. Cohn understood that I gave him the brush-off at Cannes. Because that is just exactly what I meant to give him. There is nothing in my life that requires me to associate with the likes of him."

Those smug words were written by someone who in 1912 had himself been passed over for the most prestigious senior clubs at Harvard College like Porcellian and Fly because of his own non-Yankee, immigrant background. A decade later, in 1922, he had been blackballed by Protestant snobs when he tried to join the Cohasset Country Club on the South Shore. Even late in life, as one of the richest men in America, he had been rejected by his fellow Harvard graduates for the school's Board of Overseers. Yet, as so often with the Kennedys, the irony eluded Joe.

As for calling the Jewish moguls "sterling patriots"—it was Joe Kennedy who dodged the military draft in World War I, a fact that some have speculated was what drove his chagrined son Joe Jr. to volunteer for the reckless mission in 1944 that cost him his life, to prove to the world that the Kennedys weren't "yellow."

The family retainers who try to defend Joe always stress a few Jewish names—among them, Carroll Rosenbloom, the owner of the Baltimore Colts, who became a friend of Joe's in the 1950s. Then there was Arthur Krock, his cheerleader at the *New York Times*. But Krock was more of a hireling than a pal. It was a marriage of convenience.

JOSEPH PATRICK KENNEDY
Born September 6, 1889, at East Boston, Massachusetts. Prepared at Boston Latin School. Home address, 159 Locust Street, Winthrop, Massachusetts. In college four years as undergraduate. Freshman Baseball Team; University Baseball Team, 1911. Institute of 1770, D. K. E., Delta Upsilon, Hasty Pudding Club, St. Paul's Catholic Club, Boston Latin Club.

Joe Kennedy, Harvard yearbook, Class of 1912. Note that he lists a Winthrop, rather than an East Boston, home address.

"I've often reflected since those days," Krock wrote after his retirement, "that he probably never liked me at all, but found me useful and thought he might be able to make use of me."

Of course, that's the way Joe felt about most people, Jew or gentile. For the Kennedys, life was a movie. They were the stars, and everyone else was an extra.

The apologists also cite the fact that Joe was the only, or one of the very few, non-Jewish members of the Palm Beach Country Club. But that wasn't because Joe Kennedy was any kind of civil-rights pioneer. Given his background—whatever the extent of his ties to organized crime, which is still debated—the Everglades Club would never have had him as a member under any circumstances.

There were always a few Jews at the Everglades; there seems to have been no formal policy banning them from the club on Worth Avenue or its golf club. Where the Everglades did draw the line was at gangsters. Plus, the newer Jewish golf club was on the north side of the island, much closer to the Kennedys' beachfront mansion at 1095 North Ocean Boulevard than any of the other courses, even The Breakers.

In 2016, former *Boston Globe* reporter Larry Tye published a biography of Robert F. Kennedy, another worshipful look at the man Tye considered a "revolutionary." During a radio interview in Boston, Tye was asked about RFK's well-documented anti-Semitism and homophobia.

While conceding his subject's lifelong hatred of gays, Tye, who is Jewish, said that RFK had "grown" in the last years of his life, eventually relying on Jewish aides like Adam Walinsky.

"But what I never realized," he said during the interview, "is just how anti-Semitic Joe Kennedy was until I read the book of his letters, which was edited by his granddaughter, by the way."

That 764-page book is Amanda Smith's *Hostage to Fortune: The Letters of Joseph P. Kennedy,* the publication of which in 2001 should have put to rest any further attempts to deny his anti-Semitism. But a decade later yet another family-authorized biography appeared, with the customary attempts to rehabilitate Joe's image. In a *YouTube* video in 2011, the author, David Nasaw, tried to downplay Kennedy's well-documented words during his years as an ambassador to the Court of St. James.

"When you look at Washington in the 1930s," Nasaw said, "especially in the State Department, everyone's an anti-Semite."

Up to a point, perhaps. But it's impossible to explain away Joe Kennedy's unvarnished words. For instance, in July 1941, after returning to the United States from London, he is writing in his diary about goings-on in the Roosevelt Administration.

He mentions the slowly unfolding scandal of Sumner Welles, FDR's undersecretary of state. Welles was distantly related by marriage to Roosevelt, and at the Groton School in Massachusetts, he had roomed with First Lady Eleanor Roosevelt's brother.

At the age of 12, he had been a page in their wedding. In short, Welles epitomized everything Joe Kennedy detested about WASP America—he was a blue blood, a preppie, a State Department lifer, and worst of all, a Roosevelt of sorts.

The previous year, returning to Washington, DC, by train from the funeral of a Southern politician, Welles had propositioned two black Pullman porters. That homosexual indiscretion would eventually end Welles's career, but in 1941, FDR was trying to save his friend.

Arthur Krock had the story but was sitting on it. In his diary, Kennedy first writes about FBI Director J. Edgar Hoover passing on the Welles gossip to one of Joe's political allies, U.S. Supreme Court Justice Frank Murphy. Then, Kennedy gets to his *real* obsession, listing and underlining for emphasis the names of one New Dealer after another whose loyalties he considered compromised, and why:

"Hoover told Murphy he had placed the affidavits on Roosevelt's desk on Welles' improper relations with nigger porters.

"The four men who followed me to Europe: (Harry) *Hopkins* had a Jew wife and 2 Jew children. (Averell) *Harriman* a Jew wife. (Benjamin V.) *Cohen* a Jew. (Charles Harold) *Fahey*—lawyer—a Jew mother."

This wasn't the first time Joe Kennedy had committed his anti-Semitic obsessions to paper. Apparently Murphy, the former governor of Michigan, shared his friend's paranoia about the Jewish influence in the

Roosevelt Administration. On November 4, 1940, Kennedy dictated notes to his diary:

"Murphy regards the Jewish influence as most dangerous. He said that after all, Hopkins' wife was a Jew. (Secretary of State Cordell) Hull's wife is a Jew, and (U.S. Supreme Court Justice Felix) Frankfurter and that group are all Jews, and Jackson, Attorney General, is sympathetic with the Communists."

On November 30, 1940, Joe returned to the subject of Frankfurter, again underlining one of the words for emphasis—"*He's* a Jew chiseler."

These writings didn't surface until decades later. Although his pro-appeasement sympathies as the American ambassador in London were common knowledge, they were not publicly confirmed until Nazi diplomatic papers captured by the Allies after World War II were released by the State Department in 1949.

On June 13, 1938, Herbert von Dirksen, the Nazi ambassador to the Court of St. James, reported back to Herr Hitler's foreign office on his initial conversations with the new American ambassador.

"From his whole personality," Dickens cabled, "I believe he would get on well with the Fuhrer."

When the papers were declassified, "the Ambassador," as his family deferentially called him, denounced them as "complete poppycock," but no one believed his denials. After all, in the 1940 newspaper interview that had ended his diplomatic career, Joe had been quoted as complaining that Eleanor Roosevelt was always asking him to "take care of the poor little nobodies. She's always sending me notes to have some little Suzie Glotz to tea at the Embassy."

Von Dirksen noted that Joe knew that the Nazis "had done great things for Germany," before outlining the U.S. ambassador's thoughts on what Kennedy termed "the Jewish question."

"In this connection it was not so much the fact that we wanted to get rid of the Jews that was so harmful to us, but rather the loud clamor with which we accompanied this purpose."

On the subject of FDR, Joe told his Nazi counterpart that the president was under the sway of "Jewish influence."

As events unfolded, von Dirksen cabled Berlin that Kennedy was "Germany's best friend" in London.

None of this anti-Semitism was anything new for Joe. He'd always felt this way about Jews. One acquaintance said he spoke in private the same way that popular radio priest Father Charles Coughlin spoke in public—and Coughlin was pulled off the air by the Church for his harangues against "Jewish bankers."

Before he moved to Hollywood, Joe wrote that he thought he could take the "pants pressers" who controlled the film industry. Trying to convince Gloria Swanson to let him take control of her life, both professionally and personally, he told her that she had been ill-used by "those people." (One of the Jewish producers had offered her $1 million per picture; in the end she received $50,000 per movie from Kennedy.)

When Joe bought control of his first movie studio in 1926, it was front-page news. Not because FBO was a player—it mainly churned out formulaic B movies. The reason Kennedy made the headlines was because he wasn't Jewish. Will Hayes, the former national chairman of the Republican Party, had been brought in as the head of the Motion Picture Producers Association (MPPA) to clean up the industry's tattered, scandal-scarred image in the aftermath of the Fatty Arbuckle and assorted other sordid showbiz scandals. Hooray for Hollywood indeed.

Americans loved the movies, but many of them, and not just those in the boondocks, didn't much care for the people who made them. Almost all of Hollywood's

Joe and Rose Kennedy, during his career as a Hollywood producer, 1920s.

top producers were Jews, many of them immigrant Jews, from the garment industry in New York.

As famed actor John Barrymore once said to a Hollywood mogul berating him for his chronic drunkenness, "Don't point that finger at me. I remember when it had a thimble on it."

In 1926, Hays described Kennedy, the Irish American with the big chip on his shoulder, as "exceedingly American," ironic praise indeed, considering Joe's lifelong problems "passing" in polite society.

Joe may have represented good PR for the industry in a time of trouble, but rubbing elbows with the pants pressers didn't improve his opinion of them.

In Joe's Hollywood days, Edmund Goulding was one of the producers who thought he had an understanding with Kennedy. He didn't. When Joe had needed him, they'd been friends, but there was so much to dislike about him, at least as far as Joe was concerned. He was English, he was bisexual, and he had a female attorney named Fanny Holtzman.

After Goulding threatened to sue him over a business deal gone sour, Kennedy looked him in the eye and said, "You have that Jew girl go after me and I guarantee you'll never be on a screen again. I'll tell a federal jury about some of those wild Goulding weekends and you'll be deported for moral turpitude."

In the Depression year of 1936, Paramount Pictures was struggling financially. The studio's board of directors commissioned Joe to fashion a turnaround plan. Having just wrapped up his stint as chairman of the Securities and Exchange Commission (SEC), he figured he could get away running a bluff using FDR's name. So in his report to the Paramount directors, Joe wrote that one of the industry's biggest problems was the public's distaste for what they perceived to be the control of the motion-picture industry by the Jews.

"To reduce the pressure," Kennedy wrote, the president believed that it would be appropriate for the Jewish owners of Paramount to sell—to Joe Kennedy.

Knowing Kennedy all too well, the board was skeptical. One of the directors, Edwin Weisl Sr., a New York financier, was close to Harry

Hopkins, one of the original New Deal brain trust, whom Joe disdained for his "Jew wife and two Jew children." Hopkins's desk at the White House was within shouting distance of the Oval Office. So, Weisl telephoned Hopkins and asked him to confirm what Kennedy had written about FDR's suggestion.

Hopkins yelled to the president, "What's this about Joe Kennedy and Paramount?"

"What's Paramount?" FDR shouted back.

Joe Kennedy was dismissed, with a check for $50,000, handsome recompense in those bleak Depression days, but not what he'd wanted, which was the entire studio. Joe swore revenge against Weisl.

"I'll get that dirty Jew son of a bitch if it's the last thing I do."

When Joe hitched his star to FDR's wagon, he expected to be handsomely rewarded with government appointments and favors. But over and over again, as Joe saw it, his well-earned ascension would be blocked by . . . them.

It would be a recurring theme in his correspondence until FDR's death in 1945. Joe would often use the words "Jew" and "Communist" interchangeably. Writing in his diary about the presidential election of 1944, Kennedy blamed the defection of Irish and Italian voters from the Democratic ticket on the fact that "they felt that Roosevelt was Jew-controlled. Second, they felt that the Communists were coming into control."

Joe had never been popular with the chattering classes in the nation's capital. They looked askance at his successive appointments to the SEC and then the Maritime Commission, both of which Joe considered mere stepping stones to the ultimate prize, the presidency. His critics, though, regarded his reputation as a "plunger" as disqualifying for any public service. They didn't understand that, decades before *The Godfather*, FDR was keeping his friends close and his enemies closer.

But Joe couldn't accept the fact that his own ethical shortcomings, not to mention his total inability to be a team player, were stalling his rise in politics. He identified the source of his troubles, he told his eldest son, and once again it was . . . them.

"Jewish columnists."

Joe's prejudices rubbed off on his namesake. Hitler assumed power in Germany in 1933, and a year later, at the age of 19, Joe Jr. journeyed to the Third Reich.

He was much impressed by the new salutation of the day in the Fatherland—"Heil Hitler!"

"I'm sure if I were a German," Joe Jr. wrote, "I would expend that slight effort which is required to raise my arm."

He wrote to his father about the desperation of the German people during the Weimar Republic.

"Hitler came in. He saw the need of a common enemy, someone of whom to make the goat . . . It was excellent psychology, and it was too bad that it had to be done to the Jews. This dislike of the Jews, however, was well founded. They were at the heads of all big business, in law, etc. It is all to their credit for them to get so far, but their methods have been quite unscrupulous . . . the lawyers and prominent judges were Jews, and if you had a case against a Jew, you were nearly always sure to lose it."

Many in Washington were appalled when FDR selected Joe as ambassador to Great Britain, just as they had been appalled by the earlier appointments. At a cabinet meeting, FDR acknowledged the forebodings of his friends, admitting that Joe was "a dangerous man, too dangerous to have around here."

But a diplomat is by definition an underling, a subordinate. Ultimately, the job of an ambassador is to follow orders, to carry out directives from his superiors at the State Department or the White House. An ambassador serves at the pleasure of the president.

Joe Kennedy had never really worked for anyone else, in government or business. Even more problematically, he was an unabashed anti-Semite at a moment in world history when Jews found themselves in mortal peril. Joe Kennedy didn't care.

After a few months as ambassador, he wrote one of his friends about the influential newspaper columnist Walter Lippmann.

"[He] hasn't liked the U.S. Ambassador for the last 6 months," Joe wrote, referring to himself in the third person. "Of course the fact that he is a Jew has something to do with that."

By the time he sat down with the German ambassador, Joe had already been taken under the wing of Lady Astor, the Tory MP who presided over what came to be known as the "Cliveden Set," a loosely knit group of upper-class Brits who opposed a new war with Nazi Germany.

Lady Astor was their unlikely leader, an American-born woman whose first husband had been Robert Gould Shaw II, the cousin of Robert Gould Shaw, whose service in the Civil War as commander of the all-black 54th Massachusetts Regiment is commemorated in a famous mural on the Boston Common across Beacon Street from the State House.

Lady Astor had been the first woman elected to Parliament, in 1919. She often tangled with Winston Churchill, both socially and in Parliament. According to a perhaps apocryphal story, she once told Churchill, "If you were my husband, I would poison you." To which Churchill supposedly replied, "If you were my wife, I would drink it."

Lady Astor was described by another MP as "the member from Berlin." She called Jews "the killers of Christ." (Not surprisingly, she also disliked Roman Catholics, but given their otherwise simpatico views, Joe Kennedy decided not to hold that against her.)

"I'm glad you are smart enough not to take my (views) personally," she wrote back to him.

Ambassador Kennedy made his first appearance in her salon with Rose on May 5, 1938. George Bernard Shaw was also present, but the greatest thrill for Joe was meeting Charles Lindbergh, the world-famous aviator and yet another foe of foreign entanglements. Lindbergh had recently called Hitler "a great man" who had "done much good for the German people."

Lindbergh and Kennedy got along famously and afterward, the soon-to-be public face of the America First movement wrote, "Kennedy interested me greatly."

Kennedy also hit it off immediately with Prime Minister Neville Chamberlain, who was, like Joe, a businessman who had gone into politics. They shared the same fervent opposition to a new war. That August, Joe planned to deliver a speech in Scotland, asking the question, "(Is there) any dispute or controversy existing in the world which is worth the life of your son or anyone else's son?"

He cabled the first draft of his speech back to Foggy Bottom. Appalled, the State Department ordered him not to deliver it. Then came Munich, where Chamberlain handed Czechoslovakia over to Hitler for dismemberment. He then returned to Great Britain waving the agreement in his hand and claiming he had secured "peace in our time."

A few days later, Joe sat down once more with von Dirksen, who afterward cabled a report to Berlin that "today, too, as during former conversations, Kennedy mentioned that very strong anti-Semitic feelings existed in the United States and that a large portion of the population had an understanding of the German attitude toward the Jews."

Three weeks later, Joe addressed the Trafalgar Day dinner of the Navy League. This time the State Department had signed off on his speech, even though unease over Nazi Germany was growing in the United States after the fate of little Czechoslovakia became clear.

"The democratic and dictator countries differ ideologically," Kennedy said, "but that should not preclude the possibility of good relations between them . . . After all, we have to live together in the same world, whether we like it or not."

The reaction to the speech in Washington was instantaneous—shock. FDR took to the radio airwaves to denounce it—"a stab in the back," he said, even though his own State Department had signed off on the speech beforehand.

In his unpublished memoirs, Joe tried to shrug off the criticism as coming from "a number of Jewish publishers and writers . . . Some of them in their zeal did not hesitate to resort to slander and falsehood to achieve their aims."

After the Trafalgar Day speech, even JFK, who was much less obsessed with Jews than the rest of the family, got into the act.

"The Navy Day speech," JFK wrote his parents from Cambridge, "while it seemed to be unpopular with the Jews, etc., was considered to be very good by everyone who wasn't bitterly anti-Fascist."

Less than three weeks later came Kristallnacht, a pogrom by the Nazis, in which hundreds of Jews were killed and 30,000 imprisoned, as Hitler's thugs burnt down scores of synagogues and looted Jewish-owned shops.

Ambassador Kennedy was appalled—at how bad the Nazis' savagery was making them look.

"Isn't there some way," he wrote to Lindbergh, "to persuade (Germany that) it is on a situation like this that the whole program of saving western civilization might hinge? It is more and more difficult for those seeking peaceful solutions to advocate any plan when the papers are filled with such horror."

Soon the ambassador was under surveillance by MI5, the domestic British intelligence service. They monitored his affair with a well-to-do divorcée who knew Sir Oswald Mosley, the leading fascist in the United Kingdom. His phone was tapped.

A radical weekly reported that in his frequent discussion with the Nazis, "Kennedy goes so far as to insinuate that the democratic policy of the United States is a Jewish production."

In late 1940, back in Boston, Joe sat down with several reporters in his suite at the Ritz-Carlton. It was a wide-ranging interview, during which he mentioned his view that "democracy is finished" in Great Britain. It was nothing he hadn't said privately any number of times.

All but one of the journalists ignored it in their stories, but one picked up on it. It caused a worldwide sensation, headlines across the globe. His statement that "democracy is finished" in the United Kingdom effectively ended Joe's career in government, although Joe would retain his rarefied title as ambassador to the Court of St. James for a few more months.

So he returned to Hollywood for a visit. Over lunch at Warner Bros., he spoke to 50 film moguls, almost all of them Jewish. His topic was the "European situation."

During a three-hour discussion, Kennedy told them how much Hitler enjoyed the cinema. But, he added, if you want your product shown in the new Europe, "You're going to have to get those Jewish names off the screen . . . stop making anti-Nazi pictures or using the film medium to promote or show sympathy to the cause of 'democracies' versus 'the dictators.'"

Jews in England, he told the Hollywood crowd, "are on the spot." They were being blamed for the war, he went on, and if Hollywood continued churning out anti-Nazi propaganda "then we all, and the Jew in particular, would be in jeopardy."

The more Hollywood attacked Hitler, Joe went on, the more people will believe that this is a "Jewish war."

When Kennedy returned to Washington, Roosevelt called him to the White House and formally discharged him.

"I don't want you to go back," the president told him. "You've done enough."

During his diplomatic stint in London, Joe had become close to Lord Beaverbrook, the newspaper publisher who was also a patron of Winston Churchill during his years in the political wilderness after the disaster of Gallipoli during World War I. In August 1942 Joe wrote to Lord Beaverbrook about what he described as the low wartime morale in the United States.

"There is a great undercurrent of dissatisfaction with the appointment of so many Jews in high places in Washington."

After Pearl Harbor, greatest undercurrent of dissatisfaction may have been in Palm Beach, where Kennedy was chafing at the fact that Roosevelt would have nothing to do with him, even after he wired the president on December 7, 1941.

"In this great crisis," Joe told FDR, "all Americans are with you. Name the battle front. I'm yours to command."

No calls came.

In 1944, with the war still raging, Joe Kennedy sat down in his suite at the Ritz-Carlton in Boston and gave an interview to yet another friendly reporter, Joe Dinneen of the *Globe*. The Jewish question came up, and Joe replied at some length, in the tones he had expressed a few years earlier in London to his aide Harvey Klemmer:

"It is true that I have a low opinion of some Jews in public office and in private life. That does not mean that I hate all Jews . . . I can show the names of Jews on my own books, Jews whom I have carried for years. They're all right. They're good businessmen . . . I'm sorry to say that there are, in my opinion, Jews who actually exploit anti-Semitism . . ."

Joe then pointed out that anyone in public life is fair game for criticism. But when Jews are attacked, he said, some "ascribe it to anti-Semitism, when the bald fact is that the person is being criticized and not the race. It is no secret that I have not a high opinion of Felix Frankfurter—or of Henry Morgenthau, Jr., or of a number of Jews in high places, but that doesn't mean I condemn all of them . . . There are more of them in high places than there ever have been before, and it naturally follows that there is more criticism of them. They've got to be able to take that criticism. They've got to be able to answer it. And the answer is not a charge of anti-Semitism against the critics."

The *Globe* decided not to print the interview, and Dinneen filed it away for later use.

By then, it was common knowledge in political circles that FDR was dying. Joe Kennedy dreamed of a post-FDR return to politics— "Truman will be president and will kick out all these incompetents and Jews out of Washington and ask fellows like myself and others to come back and run the government."

Truman, rumored to have once been a member of the Ku Klux Klan, had as little use for Kennedy as Roosevelt did. In Boston during the fall campaign of 1944, a few months after Joe Jr.'s death in the European theater, Joe had privately asked him, "Harry, how can you be with that crippled son of a bitch who killed my son?"

When FDR finally died in April 1945, Joe couldn't contain his gloating.

"The Jews are crying that they've lost their greatest friend and benefactor," he wrote to his daughter Kick on May 1. "It's a clear indication of the serious mistake that the Jews had made in spite of their marvelous organizing capacity."

Eventually accepting that his political career, such as it was, was over, Joe went back to wheeling and dealing. His greatest coup was buying the Merchandise Mart in Chicago from Marshall Field III, the owner of the department store as well as the newspapers that would soon be merged to create the *Chicago Sun-Times.*

Field just wanted out—he was servicing a huge mortgage, and was saddled with many long-term leases with low-paying government agencies. Kennedy knew that he could put the fix in and get out from under those leases, and he did just that. Joe had been gloomily predicting a postwar depression, but now the boom he had never seen coming would make him even wealthier.

By 1946, Joe was bragging that he was making a profit of $12 million a year—a million dollars a month!—on the Merchandise Mart, for which he had paid $11 million.

According to his biographer Ron Kessler, this was the one deal that Joe Kennedy was proudest of, justifiably so. But he described his windfall in typical Joe Kennedy terms, telling his young mistress Janet Des Rosiers: "This is the kind of deal that Jews usually get. But I got it."

With the huge cash flow being thrown off the Mart, Joe decided it was a propitious moment to sell Somerset Importers. Wryly named after the Somerset Club, the ultra-Yankee gathering place on Beacon Street in Boston that he could never, ever dream of joining, Somerset Importers had been a fabulously profitable enterprise, but with his second son running for Congress, Somerset was sure to remind voters of Joe's unsavory connections to organized crime dating back to Prohibition.

So in 1946 he sold it, not to his loyal Irish American managers (who were instead sent on their way with niggardly five-figure severance payments) but to a consortium of Jews from New Jersey, one of whom Seymour Hersh reported was Abner "Longy" Zwillman, a Newark hoodlum once described as "the Al Capone of New Jersey."

According to some sketchy, unconfirmed accounts, during Prohibition Zwillman's mob had hijacked a load of Kennedy's bootleg hootch, or vice versa. Meyer Lansky later speculated to one of his biographers that the mob's problem with the Kennedys dated back to that incident—that Joe had been angered not so much by the actual hijacking, or by the fact that some of his drivers had been killed, as he was by the demands of their survivors for money from Joe after their loved ones' deaths.

Whatever the facts, two decades later Joe had no problems selling Somerset to the group that included Zwillman. Money healed all wounds—the price was right, $8 million.

(Zwillman was another of those bold-faced names whose paths crossed and recrossed with the Kennedys. As Joe cavorted with Gloria Swanson, Longy too had had a Hollywood girlfriend—Jean Harlow. He arranged her first studio contract, a two-picture deal with Columbia Pictures, after making a huge loan to Harry Cohn, the Jewish producer whom Joe Kennedy would brag of snubbing at Cannes. In 1959, at the age of 54, Zwillman was found hanged at his suburban New Jersey mansion. He had just received a subpoena to testify in front of the Senate Rackets Committee, where he would have been questioned under oath—by committee counsel Robert F. Kennedy.)

After selling Somerset, Joe made a move on the biggest horse-racing track in Massachusetts, the only one in Boston—Suffolk Downs, in his old neighborhood of East Boston. The company that owned the track was in receivership, and a group of Jewish investors from Connecticut bought a piece of the company and then made a bid for the remaining outstanding shares.

To their dismay, however, they discovered that the fix was in, and the track was on the verge of being sold to non-investors for $1 million, perhaps a tenth of its true value. The buyer: Joe Kennedy.

According to Seymour Hersh, presiding federal Judge George Sweeney called the lawyer for the Jewish group, Milton S. Gould, into his chambers.

"You're sticking your nose where you don't belong," Sweeney told Gould. "This is a local thing and we want local people."

Gould understood what "local people" meant. It meant that the track would not go "to a bunch of Jews," as Gould later told Hersh.

Gould offered to write a brief in support of his clients, but Sweeney waved him off: "I don't need a brief. I may be wrong, but I'm never in doubt."

Sweeney then said he would deny the Jewish group's motion, but would order the receivers to buy back their stock at a premium, netting them a profit of $250,000. And, the judge said, he would also award Gould $100,000 in legal fees.

Gould and his clients rejected the offer. In the end, they didn't get the track, but neither did Joe Kennedy. Still, the whole affair sounded a lot like the German legal system in the Weimar Republic as described by the late Joe Kennedy Jr. a decade earlier, if you substituted the word "Irish" for "Jews," as in "unscrupulous" Irish lawyers and judges and how "if you had a case against an Irishman, you were nearly always sure to lose it."

Meanwhile, now that his own political dreams were behind him, Joe concentrated on JFK's prospects. In 1952, JFK was running for the Senate. Given his voting record in the House, many liberals in Massachusetts suspected that perhaps Henry Cabot Lodge, the Republican incumbent, was preferable.

A veteran New Dealer, Gardner "Pat" Jackson, was brought in by the Kennedy campaign to mend fences with the party's left wing. He quickly deduced that one big problem JFK had with some Democratic voters was his silence on Sen. Joe McCarthy. Perhaps Jackson didn't realize that Joe Kennedy liked McCarthy, socialized with him, and had contributed to him.

Jackson drafted a windy public pronouncement under JFK's name

Joe Kennedy Jr.: When it came to Jews, he was a chip off the old block.

on "the twin evils of McCarthyism and Communism." JFK had agreed to sign the statement if John McCormack would do likewise. McCormack agreed. The statement would run as an ad in the Boston newspapers.

Jackson took the statement up to JFK's apartment in the Bellevue Hotel at the top of Beacon Hill. The candidate was going out the door, but some of his top campaign aides were there, as well as Joe Kennedy. Before leaving, JFK asked Jackson to read the ad to the campaign brain trust.

As Jackson read the statement, Joe Kennedy was glaring at him, seething with rage. It was all coming back to him, all the slights he'd suffered during his years in Washington and London. Jackson was a friend of Eleanor Roosevelt, Drew Pearson, Felix Frankfurter—them!

"I hadn't gone two sentences when Joe jumped to his feet with such force that he tilted the table against the others."

Joe got in Jackson's face as he screamed at him.

"You and your sheeny friends are trying to destroy my son!"

Joe bellowed that not only was he for Joe McCarthy, he had given him money. He kept saying that the liberals, organized labor, and the Jews were conspiring against his son. He laced his tirade with obscenity after obscenity.

"I can't estimate how long he poured it out on me," Jackson recalled years later. "It was just a stream of stuff—always referring to 'you and your sheeny friends.' No one has ever shouted that way in my life."

In 1959, as JFK was gearing up his campaign for president, he okayed the family's old retainer at the *Globe* to write an authorized campaign biography—*The Kennedy Family*, a particularly obsequious tract. Dinneen decided to recycle Joe Kennedy's previously unpublished 1944 interview in which he had so candidly expressed his unflattering thoughts about the Jews. When the book was in galleys, he met JFK at a downtown hotel in Boston before the candidate left for the West Coast and handed him a set of proofs, as per their agreement. A day or so later JFK broke off campaigning in Oregon to call Dinneen back in Boston. He was frantic about his father's old anti-Semitic statements.

"You've got to take out those three paragraphs," JFK said.

Too late, Dinneen told him. The plates had been sent to the printer.

"I don't give a damn," JFK said. "I want those paragraphs out of there."

They were removed. At some expense to Dinneen, he rewrote pages 104 and 105, and the galleys were replated.

In 1960, Joe would serve as an intermediary of sorts between his son's campaign and the underworld. As the candidate's famous, or infamous, father, Joe needed a go-between, a cutout, for his dealings with organized crime. For that role Joe picked Frank Sinatra, whom he knew from the Cal-Neva Lodge in Tahoe, in which Joe held a financial interest with, among others, a Jewish underworld figure named Wingy Gober.

As the presidential field began to take shape in 1958, Joe made one of his periodic visits to Palm Springs, which is recounted in some detail in the entertaining 2003 memoir of Sinatra's black longtime valet, George Jacobs. In *Mr. S,* Jacobs wrote that he knew nothing about Kennedy when he arrived, but from his demeanor, as well as his boss's desperate eagerness to please him, he assumed Kennedy was, like Momo Giancana and so many of Sinatra's other guests, "a pillar of the underworld."

Sinatra flew in five high-priced hookers from Vegas, but Joe Kennedy wasn't satisfied. He unleashed a torrent of abuse on everybody in the Sinatra household, including his host.

"He not only told nigger jokes throughout the meals, he'd call the Indians 'savages' and the blacks 'Sambos'' and curse the hell out of anyone who served him from the wrong side or put one ice cube too many in his Jack Daniels. 'Can't you get any white help?' he'd needle Mr. S. 'Aren't you paying them enough?'

"[He] may have held a Harvard degree, but [he] was a disgrace to it, cruder and meaner and, alas, proving crime *does* pay, more successful than any of the street mobsters Mr. S ever hosted. Such was the father of our country's most captivating president."

But, Jacobs recounted, Joe dished out his worst abuse on the Jews of Hollywood.

"To him they were 'sheeny rag traders,'" Jacobs wrote. "He referred to the august Louis B. Mayer as a 'kike junkman.' The Jewish jokes didn't stop. The worst one I can recall: 'What's the difference between a Jew and a pizza? The pizza doesn't cry on its way to the oven.'"

Joe knew how to massage Sinatra's famously fragile ego. He mentioned a future ambassadorship to Italy, or perhaps a run for the U.S. Senate from Nevada. Sinatra fell into line, raising showbiz and Mafia money for JFK, re-recording hit songs like "High Hopes" as Kennedy campaign themes, serving as a conduit between the Kennedys and the underworld, especially Giancana.

But from the start, it was clear who was calling the shots—Joe Kennedy. He kept Sinatra on a short leash. In 1960, Jacobs recounted, his boss was interested in making a movie out of the book *The Execution of Private Slovik,* about the last soldier executed by the U.S. Army for desertion, in 1945. Sinatra wanted to direct the movie; it would establish him as a serious filmmaker.

To write the script, he hired veteran screenwriter Albert Maltz, who had been blacklisted a few years earlier as one of the Hollywood 10. Living in exile in Mexico, Maltz had continued working under pseudonyms, but *Slovik* would be his official comeback vehicle, penned under his own name. When the story leaked out to newspapers, Sinatra took out ads in the trades defending Maltz as well as his own First Amendment rights. But then, Jacobs wrote, Joe Kennedy called.

"What is this commie Jew shit?" he screamed at Sinatra. "You stupid guinea!"

"Yes sir," said Sinatra.

There was one more Jewish problem to deal with before the election. In 1951, JFK had knocked up a Polish prostitute in Boston whose name eventually became Alicia Darr Purdom. Obviously, the marriage didn't happen. But in 1960, she sent word to the campaign that she was planning to file a breach-of-promise suit against JFK, or so it was claimed in an FBI report that was released in 1977.

RFK was cut loose from his campaign duties, the FBI said, to deliver a half-million-dollar payoff to Purdom. According to another signed statement by JFK, discovered by Seymour Hersh in the papers of JFK's secretary Evelyn Lincoln after her death in 1995, Purdom in 1960 had offered to sell LBJ "compromising" material on her former boyfriend. According to other accounts, Kennedy had impregnated the gold digger, although she had no children. Joe was livid about the shakedowns, and there was one particular reason for his outrage.

Purdom, he said, was "another no-class Polish Jew."

After JFK's election, Sinatra was assigned the task of putting together the inaugural gala in DC. It was to be the most star-studded entertainment spectacular ever. And one of the headliners would be Sammy Davis Jr., another member of Sinatra's Rat Pack, a black nightclub superstar who had converted to Judaism a few years earlier. At Sinatra's behest, Davis had done yeoman's work for the Kennedys during the campaign.

During the Democratic convention in Los Angeles, Davis had been heckled off the stage by the all-white Alabama delegation (which was under the control of JFK's top Southern ally, Gov. John Patterson, an arch-segregationist). Davis fled back to New York in tears. He had postponed his wedding to a white Swedish actress until after the election, so as not to cost JFK votes in the South. (After the election, Davis married her in Las Vegas, in a Jewish ceremony, with Sinatra as his best man.)

When Sinatra presented the roster of inaugural performers to Joe to sign off on, the old man immediately vetoed Davis.

"Sammy was the ambassador's sum of all fears," Jacobs wrote. "He was black, he was Jewish, he was married to a blonde Aryan, he was a superstar. That drove old Joe crazy, that Sammy had beaten all the odds."

Sinatra pleaded with Joe. Sinatra pointed out to Joe that he had no reservations about all the other black performers he'd blocked, so why break Sammy's heart?

"Joe said no. Ella Fitzgerald was okay, so was Mahalia Jackson, Harry Belafonte, Nat King Cole. But to Joe, they were 'nigger niggers.' They knew their place. They kept in their place. But 'the nigger bastard with the German whore' . . . that was beyond the pale."

In 1949, one of Joe's old Jewish associates in Hollywood, Jesse Lasky, after decades of observation, made what turned out to be a prescient observation:

Joseph Patrick Kennedy
September 6, 1888 - November 18, 1969

LOOK down upon me, good and gentle Jesus, while before Thy Face I humbly kneel, and with burning soul pray and beseech Thee to fix deep in my heart lively sentiments of faith, hope and charity, true contrition for my sins and a firm purpose of amendment; the while I contemplate with great love and tender pity Thy five wounds, pondering over them within me, and calling to mind the words which David, Thy prophet, said of Thee, My Jesus: "They have pierced My Hands and My Feet, they have numbered all My Bones."

(Plenary indulgence, applicable to the Souls in Purgatory, if said before a Crucifix, after Holy Communion.)

"Let us place our hearts at the foot of the cross, and accept the death of this beloved one for the sake of Him who died on it."

Eternal rest grant unto him, O Lord!

And let perpetual light shine upon him.

May he rest in peace. Amen.

Joe Kennedy's Mass card, November 1969, with his favorite photo of himself and a prayer for the immortal soul of this devout Roman Catholic.

"He is a man of egomaniacal ambition but somehow I sense seeds of self-destruction in him. I suspect he will come to a sad end, somehow."

Eleven months after the inauguration of his son as the 35th president of the United States, Joe Kennedy would suffer a paralyzing stroke in Florida, while playing golf . . . at the Jewish-owned Palm Beach Country Club. Joe Kennedy spent his final moments as a fully functioning human being among the people he had most despised in his 70 sentient, hate-filled years—Jews.

He would linger on another eight unbearable years, speechless, crippled, watching helplessly as two more of his sons were gunned down and the youngest disgraced himself and the family, beyond redemption, as all the while Joe could do nothing more than express himself fitfully through a single grunted word: "No!"

CHAPTER NINETEEN

IN HIS OWN WORDS: PATRICK J. KENNEDY

The following comments are transcribed verbatim from the remarks of Rep. Patrick J. "Patches" Kennedy (D-RI), 1995–2011, and state representative from Providence, 1989–1995.

Patches Kennedy at the height of his career, such as it was.

Childhood

"I'd always be the one everybody got a laugh out of, because they ended up making me cry or run out of the room."

Gays in the Military

"I believe in the code of conduct that guides the conduct of all military personnel, um, that would make sure that no one, uh, should be, uh, doing anything that they shouldn't be doing."

History Lesson

"Can you imagine? This country was founded we declare—we said, uh, that Boston Tea Party 'clared our Revolutionary War because we didn't have representation."

Charitable Contributions

"I'm a proud member of United Way."

"Incentify?"

"Uh, how can you incentify someone to get off welfare? So there's, uh, more incentive for people to work and that those people who are living on the margins, trying to make ends meet, uh, have the facilities as opposed to the other way around, uh, thus incentifying people to stay on welfare."

Alcohol Among the Kennedys

"You know, it was ubiquitous. There were, there was alcohol and there's parties all the time. It wasn't like, oh, I stood out."

Depression

"I myself have suffered from depression. I have been treated by psychiatrists. Oh my God, it's out! That's another skeleton in the closet . . . I am on a lot of different medications for among other things, depression."

Racial Intolerance in the Military

"So what happens is, things don't get reported because, you know, let's not make much to do about nothing, so to speak. One of the worries I have about, you know, a really zero-defect mentality with respect to defect—I'm not talking now—I mean everyone can acknowledge that if there's a little bit of extremism, I'm not saying that isn't just grounds for, you know, expulsion from the military. But how do we address the broader issues . . . Can you answer that in terms of communication?"

Impeachment

"I myself have educated myself about the severity of the Articles of Impeachment, and I want to share with my colleagues and the American people some of the thoughts that I have learned. . . . Impeachment proceedings are just like pulling a fire alarm in a crowded room."

Agenda

"I'm on your sheet of music. I'm on a working, uh, person's agenda."

Statehood for Puerto Rico

"I think that we as American citizens ought to fundamentally be wide enough in our, in our, I our breadth of, our, uh, of our knowledge and our, uh, and our, and our, sense of other human beings to allow them their own sense of self-identification."

President Patches

"I'm pretty overwhelmed with everything I'm doing currently, but, yeah, I think I'd really like to be president."

CHAPTER TWENTY

KENNEDY COUNTRY

IT WAS A THROWAWAY line in the final days of his doomed 1994 Senate race, but Mitt Romney's quip about the legacy of Ted Kennedy stuck—"Kennedy Country" became shorthand for the ruination brought on by the policies the Senate's "Liberal Lion" had espoused over the decades.

A young Ted Kennedy campaigning in the ethnic working-class neighborhoods of Boston . . .

Romney, now a 71-year-old freshman senator from Utah, had been running neck and neck with the bloated, dissipated Teddy until Kennedy went all-negative all the time, blasting Romney's religion, his business practices, even his youthful arrest decades earlier in a national park on skinny-dipping charges.

In a preview of his hapless campaign for president against Barack Obama 18 years later, Mitt wilted. After each attack, he went into the fetal position—the classic RINO (Republican in name only) non-strategy for dealing with the politics of personal destruction, to use Bill Clinton's phrase.

. . . .which would in the coming decades be ravaged by the ruinous social programs he espoused, turning them into "Kennedy Country."

By late October, at the last debate, Teddy was cruising to another easy victory, to his sixth full six-year term. At one point, Romney mentioned a recent visit to Dorchester, the Boston neighborhood where Teddy's mother Rose was raised.

Mitt mentioned that as he campaigned, someone had informed him that he was in "Kennedy Country."

"I looked around," Romney said on statewide TV, "and I saw boarded-up buildings and I saw jobs leaving and I said, 'It looks like it.'"

Devastating—too late to turn the tide, but undeniably true nonetheless, as shown by the fact that Romney was soon under withering attack yet again from all the usual suspects—urban Democratic machine politicians, "community activists," even the *New York Times*—for his refreshing refusal to embrace Political Correctness (a habit he would "correct" in his dismal runs for the White House).

But Romney's offhand quip instantly became a local code phrase for every one of Teddy's disastrous policies—in his personal as well as his political life. But mostly the phrase referred to his catastrophic embrace of the big-government, open-borders policies that were turning the nation into . . . Kennedy country.

Everyone had their own examples of Kennedy Country, and the list is continually updated, as the breakdown of society that started in the aftermath of his brother's assassination in 1963 continues, slowed down sometimes by an election or two, but never really halted, let alone reversed.

Kennedy Country

Everyone asks not what they can do for their country, but what their country can do for them.

The only four-letter word is "work."

No one is married, but everyone has a "fiancée."

Everyone files federal income tax returns—for the "earned" income tax credits (EITC)—but no one ever files state income tax returns, because there is no state EITC program available to be fraudulently taken advantage of.

Sweatpants are considered evening wear.

The new public high school has a larger day-care center than gymnasium.

Press 2 for English.

Your date wears a life preserver, and as for fireworks laws—we don't need no stinkin' fireworks laws.

The few remaining cabbies demand the fares up front.

You see storefront churches, multi-service centers, cockfights, crack houses, pawn shops, and at least two or three satellite dishes on every three-decker.

Every back porch has jerry-built railings—to meet the regulations that make the unit eligible for Section 8.

It's always the cops' fault.

The only flags flying aren't Old Glory.

Every male under the age of 30 is an "aspiring rapper," and their deaths are inevitably commemorated with candlelight vigils.

Three words: graffiti, graffiti, graffiti.

Most stores have signs that read, "EBT Accepted Here" and "Checks Cashed" and the flashing neon beer signs in the packies read, "Cerveza."

The cars in the parking lot at the methadone clinic are better than the one you're driving.

You are judged not on the character of your soul, but on the color of your skin.

The local gas station—if one remains that hasn't yet been looted and burned out—has bulletproof glass and large hand-printed signs in the window that read, "Cashier Has No More Than $20 in Cash After 8 p.m."

At least one of the local politicians has died of a drug overdose.

The candidates for district attorney hold a debate at the local house of correction.

The local burger joints have more drive-bys than drive-throughs.

Western Union serves more than McDonald's.

Most of the product in your local liquor store is behind the counter, in nips and half-pint bottles.

And a case of beer means 24 brown paper bags.

No funerals can be held until the aspiring rapper's GoFundMe page has been set up.

The politicians invariably oppose charter schools, express total solidarity with the local teachers' unions . . . and send their own kids to private schools, if they even still live in the district at all.

There is no morning rush hour, weekends are no busier than weekdays at the local supermarket, and the busiest shopping day of the month is the first—when the EBT cards are reloaded.

At the courthouse, the interpreters are better dressed than the lawyers, all of whom are public defenders.

The adolescent girl pushing the baby carriage who looks like a babysitter usually turns out to be the mother.

The local high school student murdered in broad daylight turns out to be 20 years old, has two children by different "fiancées," and was on the high school basketball team—the freshman basketball team.

The largest social club is MS-13.

Pit bulls far outnumber golden retrievers, labs, and German shepherds—combined.

The politicians' parents haven't left the state in 12 years, but they still file their wills in Florida, so their children can avoid paying their "fair share" of the local death taxes.

Court-ordered school busing in Boston 1974—a pivotal moment in the evolution of Kennedy Country.

Guns don't have serial numbers, and drivers feel no obligation to have licenses, insurance, or inspection stickers.

Every house that hasn't been abandoned has an alarm sticker, window bars or a "Beware of Dog" sign, and the SUV in the driveway is worth more than the house itself.

The leading cause of death among infants is falling out of upstairs windows while unattended.

Kennedy Country is where you get your windshield washed at a stoplight.

Nobody drinking beer on the porch across the street is wearing a shirt.

Restrooms in the local malls install needle-disposal boxes, and claim they're for diabetics.

Every family has either (a) three jobs or (b) no jobs—usually b.

Every Spanish speaker—whether Dominican, Mexican, Guatemalan—has a birth certificate from Puerto Rico, which identifies him or her as a U.S. citizen, and thus eligible for welfare.

Everyone's favorite song from *West Side Story* is "Everything Free in America."

Most of the adults are on "disability," their minor offspring get SSI "crazy checks," and the transition to adulthood for girls isn't high school graduation, it's their first pregnancy, which enables them to get their own Section 8 apartment.

The most confusing holiday is Father's Day.

When you ask anyone the question, "Who was Sen. Edward M. Kennedy?" and the answer is, "Quien?"

CHAPTER TWENTY-ONE

VICE PRESIDENT "UNCLE CORNPONE"

SHORTLY AFTER DAWN ON the first Wednesday morning in November 1952, a young JFK finally learned that he had eked out a narrow victory over incumbent Henry Cabot Lodge Jr. in their Senate race in Massachusetts.

Almost immediately, JFK's phone rang. He answered, and one of his aides overheard Kennedy's end of the call.

"Well thank you, Senator, thank you very much," JFK said. After hanging up, he turned to the aide and said, with a puzzled expression, "That was Lyndon Johnson in Texas. He said he wanted to congratulate me. The guy must never sleep."

But, as was always the case with LBJ, there was more to his solicitude than mere good manners. Johnson had just been informed of a major upset in the Arizona Senate race—a Phoenix city councilor named Barry Goldwater had knocked off the Senate majority leader. There was suddenly a vacancy in the Democratic leadership.

"Johnson wasn't wasting any time in courting Kennedy's support," the aide, Lawrence F. O'Brien, would later explain to Robert A. Caro in his book, *Master of the Senate: The Years of Lyndon Johnson.*

JFK would go on to have an unremarkable, indeed lackluster career in the Senate. As LBJ would later say, "He never said a word of importance in the Senate and he never did a thing."

Furthermore, in Johnson's view, JFK was "malaria-ridden and yellah, sickly, sickly."

But Kennedy wasn't too incapacitated to engage in his favorite pastime: chasing poontang, as he called it. The fact that he did so with such prowess was well known to his Senate colleagues, not least of all LBJ.

LBJ, however, was in no position to judge the morality of his younger future rival. Like JFK, he had a Texas-sized sexual appetite and an ever-changing collection of paramours that LBJ's Secret Service agents referred to as his "harem."

He was also known to frequent the Chicken Ranch in La Grange, Texas, the house of ill repute that was only somewhat fictionalized in the Broadway play and movie *The Best Little Whorehouse in Texas* and the ZZ Top hit song "La Grange."

If political duties kept LBJ away from the hookers, he wasn't shy about ordering "takeout" and having the prostitutes delivered to him from the infamous brothel. Like JFK, LBJ enjoyed bragging about his conquests, referring to his penis as "Jumbo." And he was more than obliging about showing proof of it at any opportunity—sometimes in the parking lot outside the Capitol, to young congressional secretaries leaving work in the evenings.

Just as Jackie knew only too well about her husband's philandering, so, too, did LBJ's wife Lady Bird.

"My husband loved people," she said after his death in 1973. "He loved all people. Now, half the people in the world are women. You don't think I could have kept my husband away from half the people in the world, do you?"

One such person that LBJ apparently "loved" was Madeleine Brown. Brown met LBJ in 1948 and eventually hooked up with him at a party in Austin at the Driskill Hotel.

"He looked at me like I was an ice cream cone on a hot day," Madeleine later recalled. "And he said after a while, 'Well, I'll see you up in my apartment.'"

Eventually, Brown claims, she was set up with a two-bedroom home, a new car every two years, a live-in maid, and lines of credit. But according to Brown, that's not all Johnson gave her. She also claims she gave birth to LBJ's illegitimate son, whom she insisted was his only male heir. Brown said in her own book that she told LBJ she felt he owed it to his son, named Steven, to acknowledge him.

"But [LBJ] said, 'Oh, I can't do that. I've got the girls to consider, and Lady Bird.'"

Years later, Steven Brown would file suit against LBJ's estate, but the case was dismissed. Steven died of cancer just a year later.

All the while, Lady Bird knew about LBJ's floozies, according to Jan Jarboe Russell, who interviewed the former first lady late in life. LBJ "collected" women, she wrote, and felt entitled to their services. This included a "very public relationship" with Alice Glass that lasted decades.

He also had a fling with California Congresswoman Helen Gahagan Douglas, "the Pink Lady," as Richard Nixon called her when he defeated her for a Senate seat in California in 1950.

As president, LBJ was known to lock himself into a private compartment with a secretary aboard Air Force One, even when Lady Bird was on board. His wife even caught him once with his pants down in the Oval Office, which prompted LBJ to install a new alarm on the door.

Fully aware of Sen. Kennedy's reputation as a rake, Sen. Johnson saw himself as being in a competition of sorts with the younger, more handsome JFK.

"I had more women by chance than Jack had on purpose," LBJ said.

For whatever reasons, he seemed to relish keeping his own personal scorecard of his conquests versus JFK's. Which meant he always had to know who JFK was bedding.

Bobby Baker, his top Senate aide, recalled LBJ once summoning him on an urgent matter. He rushed to the Senate chamber as LBJ presided over a debate. LBJ waved him over and leaned forward as everyone—senators, reporters, tourists—all stared at them, wondering what momentous developments were afoot.

"Is ol' Jack gettin' much pussy?" LBJ whispered to Baker. The aide regaled him with a story about JFK's latest conquest as LBJ listened intently, silently, nodding occasionally.

Of course, LBJ wasn't the only major figure in Washington with a keen interest in JFK's romps. In 1941, when JFK was a 23-year-old ensign in the Navy, FBI chief J. Edgar Hoover opened a file on him, starting with his affair with married Danish journalist Inga Arvard.

Arvad was famously connected to Adolph Hitler, with whom she spent time with at the 1936 Berlin Olympic Games. Hitler had fawned over Arvad, describing her in classic Nazi parlance as "a perfect Nordic beauty."

And there was also Judith Campbell, whom JFK had met in February 1960 after a Frank Sinatra–Rat Pack show at Las Vegas's Sands Hotel. According to Campbell, soon after their first meeting, she became JFK's lover.

A month or so later, after the New Hampshire primary in March, Campbell was introduced to mob boss Sam Giancana with the help of Sinatra. That love triangle was yet another connection between the Kennedys and the underworld—two subjects of great interest to Hoover.

Hoover and LBJ had long been friends and neighbors in Northwest Washington since the 1940s. On Sundays, Hoover would often walk across the street to the Johnsons' house for Sunday brunch, along with other Capitol Hill "bachelors" like House Speaker Sam Rayburn and Sen. Richard Russell of Georgia, who would later become the only member of the Warren Commission to refuse to sign the whitewashed report.

LBJ and Hoover even used to search their neighborhood together whenever LBJ's dog, "Little Beagle Johnson," would get loose. Later, when LBJ was enduring his difficult years as an outcast in the Kennedy Administration, it was Hoover he turned to for solace. Perhaps that came in the form of Hoover's reassurance that he held vast resources of blackmail material on JFK.

"J. Edgar Hoover has Jack Kennedy by the balls," LBJ happily boasted once to friendly reporters over cocktails.

President John F. Kennedy addresses Congress, 1961. Behind him are Vice President Lyndon B. Johnson and House Speaker Sam Rayburn of Texas. Rayburn would be dead in six months.

Not that any of this was a secret to JFK. In fact, it was during the 1960 presidential campaign that JFK learned how vulnerable his womanizing had left him. According to JFK's longtime secretary, Evelyn Lincoln, sexual blackmail had long been part of LBJ's modus operandi, with the assistance of Hoover.

She told journalist Anthony Summers, "J. Edgar Hoover gave Johnson the information about various congressmen and senators so that Johnson could go to *X* senator and say, 'How about this little deal you have with this woman?' and so forth. That's how he kept them in line. He used his IOUs with them as what he hoped was his road to the presidency. He had this trivia to use because he had Hoover in his corner. And he thought that the members of Congress would go out there and put him over at the convention. But then Kennedy beat him."

JFK, J. Edgar Hoover, and RFK during one of Hoover's rare visits to the White House, March 1961.

And so, it appears that LBJ—along with his mentor Rayburn—used Hoover's 20 years of dirt on JFK to force the candidate to take the Texan as his running mate for vice president.

No one was more infuriated by the shakedown than JFK's younger brother, RFK, who was also his campaign manager. RFK's animus toward LBJ had deep roots. And as Joe Kennedy told Tip O'Neill, "You can trample all over [Jack] and the next day he's there for you with open arms. But Bobby's my boy. When Bobby hates you, you stay hated."

Their mutual contempt for one another dated back to their first meeting, back in 1953. RFK, then only 27 and fresh out of law school, was having breakfast with his boss, Sen. Joe McCarthy, and a few other staffers in the Senate cafeteria.

LBJ came in and approached their table. LBJ had no use for Tailgunner Joe, and was well aware of the fact that Joe Kennedy had gotten his son his new staff job with McCarthy. Moreover, LBJ was likewise not impressed by JFK, whom he would soon be referring to as a "sickly absentee" and "not a man's man."

Despite LBJ's evident hostility toward him, the amiable McCarthy jumped up and warmly greeted LBJ, shaking his hand and addressing him as "Leader." Bobby's colleagues did the same, but RFK remained seated, scowling up at LBJ.

RFK had heard what LBJ had been saying about both McCarthy and his father, and he always took personal offense at slights against his family.

Equally thin-skinned, LBJ took note of the snub and went over to RFK, his 6'4" frame towering over the slight, younger man. LBJ extended his hand. RFK grudgingly rose and shook LBJ's imposing paw, but his contempt was palpable. He averted his eyes and refused to look at the Senate minority leader. (LBJ would become majority leader in 1955, when Democrats regained control of the Senate.)

Despite his disdain for LBJ, in 1959 RFK drew the short straw to make the journey to LBJ's ranch in Texas in an attempt to discern LBJ's intentions in the upcoming presidential election.

The pair spoke at some length, with LBJ assuring RFK that he wasn't going to run for president. But LBJ was lying. He was not only planning a run, but in his political opinion, JFK was seeking the presidency too soon—he was, after all, barely 40.

Always scheming to gain an advantage, especially a physical one, over an adversary, LBJ took RFK out deer hunting and gave him a rifle with a powerful kick that he didn't bother to mention. RFK fired the gun and was thrown backward to the ground, gashing his forehead in the fall.

Barely suppressing a smirk, the lanky Texan strode over to the college boy now sprawled in the Hill Country dirt.

"Son," LBJ drawled, "you've got to learn to handle a gun like a man."

Some months later, in July 1960, RFK returned the insult by proxy when he and some friends ran into Bobby Baker, LBJ's all-around fixer (and the soon-to-be landlord of a new girl in town named Mary Jo Kopechne).

RFK introduced Baker to his crew as "Little Lyndon Johnson—and you should ask him why Big Lyndon won't risk running in the primaries against my brother."

Baker, who'd been working in the Senate since the age of 16, knew enough not to take the bait.

"They're supposed to make them tough in Texas," RFK said, "but Big Lyndon doesn't look tough to me."

LBJ didn't challenge JFK in the Democratic primaries in 1960. But he still had his eyes on the nomination, and he made his move at the 1960 convention in Los Angeles. He arrived on a private plane with his family. On the tarmac, reporters asked the Senate majority leader if he was interested in the vice presidency.

"The vice presidency," he replied, with an obviously well-rehearsed line, "is a good place for a young man who needs experience. It is a good place for a young man who needs training."

The inference, of course, was that he was the candidate who would be needing a running mate, and that JFK would be the right "young man" for that role.

LBJ had been making sarcastic remarks about John from the moment JFK began his campaign. LBJ would refer to him as "the boy," or "Sonny Boy," or even "Little Johnny." He would describe JFK, accurately, as "just a rich kid whose daddy was trying to buy him the nomination."

JFK, he said, "was out kissing babies while I was passing bills, including his bills."

It was at the convention in Los Angeles where RFK again vented his anger about LBJ on Bobby Baker. The pair sat down to breakfast and, during an otherwise civil meal, Baker mentioned that he thought Teddy had been rough on LBJ by saying Johnson had not recovered from his earlier heart attack. RFK's face instantly darkened.

"You've got your nerve," he growled at Baker. "Lyndon Johnson has compared my father to the Nazis and John Connally and (LBJ operative) India Edwards lied in saying my brother is dying of Addison's disease. You Johnson people are running a stinking damned campaign, and you're gonna get yours when the time comes!"

RFK went on to say that LBJ's people were no damned good, that they were crooks and a disgrace to decent Democrats—in other words, the pot was calling the kettle black.

Even though the Johnson campaign, from LBJ on down, had been brutal to the Kennedys, the candidate took it upon himself to really lay it on thick once he arrived at the convention.

"I was never any Chamberlain umbrella policy man," LBJ told Washington state delegates hours before the balloting began. "I never thought Hitler was right."

It was a direct shot fired directly at the family's Achilles' heel—the old man's failure to take a hard line against Hitler when the world was on the brink of war.

LBJ also criticized JFK's life of easy privilege.

"I haven't had anything given to me," LBJ said. "Whatever I have and whatever I hope to get, will be because of whatever energy and talents I have."

Privately, LBJ and his campaign were spreading even nastier rumors. During the convention, an LBJ operative called *Time* journalist Theodore White and said, "I think you should know that John Kennedy and Bobby Kennedy are fags."

"You're crazy," White replied, not taking the assertion seriously. (He was a Harvard classmate of Joe Jr., and also a graduate of Boston Latin—Joe Sr.'s high school.)

But the caller—who was known to White—was insistent. "We have pictures of John Kennedy and Bobby Kennedy in women's dresses in Las Vegas this spring at a big fag party. This should be made public."

When White demanded evidence—photographic proof—LBJ's operative claimed he'd have it for him within 24 hours.

No pictures ever arrived.

The Kennedys spread their own rumors about LBJ as well. RFK made the baseless accusation that Teamsters' locals in Los Angeles had been told to "whoop up" the sputtering Johnson campaign.

In fact, LBJ, as a legislator from a right-to-work Southern state, had a somewhat prickly relationship with organized labor.

But RFK's noteworthy time on the Senate Rackets Committee must have given him the idea to spread rumors about Jimmy Hoffa's Teamsters. After all, they had been expelled from the AFL-CIO, and no one seemed more qualified to comment on their nefarious activities than RFK.

This fact was not lost on LBJ. He pointed out that RFK was using a tactic he likely learned from Joe McCarthy—guilt by association. Privately, LBJ described RFK as "one of McCarthy's toadies" and a "liberal fascist."

With his convention campaign lagging, LBJ was increasingly desperate to pry delegates away from JFK. So he publicly challenged JFK to a debate at a joint session of the Texas and Massachusetts delegations in the ballroom of the Biltmore Hotel.

The family carefully considered the challenge. Joe Kennedy wanted no part of it.

"But, Daddy, how can Jack say no?" his daughter Jean Kennedy Smith asked. "The man challenged us."

JFK agreed to the debate, but was concerned.

"What shall I say?" he asked RFK.

Time's Hugh Sidey saw an uncharacteristically, visibly nervous JFK.

"I remember seeing that pant leg fluttering there, as he waited for Johnson."

As the debate was about to begin, RFK was taking no chances. Ever suspicious of dirty tricks by the Texans, RFK intercepted a glass of water that was passed to his brother on the platform. He tasted it before handing it over to JFK.

Despite the Kennedys' pre-debate anxiety, LBJ proved no match for JFK when it came to the ability to win over an audience.

LBJ's arcane, inside-baseball attacks on JFK's record on such matters as his votes on agriculture and civil-rights bills, as well as his chronic absenteeism, were total nonstarters with the delegates and the press.

The younger man simply smiled, shrugged and deflected LBJ's churlish sniping, never losing his cool.

"I don't think Sen. Johnson and I disagree on the great issues that face us," he said more than once.

When it was over, even LBJ's closest friends knew that his campaign for president was over.

"I yield to no man in my love and affection for Johnson," said Jack Valenti, "but he was handled with such skill by Kennedy, who was like some great toreador handling one of the great Andalusian bulls. Kennedy just massacred him."

"That," admitted John Connally, "was our last gasp. It was the end of the road."

That JFK, a complete lightweight his entire career in Congress, was running away with the nomination infuriated LBJ. He complained to Sam Rayburn that JFK "[p]robably got himself a half dozen starlets."

"Now, now," replied Rayburn, fully aware of both LBJ's similar proclivities and his competitive nature. "Don't be jealous, Lyndon."

"Jealous?" LBJ spat back. "Chickenshit! I'm not jealous, I'm just pissed off that I'm working my ass off and he's playing Tiddlywinks."

LBJ fancied himself a self-made man. (He'd knuckled the FCC into approving his applications for radio- and TV-station licenses in Austin.) And now he was becoming obsessed with JFK, whose father had made his fortunes in much the same dodgy way LBJ had—only a generation earlier.

"I am not going to go elbowing through 179 million Americans," LBJ sneered, "pushing aside other senators and governors and Congressmen to shout 'Look at me—and nobody else . . . Those who have engaged in active campaigns since January have missed hundreds of votes . . . This I could not do—for my country or my party. Someone has to tend the store."

So he briefly threw his support to Adlai Stevenson. This incensed RFK, who hated Stevenson almost as much as he hated LBJ—for years RFK had gleefully passed along rumors, unconfirmed, about the former Illinois governor's alleged homosexuality. RFK also resented the fact that Stevenson hadn't selected his brother as his running mate in 1956.

But LBJ's political dalliance with the dithering Stevenson was short-lived, and he knew that his best—indeed, his only shot at the White House would be on a Kennedy-Johnson ticket.

However, by then the Kennedys had already settled on their ideal running mate—Sen. Stuart Symington of Missouri.

Among other things, Symington's selection would have represented an olive branch of sorts to former president Harry S. Truman, another Missourian who had never hidden his disdain for Joe Kennedy, whom he once described as "the biggest crook in America."

To deliver the news to Symington, JFK picked Clark Clifford, another Missourian, who had recently proven his mettle to the family. Clifford, a well-connected DC lawyer, had successfully threatened Washington columnist Drew Pearson with a lawsuit after Pearson (correctly) accused JFK of falsely claiming that he had authored *Profiles in Courage.* The best seller was actually written by JFK aide Ted Sorensen, who as his end of the deal received 100 percent of the royalties.

After the book was published, Joe Kennedy had ordered Arthur Krock, his man at the *New York Times,* to make sure that his son got the Pulitzer Prize for nonfiction. As usual, Krock came through for his boss. It was quite an honor for JFK, whose interest in literature was mostly confined to the show-biz magazine *Confidential,* where he eagerly read about the latest sex scandals of the Hollywood starlets he was planning to bed.

Pearson had described JFK as "the only man in history that I know of who won a Pulitzer Prize on a book which was ghostwritten for him, which indicates the kind of public-relations build-up he's had."

Clifford had forced Pearson to retract his accurate expose of JFK's intellectual fraud, although the Kennedys would eventually pay a price for their humiliation of the powerful newspaperman. But now Clifford was back running errands for the Kennedys.

"We've talked it out," JFK told Clifford on July 13, "me, dad, Bobby—and we've selected Symington as the vice president."

Kennedy insider Hy Raskin told Seymour Hersh that "Johnson was not being given the slightest bit of consideration by any of the Kennedys."

But, abruptly, the Kennedys reversed their decision. Suddenly, rumors swept the convention in Los Angeles that LBJ would be JFK's running mate.

JFK did not embarrass easily, but he was chagrined by what had happened—whatever happened.

"I must do something I have never done before," he told an aide. "I made a serious deal, and now I have to go back on it. I have no alternative."

As Raskin told Hersh, "It was obvious that something extraordinary had taken place. During my entire association with the Kennedys, I could not recall any situation where a decision of major significance had been reversed in such a short period of time . . ."

Exactly what transpired will never be known with certainty—if indeed it was blackmail, and it seems more than likely that it was, neither side would have wanted to commit any details to paper. RFK later told close aides that no one would ever know what had occurred—and so far, apparently, no one does.

What information could LBJ and Rayburn have used to compel the Kennedys to put LBJ on the ticket? Again, no one can be certain. But in addition to all of his agents' field reports about JFK's liaisons with starlets, showgirls, and married women, not to mention his and his family's associations with mobsters in both the United States and Cuba, Hoover possessed at least two audiotapes of JFK having extramarital sex.

The earlier one was recorded by FBI agents in the early 1940s when Ensign Kennedy was shacking up with Inga Arvad at the Fort Sumter Hotel in Charleston, South Carolina. The more recent tape proved that Sen. Kennedy had seduced his 22-year-old Senate aide Pamela Turnure in Washington in 1958.

The Kennedys had been paying off much of the press for decades, with both money and access (and in the case of Arthur Krock, women). But they didn't own everyone, and thus they couldn't risk allowing such scandalous information to be shopped around by their political enemies, not with the presidency on the line.

Whether it was blackmail, or something else, the Texans had the Kennedys over a barrel, and both sides knew it.

On the morning the vice-presidential decision was to be announced, JFK called LBJ with a tentative offer. But apparently JFK was somewhat vague in his offer—for obvious reasons. Sam Rayburn told LBJ to play it cool.

"I don't think you ought to have to fight for the nomination," Baker quoted Rayburn as advising his boy. "If Kennedy wants you, let him draft you. Let him pave the way and do the sweating."

In fact, everyone was sweating. By midafternoon, LBJ was huddling privately in his room with his wife and *Washington Post* publisher Phil Graham. Meanwhile, RFK was meeting with Rayburn and John Connally in a nearby room to make a firm offer of the vice presidency.

Perhaps hoping to placate his brother's blackmailers with a lesser prize, RFK at first dangled a counter offer of the chairmanship of the Democratic National Committee.

"Shit!" said Rayburn with a sneer.

RFK got the message. He knew he was beat. He then formally offered the vice presidency to LBJ.

Rayburn walked over to LBJ's room and informed him of the surrender, or offer, or whatever it was. Lady Bird thought that hearing it from the candidate's brother was insufficient.

"I've never argued with you, Mr. Sam," Lady Bird Johnson said, "but I don't think Lyndon should talk to him."

Graham agreed with Lady Bird.

"You don't want it," Graham advised LBJ to tell RFK. "You won't negotiate for it, you'll take it only if Jack drafts you, and you won't discuss it with anyone else."

LBJ concurred with Graham's advice and the publisher left the room to call JFK directly to inform him of LBJ's position.

After some delays caused by the badly overburdened hotel phone lines, JFK and Graham finally spoke.

"It's all set," JFK said. "Tell Lyndon I want him and I'll have (Gov.) David Lawrence [of Pennsylvania] nominate him."

Between all the proxies and the telephone problems, LBJ was still anxious. He nervously waited to hear from JFK directly. RFK assured Rayburn his brother would soon call.

All of this uncertainty and chaos was unfolding as if JFK and LBJ hadn't spoken directly a few hours earlier, in the morning.

"It appears," Bobby Baker later wrote, "that Jack Kennedy did not tell his people he'd called on Lyndon and thus added to the confusion; it also appears that JFK several times waffled during the day under the fire of red-hot liberals. Either that, or he had not made as firm an offer at the morning meeting as LBJ had said he did."

A half hour had passed since RFK said JFK would call. Bill Moyers, another LBJ aide from Texas, arrived to report that RFK had just come in and told Rayburn and Graham that the liberals were threatening an open rebellion if LBJ were added to the ticket. LBJ, RFK suggested, should withdraw, for the good of the party.

Stunned, Graham said, "That can't be right. Jack Kennedy just told me it's all set and David Lawrence agreed to nominate you."

"Phil," Rayburn barked, "call Jack Kennedy and straighten out this mess."

LBJ must have been furious. He knew RFK was JFK's alter ego, his mini-me. As he had once told a group of senators, "Why, don't you know Bobby Kennedy won't get to go to the bathroom unless Jack Kennedy feels like takin' a pee?"

All of the commotion caused Baker to have "a fleeting thought of how the press had written of the 'smooth Kennedy machine.' Hell, they're as confused as we are."

At long last, Graham got through to JFK. He told him of RFK's hesitancy, and JFK said that his brother had been out of touch with the campaign. RFK had misunderstood his 100 percent commitment to LBJ, JFK said.

LBJ would never forget how RFK had tried to deny him what he considered his rightful place on the ticket. After speaking directly with JFK for the second time that day, LBJ met with reporters and spoke angrily of RFK off the record, calling him "that little shitass" and worse.

If LBJ was naturally upset by the whole process, RFK was devastated.

"Yesterday was the best day of my life," RFK would tell a journalist friend later that night, "and today is the worst day of my life."

In the end, though, it was a victory for LBJ—the ultimate prize, as it would turn out three years later.

At the inauguration in 1961, Clare Booth Luce, the ex-congresswoman who had been the girlfriend of both Joe Kennedy and LBJ, asked Johnson why he would give up running the Senate to become JFK's second banana.

"Clare," he said. "I looked it up: one out of every four presidents has died in office. I'm a gamblin' man, darlin,' and this is the only chance I got."

After the election, LBJ had floated a trial balloon—he had proposed to remain in the Senate as majority leader while simultaneously serving as vice president.

LBJ would have theoretically had two votes in the Senate—one as a senator from Texas, the other as vice president (in the case of ties). Obviously, that was not possible under the Constitution or any other circumstances. Almost as important, everyone in the Senate Democratic leadership, starting with majority whip Mike Mansfield, wanted LBJ "up or out" so they could each advance a slot.

Johnson was initially enthusiastic about the vice presidency, or at least tried to be. He weighed his strengths, fully aware of the power he had accumulated in the Senate.

"I've been thinking about where I can do Jack Kennedy the most good," he told an aide. "And it's right here on this Hill, the place I know best. Jack, you know, was an indifferent senator. He never learned how things operate around here and he still doesn't know. All those Bostons and Harvards don't know any more about Capitol Hill than an old maid does about fuckin' . . . I'm gonna keep this office . . . and help (Sens.) Mike Mansfield and Bob Kerr and Hubert Humphrey pass the Kennedy program."

His optimism, however, was soon dashed by the dismal reality of the job. As an earlier vice president from Texas, John Nance Garner, had observed 20 years earlier, "The vice presidency isn't worth a pitcher of warm piss."

Even now-President Kennedy sympathized, telling Bobby Baker, "I really feel sorry for Lyndon. I know he's unhappy in the vice-presidency. It's a horseshit job, the worst fucking job I can imagine."

The president told Baker his old boss wasn't speaking up enough at the cabinet meetings, and Baker concurred.

"I think he's afraid to," Baker said. "I think he feels that some of your cabinet members and the 'palace guard' are looking to cut his throat and dump him from the ticket in 1964."

"Shit, I've read all that crap in the papers," JFK said. "It distresses me and I've told my people I'll kick ass if I hear them spreading that horseshit around. What I want you to do is tell Lyndon how much I truly appreciate him as vice-president. Get it across that he's a valuable man to me and that he has nothing to fear."

Of course, that was bullshit too. The Kennedys had as much contempt for LBJ as he had for them and the rest of the "Harvards."

As for the Kennedys, they had a new nickname for the vice president—"Uncle Cornpone." It didn't help LBJ's position that the "little shitass," Bobby, was now his brother's attorney general, even though he had never tried a single case after graduating for the University of Virginia Law School.

His appointment had been dictated by Joe, the old man. At the time, LBJ didn't seem that worked up about the breathtaking nepotism involved in appointing someone so utterly unqualified to the nation's top law-enforcement job.

"Well," LBJ told Baker, "since the old bastard bought the office I guess he's got a right to get his money's worth."

JFK, however, seemed more bothered by his father's direct order. After all, he, not Joe, was going to have to absorb the slings and arrows involved in such a preposterous selection. So JFK dispatched two members of his own generation whom his father liked and respected—George Smathers and Clark Clifford—to argue with Joe against Bobby's selection as AG. A better starting appointment, they both told the old man in different visits, might be . . . assistant secretary of defense.

Joe had the same reaction to that as Sam Rayburn had to the Kennedys' offer to LBJ of the chairmanship of the Democratic National Committee: "Shit!"

In his book, *Counsel to the President: A Memoir*, Clifford wrote of his unsuccessful visit to Palm Beach:

"For a moment I had glimpsed the inner workings of that remarkable family, and, despite my admiration and affection for John F. Kennedy, I could not say I liked what I saw."

After the inauguration, "Uncle Cornpone" was increasingly shunned by the hated "Harvards."

Baker said he told JFK that LBJ felt "excluded and snubbed him socially." What LBJ wanted, Baker wrote, was "nothing so much as to relax with Jack Kennedy over a few drinks in the family quarters, kick off his shoes, and talk politics in the informal way he'd always done as Senate majority leader."

But that wasn't how JFK and his team of Ivy Leaguers operated, and even if it were, how much warmth could there be between the two men, given the circumstances of their shotgun political wedding in Los Angeles in the summer of 1960?

Baker reported back to LBJ about his conversation with JFK, telling the vice president about JFK's sympathy, as insincere as it may have been, which was clearly how the vice president regarded it.

"LBJ had a glum hang-dog air about him," Baker said. "He was almost impossible to cheer up. 'If I speak one word of disagreement with the cabinet and White House staff looking on,' he said, 'then they'll put it out to [columnist] Joe Kraft and [network TV reporter] Sander Vanocur and everybody that I'm a damned traitor. You don't know how they treat me over there. Oh, sure, Jack Kennedy's as thoughtful and considerate of me at those meetings as he can be. But I know his snot-nosed brother's after my ass, and all those high-falutin' Harvards, and if I give 'em enough rope they'll hang me with it.'"

Baker himself would run into trouble late in the Kennedy presidency. In September 1963, Republicans on the Senate Rules Committee began an investigation into allegations of Baker's unsavory rackets—specifically, bribery and arranging sex for members in return for votes and government contracts. Within a month, Baker would be forced to resign from his longtime job as secretary to the majority leader.

The sexual trysts that Baker had arranged included hooking up Ellen Rometsch, a suspected East German spy, with President Kennedy. Baker later said that JFK described Rometsch as "the best blow job he ever had in his life."

The pending investigation spelled serious trouble for the president. So his brother begged J. Edgar Hoover to keep the Rometsch story out of the Senate investigation. Hoover went back to his usual stock in trade: dangling some of his infamous secret dossiers over the senators' heads.

Hoover met at Mansfield's home with the Democratic leader and his Republican counterpart, Sen. Everett Dirksen of Illinois. Hoover had two words for the Senate leaders to pass on to their members.

Hoover's words were: "Negro girlfriends."

The Senate probe of Rometsch and the president ended as abruptly as it had begun.

But the director's favor to the Kennedys came with a heavy price. Hoover had already guaranteed himself life tenure the previous year when he obtained the final telephone records of Marilyn Monroe before her mysterious death in Brentwood during a visit to Los Angeles by RFK.

And now, in return for quashing this latest Kennedy sex scandal, Hoover had a new demand: he wanted authorization to surveil Dr. Martin Luther King Jr.

RFK granted Hoover's wish instantly—a decision that would forever tarnish his record as attorney general.

Between her deportation and Hoover's files about Negro girlfriends, Rometsch may have been eliminated as a target for Senate Republican investigators, but Baker remained in the crosshairs. And his wheeling and dealing had ensnared the vice president in a growing number of criminal probes, even though LBJ had not been involved in Baker's affairs after 1960.

By the fall of 1963, whispers were growing ever louder that LBJ would be dropped from the 1964 ticket. JFK had even mentioned the name of his likely replacement to his secretary, Evelyn Kennedy: North Carolina Governor Terry Sanford, a moderate who might be able to keep the increasingly not so "Solid South" in the Democratic column.

LBJ was becoming persona non grata, even in the Lone Star State. Planners for the motorcade scheduled for Dallas on November 22 asked Governor Connally and Sen. Ralph Yarborough if they wanted to ride in the vice president's limousine.

Both flatly refused.

A few days later, LBJ was president. As leader of the free world, especially under such dire circumstances, he would never again have to worry about being prosecuted for the crimes that others had been testifying under oath that he had committed—all sorts of shakedowns, laundered through "advertisements" on his radio and TV stations in Austin.

LBJ had caught another break, even if his old friend Baker didn't. He would be convicted of tax evasion and spent 18 months in prison.

With President Kennedy dead and LBJ in the Oval Office, the 1964 presidential election was less than a year away. LBJ would surely seek reelection, but he would need a running mate, and the prospect of being vice president briefly mesmerized RFK.

By early 1964, LBJ was angered to learn that overtures were being made on RFK's behalf in New Hampshire, site of the first presidential primary.

The man behind the draft-Bobby movement was Paul Corbin. Corbin was the widely disliked henchman for RFK on the Democratic National Committee, who just before the assassination had been investigating Kenny O'Donnell's reported embezzling. Corbin was known to be "abrasive and intemperate" and a "constant liability and frequent embarrassment to RFK."

Nevertheless, RFK valued Corbin as a ruthless politico who delivered for JFK in the 1960 primaries.

LBJ wanted the Bobby-for-VP effort stopped, and he ordered O'Donnell to tell RFK to end it. When O'Donnell delivered the message, RFK snapped, "Tell [LBJ] to go to hell."

With the New Hampshire primaries just a month away, LBJ summoned RFK to the Oval Office. Recounting the meeting, RFK would say, "It was the meanest tone I'd ever heard . . . The substance wasn't that drastic, but the tone was so . . ."

LBJ demanded that Corbin be removed from the Democratic National Committee. RFK protested, extolling Corbin's usefulness to his brother's campaign.

"He was appointed by President Kennedy," he told LBJ, "who thought he was good."

But LBJ wanted him gone. That was his order to his underling, the little shit-ass.

"Do it," LBJ demanded. Then he delivered the words that were the hardest for RFK to hear: "President Kennedy isn't president anymore. I am."

Following LBJ's direction, and without RFK's knowledge, the FBI had already investigated Corbin. FBI documents referred to him as "Paul Corbin also known as Paul Kobrinsky" and described his "former association with the Communist movement."

The file on Corbin's "completely un-American activities background" was said to be "seven inches thick."

LBJ didn't keep RFK out of the loop on all of the FBI's counterintelligence operations. The bugging of Martin Luther King Jr., for instance, was producing a torrent of what the FBI director and the new president valued most—blackmail material.

Until a falling out with J. Edgar Hoover late in his career, William C. Sullivan was one of the director's top aides at the FBI. In 1977, days before he was to testify before the House Select Committee on Assassinations, Sullivan was shot to death at the age of 65 in a predawn hunting accident in New Hampshire. He had been working on his memoirs, which were posthumously published in a severely expurgated version.

The original proposal, however, which was shopped around before Sullivan's death, included some purported transcripts of King's drunken chatter in an LA hotel room. The room had been bugged shortly after JFK's assassination, Sullivan wrote, and King was recorded speculating that JFK "got even more poontang than me."

According to Sullivan, King had drunkenly told his fellow black ministers that Jackie Kennedy was one "white woman" he'd love to bed, because "she probably wasn't satisfied by her husband's little weenie."

The accuracy of those quotes provided by Sullivan is unknown. The FBI records on King were sealed under a court order for 50 years, until 2027. Given the nature of the civil-rights leader's un-PC remarks, it appears unlikely that the real Martin Luther King Jr. transcripts will ever be released.

But Hoover—perhaps at the direction of LBJ—did make the FBI transcripts available to RFK, and he informed Jackie. This is confirmed by her comments in an oral interview just a few months after the assassination. Those interviews were released in 2011. She mentioned how RFK had told her about the orgies King had participated in while on the road leading civil-rights demonstrations.

"I just can't see a picture of Martin Luther King," she said, "without thinking, you know, this man's terrible."

She also mentioned what RFK had told her about how King described her husband's funeral—"He made fun of Cardinal Cushing and said that he was drunk at it. And things about how they almost dropped the coffin and—well, I mean Martin Luther King is really a tricky person."

Everything President Johnson did infuriated RFK. JFK had a hobby of having himself photographed while having sex—Peter Lawford handled the chores when JFK trysted with Marilyn Monroe in Hollywood.

In Washington, DC, Seymour Hersh discovered, White House photographers were assigned the pornographic chore, with Secret Service agents tasked with getting the XXX-rated photographs developed.

Before leaving the White House in November 1963, RFK and other JFK loyalists apparently managed to find and dispose of most of the embarrassing photos—not to mention the White House logs showing how many harlots had visited the president during "Camelot."

But after moving into 1600 Pennsylvania Avenue, LBJ discovered at least a few of the photos—and he recognized some of the late president's secretaries.

He arranged for one of the women to be called into the Oval Office, where she saw the new president perusing a graphic photograph of herself being mounted by JFK. LBJ apparently enjoyed seeing the woman's shocked reaction.

With his closest aides, LBJ would remark how his predecessor had at the very least acquiesced in the assassinations of two foreign leaders who had supported him—Rafael Trujillo of the Dominican Republic and, more recently, the Diems in South Vietnam. They were Roman Catholics, too, like the Kennedys, and JFK had betrayed them.

"Was it divine retribution?" LBJ mused of the assassination in Dallas.

RFK remained attorney general for a few months more, but he was obsessed with his own sense of guilt over the death of his brother—did the Mafia murder JFK to put an end to RFK's crackdown on organized crime?

Another obsession of RFK as the months went by: his ever-growing hatred of LBJ.

"[He] lies all the time," RFK told friends. "He just lies continuously about everything . . . In every conversation I have with him, he lies . . . He lies even when he doesn't have to."

LBJ would never run on the same ticket with RFK, but Bobby did manage a star turn at the Democratic national convention in Atlantic City in August 1964.

His emotional address to the convention brought loud, impassioned, sustained ovations from the crowd that was vicariously cheering for his martyred brother. But even in remembering JFK, RFK took a not-so-veiled shot at LBJ.

"I realize that as individuals we can't just look back, that we must look forward. When I think of President Kennedy I think of what

Shakespeare said in Romeo and Juliet, 'When he shall die, take him and cut him out in little stars, and he shall make the face of heaven so fine that all the world will be in love with night and pay no worship to the garish sun.'"

The garish sun!

LBJ was incensed. It was so clearly a reference to the sitting president, a man RFK detested. RFK had so gotten under LBJ's skin that the president, according to historian Michael Beschloss, "had nightmares that he would get to the Democratic Convention in 1964, and in would come Bobby Kennedy and Jackie Kennedy—stampede the delegates to vote for not LBJ but RFK for president."

Ultimately, LBJ would be reelected and RFK would have to defer his dream of sitting behind his brother's desk in the Oval Office. He was elected to the Senate from New York in the Democrat landslide of 1964. As the sixties wore on, RFK began to turn against the war in Vietnam that was so vexing LBJ.

He began making antiwar speeches, which was when his family's old foe Drew Pearson began writing columns pointing out RFK's hawkishness when his brother was president. Obviously, it was LBJ leaking to Pearson.

In 1968, Sen. Eugene McCarthy's insurgent antiwar campaign for president caught fire, and RFK abruptly decided to run for the Democrat nomination for president himself. LBJ quickly announced he would not seek reelection, but he still wanted revenge on Sonny Boy.

In April 1968, after Martin Luther King Jr. was assassinated in Memphis, RFK was a strutting presence at the funeral, wearing his grief on his sleeve. He even dragged Jackie along with him, despite the horrible things the slain preacher had said about her and her late husband.

Well aware of the sordid backstory about the Kennedys and King, LBJ sensed an opportunity to torpedo the born-again liberal RFK. As RFK campaigned against McCarthy in Oregon, Pearson ran a column revealing that RFK had approved the FBI's "wiretaps" against King.

It was a devastating story, putting the lie to the former Joe McCarthy acolyte's attempt to remake his image as some kind of counterculture crusader. His shocked aides asked how to respond, and RFK dictated a tepid statement saying he had never authorized "wiretaps." (He had approved the planting of bugs in the room, not taps on King's phones.)

Nobody believed his parsed words, and a few days later, in Oregon, RFK did what JFK had never done eight years earlier. He lost a primary.

A week later, though, RFK rebounded, edging McCarthy in the California primary. He probably wasn't going to defeat LBJ's candidate, Vice President Hubert Humphrey, at the national convention in Chicago, but he had managed to stave off elimination before August.

RFK's California campaign headquarters were in Los Angeles, the same city where he and LBJ had tangled so acrimoniously less than eight years earlier, and where he had loudly argued with Marilyn Monroe on the last evening of her life in August 1962.

RFK spent election night watching TV, complaining to aides about the endemic anti-Catholicism of the *New York Times*—"their idea of a good story is 'More nuns leave church,'" he said. But finally he could declare victory. He went downstairs to the ballroom of the Ambassador Hotel to address his supporters.

"And now it's on to Chicago," he told his fans before heading out through the hotel kitchen on his way to his former brother-in-law Peter Lawford's club, The Factory, in West Hollywood.

And then a Palestinian immigrant stepped out and shot RFK in the head. He was brain-dead, placed on life support.

After hearing news of the shooting, LBJ incessantly pestered his aide Joseph Califano.

"Is he dead?" LBJ kept asking in the Oval Office. "Is he dead yet?"

Califano ordered his assistant, Larry Levinson, to keep an open line to the Secret Service in Los Angeles. By the time Jackie Kennedy signed the necessary papers to remove her brother-in-law and lover from life support, Califano had made so many calls that Levinson finally asked him about the president:

"Joe, is this something that he's *wishing* to have happen?"

(Of course LBJ wasn't the only one gleeful over RFK's murder. Aristotle Onassis knew that he could now marry Jackie Kennedy. And in Palm Springs, Frank Sinatra was at first excited, but later somewhat disappointed that the killer was an Arab, rather than an Italian—preferably a Mafia member, settling all the family business at once, as far as the Chairman of the Board was concerned.)

Even in death, LBJ couldn't let go of his grudge against RFK. Though he promised the Kennedys to do "anything I can do to help," he delayed their request to have the federal government pay for a permanent grave site for RFK next to JFK at Arlington National Cemetery.

Ironically, it would be President Richard Nixon who granted the family their request in 1969.

Near the end of his life in late 1972, LBJ's decades-old obsession with the Kennedys was still evident. Bobby Baker, now on parole after finishing his prison term, visited his old boss at his ranch in Texas for the last time. LBJ was still talking about his old feud with the Kennedys.

"Well," Uncle Cornpone told Baker, "they're all dead except Teddy and I never knew him well. He's still the fair-haired boy where the national press is concerned. You know, if I'd killed a girl like he did then, they'd have wanted to send me to the electric chair."

CHAPTER TWENTY-TWO

JFK: THE FINAL DAYS

THE GENESIS FOR PRESIDENT Kennedy's fateful trip to Dallas in November 1963 came a little over a year earlier, on the Wednesday after the midterm elections in 1962.

JFK was well-aware of how narrowly he had carried Texas in 1960—by 46,233 votes. And he also knew that LBJ was facing some serious corruption issues—namely, his crooked former Senate aide Bobby Baker.

Looking ahead, perhaps, to a post-LBJ campaign for reelection in 1964, Kennedy was talking politics with the ambitious Fort Worth lawyer, who would someday run for president himself, as a Republican.

They were not exactly close friends. During the acrimonious 1960 primary campaign, Connally had accused the future president of having Addison's disease. He did, but no one was supposed to know.

But politics makes strange bedfellows, as they say, and now the president was calling to congratulate the governor-elect of a large, increasingly swing state with 25 electoral votes. Their conversation about the previous day's election returns, like all Oval Office conversations, was recorded on a Dictabelt. Connally was crowing about his victory—"I carried 205 out of 254 counties."

JFK: "What about Dallas?"

CONNALLY: "Dallas? I lost the hell out of it. I lost the hell out of it. I lost it by 21,000 voters."

JFK: "What did we lose Dallas by, do you remember? In '60?"

CONNALLY: "Yes sir, you lost [by] over 60,000 votes."

JFK: "Sixty thousand votes? Hell, I got uh . . . you know, they're up there talking to me about, remember having that federal building down there and all the rest of that stuff. I don't know why we do anything for Dallas."

CONNALLY: "I'm telling you, they just murdered all of us. But we're gonna change that now."

In retrospect, the last year of JFK's presidency—and his life—has a kind of fin de siècle poignancy about it—the end of an era, one ominous portent after another.

Years later, trying to talk Paul Newman into abandoning Sen. Eugene McCarthy's presidential campaign for RFK, Jackie would tell Paul Newman that JFK could never have been reelected—"his indiscretions had become so plentiful."

The problem was that everyone who was anyone knew. Most had their reasons for remaining silent—the Mafia, J. Edgar Hoover, the ex-girlfriends, the LAPD. As long as they had information to threaten the president of the United States with, they had leverage. Once the dirt was out there, they would have no clout. It was the eternal problem of blackmail.

The brothers pose for a portrait at the White House, April 1963.

Phil Graham was the publisher of the *Washington Post,* and he knew everything about everybody in the District. He was wired into both the president and the vice president. His wife's family owned the only morning paper in the nation's capital, having bought the rival *Times-Herald* in 1954. He had recently purchased *Newsweek,* at the urging of Washington bureau chief Ben Bradlee, JFK's great friend from Boston, the future editor of the *Post.*

Bradlee's sister-in-law was Mary Pinchot Meyer, and the previous year, she had become the latest, and perhaps most serious, of the president's blue-blooded girlfriends.

The only problem was that Graham, at age 48, was an alcoholic, and he was going insane. He left his wife Katherine to run off with an Australian stringer for *Newsweek,* a woman named Robin Webb, and was gallivanting around the west with her in January 1963 when he heard that some society of newspaper editors was holding its winter convention in Phoenix.

Graham blew into town and, although accounts vary as to what happened, it appears clear that he was drunk and disorderly at the conference. He hijacked an evening meeting with a lengthy harangue that he began by informing the assembled editors and publishers that he "wouldn't wipe his ass with their papers."

According to Carol Felsenthal, author of *Power, Privilege and the Post: the Katherine Graham Story,* Graham mocked and mimicked several of the self-important newspapermen in attendance. He then announced he was next going to name "who in Washington was sleeping with whom, and that he might as well start with John Kennedy, who was sleeping, in the White House, with Mary Meyer."

After telling his fellow publishers that they were "fat bastards" who were afraid of the truth, Graham sneered, "I don't know what you other sons of bitches are going to do, but I'm going to go home and screw my girl."

Not a word of his outburst ever appeared in any of the newspapers whose publishers and editors Graham had insulted. But the next day, President Kennedy dispatched a military transport out to pick up Graham.

He was brought back to Washington, DC, in a strait jacket, and when he was taken off the flight on a stretcher, he yelled at an old lady who seemed frightened to see him in the terminal:

"It's okay, ma'am, I'm only dying."

White House phone logs show that his girlfriend, Robin Webb, called the White House that evening at 6:18 p.m. and asked to speak to the president, although there is no record if she ever did.

On August 3, 1963, on a day pass from a mental institution, Phil Graham killed himself with a shotgun.

The next Kennedy confidante to die was James McInerney, the former FBI agent and attorney general whose private practice of law for the last decade had mostly involved getting JFK out of one sexual scandal after another.

He'd worked on the Pamela Turnure affair—offering her landlords valuable paintings in return for the photos and audiotapes of JFK's adultery with his 22-year-old secretary. (They'd turned him down and given everything to J. Edgar Hoover.)

In 1960, he seems to have been instrumental in stopping Alicia Darr Purdom from releasing whatever it was she had on JFK. (There are conflicting reports about that sex scandal, and the veracity of the contemporaneous FBI reports about RFK's role in paying off the gold-digging ex-prostitute during the 1960 campaign have been questioned.)

James McInerney, former FBI agent who became the family's "fixer" in the 1950's, handling various scandals, mostly involving JFK. Died at age 58 in 1963.

In the spring of 1963, McInerney made some of the calls to the management of the Hearst newspapers as RFK was trying to kill a story in the *New York Journal-American* about the president's assignations with "V girls"—prostitutes—involved in the Profumo scandal in the United Kingdom. The prostitute in question said her services had been procured for the president by Peter Lawford.

McInerney knew the Hearst management because, as a prime fixer for the new administration, he'd helped smooth the antitrust concerns of the Justice Department over the divvying up of the LA newspaper market between the Hearst and Chandler families.

The Hearsts' JFK scandal story had been killed after running in just one edition of the *Journal-American*, as the president was shacked up in a remote Italian villa on Lake Como with Marella Agnelli, the wife of an Italian tycoon. But that was to be McInerney's final service to the Kennedys.

Shortly afterward, he was killed in a car accident. He was 58 years old.

As 1963 wore on, JFK's favorability ratings were dropping in the South. The civil-rights movement was tearing apart the Democrat party of Jim Crow, separate-but-equal, massive resistance, and the Ku Klux Klan. And JFK remained a most reluctant warrior in the black man's struggle for equality.

In his book, *The Politics of Deception: JFK's Secret Decisions on Vietnam, Civil Rights, and Cuba,* author Patrick J. Sloyan recounts a campaign swing JFK made that year through Pennsylvania.

During a stopover in Pittsburgh, he met with local Democratic politicians. Discussing the fears of the white working classes about blacks moving into their neighborhoods, the president had a knock-knock joke to share with, among others, former Gov. David Lawrence.

"Knock, knock," the president said, according to Lawrence's later recollection.

"Who's there?"

"Izya," Kennedy said.

"Izya who?"

"Izya new neighbor," the president said, chuckling.

The next scandal of 1963 involved Bobby Baker, LBJ's fixer. His connection to JFK was, of course, women. He had provided Ellen Rometsch, the suspected East German spy, to the president. She was summarily deported, but wanted to return to the States. Implausibly, she had fallen in love with one of her government handlers.

To keep Rometsch quiet, the Kennedys needed money, lots of money. According to Seymour Hersh, the president called on Grant Stockdale, a former aide to Sen. George Smathers. JFK had appointed Stockdale ambassador to Ireland as a reward for his fund-raising prowess in the Southeast in the 1960 campaign.

Now, Stockdale was back at his real estate business in Miami when the president called and told him he needed $50,000 in cash. He would have to raise it from his friends, the president told Stockdale, but he could never acknowledge the contributions. This, of course, put Stockdale in an untenable position. He asked JFK what he needed the cash for.

"For personal use," Hersh quoted the president as telling him.

Stockdale somehow gathered the money, put it in a satchel, and went from Miami to Palm Beach to deliver the money.

Stockdale's son told Hersh: "Kennedy said, 'Thank you,' opened a nearby closet door, and threw the briefcase in there . . . The closet was full of briefcases."

When JFK was murdered in Dallas, Stockdale realized he would never be able to convince any of his friends in Miami that he hadn't been running a grift for himself. Ten days after the assassination, he jumped to his death from his Miami office building at the age of 48.

Kenny O'Donnell, the president's longtime aide and sometime procurer, was likewise coming apart at the seams in 1963. His drinking, which would eventually claim his life in 1977, was increasingly out of control. He was overheard by Secret Service agents that summer at a bar on Cape Cod, drunkenly telling patrons that he was the real power behind the Kennedy throne. He suddenly had enough cash to make a bid on an expensive home in Georgetown.

Paul Corbin, RFK's eyes and ears who would soon be running the draft-Bobby campaign in New Hampshire, began to do a little sleuthing. Among his many duties for the president, O'Donnell was of course a bagman—he handled cash contributions to his boss's campaigns.

The problem with bagmen, as an old-time Boston pol named Sonny McDonough once observed, is that you never know how much they're skimming for themselves.

"When a cop hands me $300," Sonny used to say, "I never know if he's stolen $200 or $700."

Corbin came to the conclusion that O'Donnell was stealing big bucks. He kept digging and digging all through the summer. Finally, in November, he thought he had the smoking gun. He handed over his research to RFK on November 21, the day JFK flew to Texas. RFK was finally ready to take action against the president's fixer-pimp-bagman.

"We'll do it Monday," RFK told Corbin. But Monday never came.

Another of JFK's old Massachusetts associates had his head on the chopping block—Henry Cabot Lodge, who JFK had defeated for the Senate in 1952, and who had been Richard Nixon's running mate in 1960.

Now he was the ambassador to South Vietnam, a thankless position. The Diem brothers were losing control of their country. The Vietcong and the North Vietnamese were on the march. The *New York Times,* in the person of David Halberstam, was lobbying for the brothers' overthrow.

At the White House, JFK had his own questions for Lodge about the Diems—specifically, about Diem's wife.

Ambassador Henry Cabot Lodge, 1963.

"What about Madame Nhu?" he asked his old rival in the Oval Office on August 15. "Is she a lesbian or what? She's awful masculine."

Lodge, knowing the president's fondness for prurient gossip, mentioned how she had lived in Washington with her mother years earlier.

"I think she was very promiscuous, a nymphomaniac," Lodge told JFK. "When she was here in Washington a couple of years ago, she took an overdose of sleeping pills and they had to pump her stomach."

In September, the president was back on the subject of Madame Nhu.

"I never saw a more featherheaded dame in my life than this bitch," he raged at a White House meeting September 23.

In September, he sent his old Harvard College roommate, Cong. Torbert MacDonald, to Saigon to warn the Diems that a coup was afoot, as if they didn't already know. MacDonald delivered the message, but the brothers seemed strangely unconcerned. On November 1, 1963, the Diems were ousted, and shot to death in the back of a car as they finally tried to flee—too little too late.

"The Nhu family has been treacherously killed," the woman JFK thought was a lesbian told reporters of her husband and brother-in-law. "That will only be the beginning of the story."

At the U.S. embassy, Lodge's top aide was yet another Massachusetts native, an Irishman named Dunn. On November 1, after the murders, Dunn was distraught, and tried to start a conversation with his boss. Lodge waved him off and looked at his watch.

"What time are cocktails?" the ambassador said.

Someone had to take the rap for the death of the Diems, and Lodge knew who the fall guy would be.

"They're going to try to blame this on me," Lodge told Bob Healy, the *Boston Globe* reporter who was also an operative for the Kennedy family.

RFK admitted as much in an oral interview he gave to the John F. Kennedy Presidential Library in 1964.

"We were going to try to get rid of Henry Cabot Lodge," he said. "He was supposed to come home . . . and we were trying to work out how he could be fired, how we could get rid of him."

Lodge had been ordered to report to the White House for a sit-down with the president . . . on Monday, November 25. O'Donnell, Lodge—the Kennedys were planning on taking care of all family business, Godfather-style, on the Monday after JFK returned from Texas.

President Kennedy made his final visit to Massachusetts in late October 1963. He went to the Harvard-Columbia football game, and visited the grave in Brookline of his infant son Patrick, who had died that summer after being born prematurely. He called his 19-year-old White House intern, Mimi Alford, and invited her to come up to his suite at the Sheraton, where he asked her to fellate his brother Teddy. As detailed in Chapter 16, she refused.

The two brothers then headlined a major black-tie fund-raiser for New England's four Democratic governors at the Commonwealth Armory. On Sunday, the president visited Hyannis Port for the last time, kissing his incapacitated father on the head. He wept openly in front of his aide Dave Powers as he waited for the helicopter at the compound.

"He's the one who made this all possible," a tearful JFK told his pimp, "and look at him now."

As the date for the trip to Dallas neared, JFK began to have misgivings. The Rev. Billy Graham tried to reach the president to warn him that he had a premonition of doom. The wife of NBC news anchor David Brinkley likewise told her friends she had a very bad feeling about the trip. JFK himself asked George Smathers if he thought there was any way he could back out of the trip.

The route through Dealey Plaza was finalized November 15, and was printed in the Dallas newspapers on November 18.

On November 19, the president's secretary Evelyn Lincoln wrote in her 1968 book, *Kennedy and Johnson*, JFK told her that he was going to make a change at the top of the ticket in 1964.

"At this time," she quoted him as saying, "I am thinking about Gov. Terry Sanford of North Carolina, but it will not be Lyndon."

The presidential party spent the final night of JFK's life in Fort Worth. It was rainy, and he mused about how it would have been a good night to kill a president, with all the fog and everyone wearing overcoats. The next morning JFK made the final speech of his life, hatless, with LBJ, Gov. John Connally, and Sen. Ralph Yarbrough standing behind him.

"There are no faint hearts in Fort Worth," he said.

As they made the short hop on Air Force One from Fort Worth to Dallas, JFK glanced at the *Dallas Morning News,* which carried a full-page ad with black borders excoriating him and his administration.

"We're really heading into nut country today," he said to no one in particular.

LBJ was planning to host the Kennedys at his ranch over the weekend. He had even stocked up on Jackie's favorite brand of cigarettes, L&Ms. Before heading to Johnson City, there would be another speech, in Austin. LBJ had already prepared his introduction.

"Thank goodness, Mr. President," the vice president would say, "you made it out of Dallas alive."

In Dallas, as always, JFK instructed the Secret Service that he wanted no bubble top on his limousine. He said he wanted an open car "so these Texas broads can see how beautiful Jackie is."

JFK's last speech, November 22, 1963, in Fort Worth, with Sen. Ralph Yarborough, Gov. John Connally, and Vice President Lyndon Johnson.

JFK always loved riding in an open car, especially with Jackie.

Some of the Secret Service agents were moving a little slowly this morning. They'd been up until the wee hours of the morning, carousing at the Carousel Club, the strip joint owned by a strange mob wannabe from Chicago named Jack Ruby.

Meanwhile, in New York that Friday morning, *Time-Life* editors were giving the go-ahead to some of their top investigative reporters to begin an in-depth probe of Vice President Johnson and the burgeoning scandals around the myriad shady business dealings of his bagman Bobby Baker.

At that same moment, in Washington, DC, on Capitol Hill, an insurance broker named Donald Reynolds was telling Republican Senate staffers about some of these payoffs and gifts that he'd made, at Bobby Baker's direction, to LBJ. His closed-door testimony was still going on in the afternoon when a secretary burst into the hearing room with news from Dallas.

The president was wearing a back brace that stiffened his spine. Months earlier he had injured his back grabbing for a woman in the White House pool. When the shots were fired, the brace would keep him upright, unable to drop to the floor of the limousine as the others did.

As Air Force One began its descent into Dallas, the rain finally ended. The clouds were parting.

The president nodded at Governor Connally.

"Our luck is holding," JFK said. "It looks like we'll get sunshine."

The motorcade appeared routine. Behind the president and the governor and their wives was a car carrying JFK aide Dave Powers and Kenny O'Donnell, who seemed oblivious to the fate that was planned for him on Monday. As the motorcade approached Elm Street and the Texas School Book Depository, Nellie Connally, the first lady of Texas, smiled sweetly at JFK.

"Mr. President," she said, "you can't say Dallas doesn't love you."

"That's obvious," he replied.

Suddenly shots rang out. The governor grasped his chest, wounded. Jackie began wildly climbing out of the backseat onto the trunk. The first shot hit the president.

"My God," he said. "I'm hit."

Those were his last words before the head shot from the grassy knoll blew his brains all over Jackie's pink suit, fulfilling John Connally's eerie prediction a year earlier. JFK was indeed murdered in Dallas.

CHAPTER TWENTY-THREE

FAMOUS KENNEDYS I HAVE KNOWN

IKE EVERYBODY ELSE IN America in 1980, I'd been watching the Kennedys my entire life. But I never felt like I was actually close to the continuing saga of America's First Family, so called, until that winter.

I was a reporter for the *Boston Herald American.* Rupert Murdoch's purchase of the paper was more than two years in the future. It was still a broadsheet, an anemic, advertising-starved daily losing at least $1 million a month for the Hearst corporation.

But Rupert Murdoch already owned the *New York Post,* and Ted Kennedy was running for president against the incumbent Democrat in the White House, Jimmy Carter. The *Post* had been running a devastating series of articles about Kennedy's dissipated lifestyle—"Teddy's Wild Weekends"—and in those pre-Internet, pre–Fox News days, Murdoch wanted to spread the story more widely into Kennedy's home state of Massachusetts.

So he made his star witness against Teddy—his former mistress Lana Campbell—available to the *Herald American.* She'd been on the front page of the *Post* for days, usually identified as "the Countess." I was working at City Hall when I was told to come down to the paper's main offices in the South End of Boston. I'd been picked to write the hit piece.

I sat in the newsroom waiting for the phone to ring. Finally it did. I spoke to one of the *Post* reporters who'd been working on the series.

"Howie?" he said. "I've got the Countess for you."

I asked her a couple of questions. My editors were interested in the drug angle.

"Teddy and I took LSD," she told me, "and then we made beautiful love together."

Of course that wasn't my first brush with a Kennedy. My father started working at The Breakers hotel in Palm Beach in the late 1920s. He used to tell a story about a beautiful young woman who worked in one of the hotel's lobby shops in the early 1940s.

One day she came up to my father, who by then was one of the managers, and asked if he could give her a ride to the train station in West Palm the next morning. He was surprised—in those days, when The Breakers was only open three months a year, in the winter—all workers signed up for the duration of the season. Anyone who quit early would be blackballed in the resort-hotel industry.

The Depression wasn't quite over. Jobs were hard to come by, especially good, Breakers-type jobs. My father asked the attractive young woman why she was walking away from a decent career.

"I can't take it anymore," she told my father. "Joe Kennedy is chasing me all over town. He won't leave me alone."

By the way, my father voted for JFK for president in 1960. He wanted that Catholic monkey off his and everyone else's back. He said he'd voted for Al Smith in 1928 for the same reason, in the first presidential election he cast a ballot in. The only difference was, he'd actually liked Al Smith. My father always said he'd held his nose to vote for JFK.

My father knew Honey Fitz too. Teddy told me once, back when he was still talking to me, that he learned to drive taking Honey Fitz down to The Breakers in the morning where he would sit in the lobby and schmooze for hours. The politician who ended Honey Fitz's career, James Michael Curley, was likewise a late-in-life habitué of The Breakers lobby—as a jailbird, he wasn't allowed to stay there.

In the 1940s my father was the reservations manager. They checked out people they didn't know who wanted to stay there. One day he got an inquiry from some wealthy family in the Midwest, the Skakels. He called the agency in New York that kept tabs on people, and they warned him that the Skakels were trouble—big, big money, but big, big trouble.

My father took a chance.

"Terrible mistake," he used to say. "They trashed their rooms like nothing I ever saw. Total animals, alcoholics."

As the years went on, I met what seemed to be an endless number of Kennedys. I used to have lunch at the Algonquin Club on Commonwealth Avenue with Michael Kennedy, the one who was married to Frank Gifford's daughter. At the time I met him, he hadn't yet started having sex with his children's 14-year-old babysitter. At least I don't think so.

I was introduced to Michael by Nick Rizzo, who later went to prison for embezzling millions from Sen. Paul Tsongas's campaign account. Michael died when he skied into a tree in Colorado shortly after beating a statutory-rape rap. Rizzo was convicted, imprisoned, and then paroled. He ended up bagging groceries in a supermarket in Essex County, after which he moved into an assisted-living facility and burned himself to death in 2018 by smoking in an oxygen tent.

Oh yeah, Nick's son-in-law was the chief aide to the first Hispanic mayor of Lawrence. He went to prison, too—Nick's son-in-law, not the mayor.

Wherever I turned, I ran into Kennedys. At the *Herald,* one of the interns was Dougie Kennedy—Douglas MacArthur Kennedy, who would later be arrested for allegedly striking a nurse at the hospital in New York where one of his children had just been born. (He was acquitted.)

Dougie and I were both friendly with a recovering junkie who, it turned out, wasn't so recovered. The last time I ever talked to Dougie, he called me to tell me our friend had ODed in New York. I was sorely tempted to tell Dougie what I was thinking: "Dennis can't be dead, he owes me 13 bucks."

When I left the *Herald American,* I went to work at what was then the CBS affiliate in Boston, WNAC-TV. One of the tape editors was Bob Dinneen, the son of Joseph Dinneen, one of the Kennedy family apologists at the *Boston Globe* whom you've read about in Chapter 18.

I worked at a Boston TV station with Peter McKelvy, right, who married Sydney Lawford, second from right. Also present are Kara Kennedy, now deceased, and Joan. The man in the middle is unidentified.

Another editor at Channel 7 was Peter McKelvey, who married one of Peter Lawford's daughters. She came by the station one Saturday. She was one hot Kennedy back in the day, Sydney was.

Later on, I began getting work in Boston radio. The morning guy at one of the places I worked at was Andy Moes. He'd started out as a part-time undercover cop in Hyannis. He got Bobby Shriver and RFK Jr. to sell him a couple of joints and they ended up busted. That was a long time ago. Marijuana is now legal in Massachusetts.

When I was a kid in Palm Beach, my parents used to check the papers to see if President Kennedy was flying in for the weekend. If he was in town, Mass at St. Edward on Sunday morning would be swarming with tourists, so we'd go across Lake Worth to St. Ann in West Palm.

Now I own a condo a block from St. Edward. As I walk to the beach past the church on Sunset, I pass a bank on the corner of North County Road. It used to be a parking lot. RFK would go to 7 o'clock Mass at St. Edward, and he'd park in that little lot. One morning after Mass he was sitting in his car, talking to somebody, and my mother handed me a pen and the church bulletin and told me to go get RFK's autograph.

I got it. But I haven't seen that church bulletin for years. I'm pretty sure it's gone for good.

When I went back to the *Herald,* it was as a columnist. Rupert Murdoch was now the owner, a media mogul in the making, with newspapers and TV stations in both Boston and New York.

It was a good time to be working for a newspaper. In the other paper in Boston, the *Globe,* seldom was heard a discouraging word about the Kennedys, which left me a lot of running room. I took full advantage of it.

I remember one editorial-board meeting Teddy had at the *Herald* when he was running for reelection in 1988. I waited my turn to ask a question. Finally, I recalled my conversation with the Countess eight years earlier and asked Teddy if he'd ever used drugs.

He looked down. "No," he said. "Never."

Later on, I asked him another question. I forgot what it was, but it had two parts.

"That's two questions," Teddy pointed out wearily.

"Yeah," I said. "Two for one. It's happy hour."

"Not quite," he said, pointing at the clock on the wall. It was 4:45.

As the years went by, Teddy got fatter and fatter. Alcohol will do that to you. Empty calories, thousands upon thousands of them, day after day after wasted night. I started calling Teddy "Fat Boy." He took extreme umbrage to my sobriquet. In late 1987, a rider was mysteriously added to a budget bill in the Senate. It would have forced Rupert Murdoch to divest himself of either his newspaper or his TV station in both New York and Boston.

The rider had been attached by one of Teddy's buddies, Sen. Ernest "Fritz" Hollings of South Carolina. As governor of South Carolina, he'd started flying the Stars and Bars—the Confederate flag—above the state capitol in Columbia. Nobody ever mentioned this, of course, because Hollings was a good Democrat, not to mention Teddy's boon companion, just like Sen. Robert Byrd of West Virginia, the former Grand Kleagle of the Ku Klux Klan.

I was in all the newspapers, identified as the scribe who'd brought down the wrath of the Kennedys on Murdoch. But I figured Rupert would back me up. I hadn't done anything wrong, and I was selling lots and lots of newspapers.

I wrote a column addressed directly to Teddy.

"Was it something I said, Fat Boy?" was the lead.

That was apparently a bit too nasty for the *New York Times*, but in a backgrounder about the feud between Murdoch and Teddy, the paper quoted another part of my Fat Boy column:

"One writer, Howie Carr, in a column last week about the furor, criticized Mr. Kennedy's actions and lampooned the Senator about his weight. He wrote, 'Really, Sen. Kennedy, do you truly believe that this newspaper employs the only people in the world who notice your periodic resemblance to the Goodyear blimp?'"

Murdoch ended up selling the *New York Post* (he later bought it back, out of bankruptcy) and he sold his TV station in Boston. (He reacquired that eventually as well.)

I spent two weeks in Palm Beach in December 1991 covering the Willie Smith rape trial. Every morning different Kennedys would arrive at the courthouse in West Palm Beach in support of their young kinsman. One day it was Eunice Shriver, looking like the Bride of the Mummy.

After a brief statement, as she walked into the courthouse, one of my old cameramen at Channel 7 turned to me and said, "Do you think Sargent Shriver cheats?"

I didn't know but I was very much aware that when the Shrivers came to town to visit Rose, Eunice stayed at La Querida—Comfortably Numb by the Sea—and Sarge checked into The Breakers.

Every Sunday during the rape trial, the family would appear, as in days of yore, at St. Edward for the 10:30 Mass. For some reason, all the Fleet Street types covering the trial for the Murdoch empire balked at going inside the church. It didn't bother me, though—I'd been confirmed at St. Edward, back in the day when it was in the diocese of Miami.

One Sunday I strolled in and planted myself in the pew behind Willie Smith and Cong. Joe Kennedy. They didn't notice me until it was time for that "peace-be-with-you" moment. Joe didn't seem too happy to see me. They made for the side exit, on Sunset, and I ran out the front door to alert the camera crews to scramble.

Those were the days.

After that I was always one of the go-to guys if you wanted to get out some bad news about the Kennedys. One day in 2005 I picked up the phone and it was Pam Kelley, whom Joe Kennedy had crippled in that infamous Jeep accident on Nantucket in 1973. He'd been fined $100 for putting her in a wheelchair for life.

Now, Pam Kelley was 50 and badly in need of cash. She had called Joe and asked for more money, and he had told her that he too was "broke." He owned three houses, and he and his second, trophy wife both made six-figure salaries at the "nonprofit" he operated. (It's now up to $824,979 a year,

Pam Kelley called me when she needed money from Joe Kennedy II.

according to his most recent filings with the state of Massachusetts, and his wife is paid more than $316,573 annually. That's quite the "nonprofit" they operate.)

"The Kennedys," she told me, "are cheap, self-centered people."

In 1973, Pam Kelley had been the girlfriend of David Kennedy, Joe's younger brother. A year before he died of a drug overdose in Palm Beach in 1984, David had called Pam.

"He told me he wanted what I had, which was sobriety. Then he said he wanted to walk down the beach with me, like he forgot what had happened to me."

I couldn't believe Pam Kelley was telling me this stuff, on the record. I asked her about the aftermath of the accident, when she was hospitalized for months as the Kennedys offered her hundreds of thousands of dollars for her eternal silence.

"I was 18, and my father's sitting by my hospital bed asking me what do I want to do, and all I can see is that wheelchair next to the bed."

I asked Pam Kelley what she would say to Joe Kennedy.

"I'd say, 'Fuck you, you and your three houses.' Broke! I'd say, 'Why won't you help me? How can you just bullshit me like that?' It's not like he's never seen me in a wheelchair."

In my column, I called her "the Mary Jo Kopechne who got away."

After the story appeared in the *Herald*, Joe Kennedy cut her a big check. I guess he wasn't all that broke.

I've always picked up a lot of dirt about the Kennedys over the years. Haven't always been able to get everything into the paper, but I always try my best.

In the winter of 2018, the movie *Chappaquiddick* was about to be released. I was in Palm Beach when my cell phone rang. It was one of the Hollywood people involved in producing the film.

"What would you think," he said, "if I told you that someone very close to the Kennedys tried to kill this movie?"

"You mean Chris Dodd?" I asked.

"I didn't say that!" the guy said. "You said that, not me."

But who else could it have been? Until the end of 2017, Chris Dodd had been the head of the Motion Picture Association of America (MPAA). Yes, that Chris Dodd, the other half of the infamous waitress sandwich with Ted Kennedy, the drunken oaf Teddy had asked actress Carrie Fisher to sleep with, the inspiration for Patches Kennedy to follow in his footsteps to Providence College . . .

This is what the Kennedys have always done when they are threatened with bad publicity (i.e., the truth). From Drew Pearson to Leo Damore to Richard Burke (author of *The Senator*), they punish anyone in the media who is not a slobbering sycophant—or try to, anyway.

I should know, right?

The Hollywood guy wanted me to write the story of how Chris Dodd had tried to spike the movie about his fellow tosspot's bad ice cube on Martha's Vineyard in 1969. I told the Hollywood guy I'd try.

Ex-Sen. Chris Dodd: I got a call from Hollywood when the head of the MPAA allegedly tried to shut down the movie about his drinking buddy Ted, Chappaquiddick. *(Dodd denied it—unconvincingly.)*

I called the MPAA and asked for a comment. When the phone didn't ring, I knew it was Chris Dodd.

Fox News called and wanted me to discuss the film on camera, as well as the attempts to kill it. I went on and pointed out that the MPAA was refusing to say one way or the other whether pressure had been applied— yet again—to keep the truth about the Kennedys from coming out.

The next day, the MPAA officially denied that Sen. Chris Dodd had ever applied pressure to halt the release of *Chappaquiddick*. Which was when the producer finally stepped up and publicly described, on the record, Dodd's attempts to sink the picture before it was released.

Not that all the Kennedys are bad, of course. Joe Kennedy's son, Joe III, he's my congressman now. I don't know what possible future he can have in the modern Democratic party. He's a white, Irish-Catholic heterosexual. That's a lot of baggage for any Democrat politician these days, a well-nigh insurmountable hurdle.

My mother died the year he was first elected to Congress, in 2012. He sent me a handwritten note, which I've kept.

"I was so sorry to hear about your mother's passing and wanted to offer my condolences. One thing we can always agree on is the importance of family and how much we owe those who raised us. I'm sure your career as a 'Happy Warrior' in the political fray comes in part from her love, guidance and spirit—standing up for what you believe, no matter what.

"Please know that my thoughts are with you and your family at this time."

Like I always say about Joe III, the Kennedy's about been bred out of him.

Did you notice how he called me a "happy warrior?" That's an old phrase from Wordsworth that's been used to describe a lot of politicians, but I associate it with my father's favorite national Irish-Catholic Democrat, Gov. Al Smith of New York. Of course Barack Obama once called Ted Kennedy the Happy Warrior, but surely he meant the Happy Hour Warrior.

As I write this, in the fall of 2018, word comes that Chris Lawford is dead of a heart attack at a hot yoga class in Vancouver. He was 63. It's been a bad year for the family. First Joe III delivers the Democratic response to the State of the Union from a vocational education center in Fall River, standing in front of what looked like the wreckage of his uncle Ted's 1967 Oldsmobile Delmont. (And now the mayor of Fall River has just been indicted on federal charges of tax fraud and swindling investors out of $231,000. Joe demanded that the mayor resign, and the newspaper story was illustrated with a photo of young Joe and the crooked mayor—another Providence College grad, like Patches and Chris Dodd—huddling together.)

Then Joe's cousin Ted Jr., a state senator in Connecticut, decides not only not to run for governor of the ruined state, but not to even seek re-election to the legislature in Hartford. And of course Chris Kennedy got smoked in the Illinois primary for governor.

And now Chris Lawford is gone, another Kennedy Everyman. Went to law school but never practiced. Arrested for drugs of course—trying to pass a forged prescription for Valium in Aspen in 1980. Had a showbiz career, in the soap opera *All My Children,* 20 years after one of JFK's girlfriends had a role in the same show.

It's a small world, as I'm sure Chris's father Peter told him on one of their LSD trips together, or maybe when they swapped girlfriends, which they did occasionally.

"Alcoholism doesn't run in my family," Chris once said. "It gallops."

Teddy Kennedy Jr. didn't run for reelection to the state Senate in Connecticut in 2018.

I remember one Saturday afternoon in Palm Beach. It must have been the winter of 1962. The phone rang and my Aunt Doris answered. My father was on the line from the front desk at The Breakers. The president was playing a round of golf at The Breakers's nine-hole course in the middle of town. My father wanted me and my younger brother to walk over to the clubhouse so that we could see him up close, without the thronging crowds of tourists outside St. Edward.

We walked up South County Road, past Worth Avenue, then cut down Royal Palm Way, where Rush Limbaugh now broadcasts from daily. We turned right onto Coconut Row at our school, Palm Beach Public, and walked to the old Breakers clubhouse, long since replaced by a plusher, air-conditioned building on South County with a fabulous steak house on the second floor.

We stood outside in the small parking lot, my brother and I, along with a couple of Secret Service agents. I peeked in one of their golf bags and saw what looked to my 10-year-old eyes like a Thompson submachine gun. The president sauntered out, in a polo shirt and khakis, his hair wet. He must have just showered. He smiled at us, waved, and then jumped into a Cadillac—a convertible of course—and took off by himself. The president of the United States, all alone, no protection . . . and no prying eyes.

He turned left, south, even though his home was north, a right turn. I still wonder where he was headed that sunny Florida afternoon. Correction: I wonder who he was heading to see that sunny Florida afternoon.

I never went to school with any of the Kennedys. One of my daughters did, though. She went to Deerfield Academy, my old prep school. She was in the same class with Bobby Kennedy Jr.'s kid, Conor, who, like his cousin Chris Lawford, would someday be arrested in Aspen, Colorado.

One day in the spring of 2014, I got a call from my daughter at Deerfield.

"Guess where we're having our class party after graduation?" she asked, and my heart sank. There was only possible reason she would be calling me about this.

"Where?" I asked.

"The compound," she said. "In Hyannis Port."

Fortunately, common sense prevailed. The party was moved. My daughter is still alive. So is everyone else in the Deerfield Academy Class of 2014. And so far at least, only one member of the class has been arrested—Conor Kennedy.

It never ends with the Kennedys. As I started writing this chapter, in September 2018, Judge Brett Kavanaugh was struggling to win confirmation in the Senate to the Supreme Court. (He was confirmed of course.) When Sen. Lindsey Graham of South Carolina lashed out at one of the female witnesses who was accusing Kavanaugh, without corroboration, of assaulting her, Maria Shriver, Ted Kennedy's niece, decided to tweet out her outrage:

"Oh my God, this is every woman's nightmare. This is a terrifying image." Someone named Cam Edwards tweeted back to Teddy's niece:

"Just asked my wife. She said being left to drown in a car like your uncle did to Mary Jo Kopechne is a bigger nightmare than being yelled at by Lindsey Graham."

Come to think of it, I can think of another worse nightmare for a woman than being yelled at by Lindsey Graham: having your husband, the governor of California, Arnold Schwarzenegger, basically aping his male in-laws and knocking up the family's Guatemalan maid.

I've had quite enough of the Kennedys, their in-laws, their minions, their assorted other apologists, and yes-men. Like the rest of America, I'm ready to move on.

Let the word go forth, as JFK might have said, to a new generation. Here is the message, as seen on the wall behind the bar of the Quarterdeck Lounge in Hyannis:

Works Cited

Andersen, Christopher P. *Jackie after Jack: Portrait of the Lady*. New York, William Morrow,1998.

Baker, Bobby and Larry L. King, *Wheeling and Dealing: Confessions of a Capitol Hill Operator,* New York, W.W. Norton and Company, 1978.

Beauchamp, Cari, *Joseph P. Kennedy Presents His Hollywood Years,* New York, Alfred A. Knopf, 2009.

Blair, Joan, and Clay Blair. *The Search for JFK*. New York, Berkley Pub. Corp., 1976.

Bly, Nellie, *Kennedy Men: Three Generations of Sex, Scandal and Secrets.* New York, Kensington Books, 1996.

Boyd, James, *Above the Law: The Rise and Fall of Senator Thomas J. Dodd,* New York, The New American Library, 1968.

Brown, Madeleine Duncan, *Texas in the Morning: The Love Story of Madeline Brown and President Lyndon Baines Johnson,* Baltimore, Conservatory Press 1997.

Bryant, Traphes, and Frances Spatz Leighton. *Dog Days at the White House: The Outrageous Memoirs of the Presidential Kennel Keeper*. New York, Macmillan, 1975.

Burke, Richard E. The Senator: *My Ten Years with Ted Kennedy*. New York, St. Martin's Press, 1992.

Caro, Robert A., *Master of the Senate: The Years of Lyndon Johnson Vol. III,* New York, Alfred A. Knopf, 2002.

Caro, Robert A., *The Passage of Power: The Years of Lyndon Johnson Vol. IV,* New York, Alfred A. Knopf 2012.

Clifford, Clark M., and Richard C. Holbrooke. *Counsel to the President: A Memoir*. New York, Random House, 1991.

Collier, Peter, and David Horowitz. *The Kennedys: An American Drama*. New York, Summit Books, 1984.

Dallas, Rita, and Jeanira Ratcliffe. *The Kennedy Case*. New York, Putnam, 1973.

Damore, Leo. *Senatorial Privilege: The Chappaquiddick Cover-Up*. Washington, D.C., Regnery Gateway, 1988.

David, Lester. *Good Ted, Bad Ted: The Two Faces of Edward M. Kennedy*. Secaucus, NJ, Carol Pub. Group, 1993.

Dinneen, Joseph F. *The Kennedy Family*. Boston, Little, Brown, 1959.

Doyle, William. *PT 109: An American Epic of War, Survival and the Destiny of John F. Kennedy,* New York, William Morrow, 2015.

Exner, Judith, and Ovid Demaris. *Judith Exner: My Story*. New York, Grove, 1977.

Felsenthal, Carol, *Power, Privilege and The Post: The Katherine Graham Story,* New York, Seven Stories Press 1999.

Friedman, Stanley P., *The Magnificent Kennedy Women,* Derby CT, Monarch Books, Inc., 1964.

Gibson, Barbara, and Ted Schwarz. *The Kennedys: The Third Generation*. New York, NY, Thunder's Mouth Press, 1993.

Gibson, Barbara and Ted Schwarz. *Rose Kennedy and Her Family: The Best and Worst of Their Lives and Times*. New York, Birch Lane Press, 1995.

Hamilton, Nigel. *JFK: Reckless Youth,* New York, Random House, 1991.

Herken, Gregg. *The Georgetown Set: Friends and Rivals in Cold War Washington,* New York, Alfred A. Knopf, 2014.

Hersh, Seymour M. *The Dark Side of Camelot*. Boston, Little, Brown, 1997.

Jacobs, George. *Mr. S: My Life with Frank Sinatra*. New York, Pan MacMillan, 2003.

Kaplan, James. *Sinatra: The Chairman*. New York, Doubleday, 2015.

Kennedy, Joseph P., and Amanda Smith. *Hostage to Fortune: The Letters of Joseph P. Kennedy*. New York, Viking, 2001.

Kennedy, Patrick, *A Common Struggle: A Personal Journey Through the Past and Future of Mental Illness and Addiction,* New York, Blue Rider Press, 2015.

Kennedy, Sheila Rauch, *Shattered Faith: A Woman's Struggle to Stop the Catholic Church from Annulling Her Marriage*, New York, Pantheon Books, 1997.

Kessler, Ronald. *The Sins of the Father: Joseph P. Kennedy and the Dynasty He Founded.* New York, Warner Books, 1996.

Lasky, Victor. *J.F.K.: The Man and the Myth.* New York, Macmillan, 1963.

Lasky, Victor. *Robert F. Kennedy: The Myth and the Man.* New York, Trident Press, 1968.

Lawford, Patricia Seaton, and Ted Schwarz. *The Peter Lawford Story: Life with the Kennedys, Monroe, and the Rat Pack.* New York, Carroll & Graf Publishers, 1988.

Leary, Timothy. *Flashbacks: An Autobiography.* Los Angeles, J.P. Tarcher, 1983.

Lertzman, Richard A., and William J. Birnes. *Dr. Feelgood: The Shocking Story of the Doctor Who May Have Changed History by Treating and Drugging JFK, Marilyn, Elvis, and Other Prominent Figures.* New York, NY, Skyhorse Publishing, 2014.

Lincoln, Evelyn, *Kennedy and Johnson,* New York, Holt, Rinehart and Winston, 1968.

Nasaw, David, *The Patriarch: The Remarkable Life and Turbulent Times of Joseph P. Kennedy,* New York, The Penguin Press, 2012.

Nelson, Garrison, *John William McCormack: A Political Biography,* New York, Bloomsbury Academic, 2017.

O'Donnell, Kenneth P., and David F. Powers. *Johnny, We Hardly Knew Ye; Memories of John Fitzgerald Kennedy.* Boston, Little, Brown, 1972.

Oppenheimer, Jerry, *RFK JR.: Robert F. Kennedy Jr. and the Dark Side of the Dream* New York, St. Martin's Press 2015.

Parmet, Herbert S. *Jack: The Struggles of John F. Kennedy.* New York, Dial Press, 1980.

Piereson, James. *Camelot and the Cultural Revolution: How the Assassination of John F. Kennedy Shattered American Liberalism.* New York, Encounter Books, 2007.

Pitts, David. *Jack & Lem: John F. Kennedy and Lem Billings: The Untold Story of an Extraordinary Friendship.* New York, Carroll & Graf, 2007.

Quirk, Lawrence J. *The Kennedys in Hollywood.* Dallas, Taylor Publishing Company, 1996.

Reeves, Thomas C. *A Question of Character: A Life of John F. Kennedy,* New York, The Free Press, 1991.

Roemer, William E. Jr., *Roemer: Man Against the Mob,* New York, Ivy Books, 1989.

Schwarz, Ted. *Joseph P. Kennedy: The Mogul, the Mob, the Statesman, and the Making of an American Myth.* Hoboken, NJ, John Wiley & Sons, 2003.

Shaw, Mark. *The Poison Patriarch: How the Betrayals of Joseph P. Kennedy Caused the Assassination of JFK.* New York, NY, Skyhorse Publishing, 2013.

Shearer, Stephen Michael. *Gloria Swanson: The Ultimate Star.* New York, Thomas Dunne Books/St. Martin's Press, 2013.

Sloyan, Patrick J., *The Politics of Deception: JFK's Secret Decisions on Vietnam, Civil Rights, and Cuba.* New York, Thomas Dunne Books, 2015.

Spada, James. *Peter Lawford: The Man Who Kept the Secrets.* New York, Bantam Books,1991.

Summers, Anthony. *Goddess: The Secret Lives of Marilyn Monroe.* New York, NY, 1985.

Thomas, Evan, *Robert Kennedy: His Life,* New York, Simon & Schuster, 2000.

Tye, Larry. *Bobby Kennedy: The Making of a Liberal Icon.* New York, Random House 2016.

Index